Bullying

How to spot it, how to stop it

A guide for parents and teachers

Karen Sullivan

RODALE®

D0064227

This edition first published in the UK in 2006 by
Rodale International Ltd
7–10 Chandos Street
London W1G 9AD
www.rodalebooks.co.uk

Printed and bound in the UK by CPI Bath using acid-free paper from sustainable sources.

1 3 5 7 9 8 6 4 2

A CIP record for this book is available from the British Library

ISBN-13: 978-1-4050-8776-6
ISBN-10: 1-4050-8776-5

This paperback edition distributed to the book trade by Pan Macmillan Ltd

Notice
Mention of specific companies, organisations or authorities in this book does not imply
endorsement by the publisher, nor does mention of specific companies, organisations or authorities in the book imply that they endorse the book.

Addresses, websites and telephone numbers given in this book were accurate at the time
the book went to press.

We inspire and enable people to improve their lives and the world around them

For Marcus,
my unexpected little ray of light

Contents

Contents

Acknowledgements 7
Foreword 9
Introduction 11

Chapter 1
What Makes a Bully? 15

Chapter 2
They Will Find You: The Different Types of Bullying 41

Chapter 3
What Makes a Victim? 57

Chapter 4
Tackling Bullying 81

Chapter 5
When Your Child Is the Bully 125

Chapter 6
The Stress Equation 165

Chapter 7
Getting It Right at Home 199

Chapter 8
Bullying Initiatives 225

Chapter 9
A Little Extra Help 273

Resources 293
Index 313

Acknowledgements

This has been a mammoth book to write and many, many people have given their time, wisdom and expertise over the past year or so. First of all, I'd like to thank Adrian Brown and his colleagues at ChildLine, who have supplied me with case histories, information and insight into what kids are really thinking and feeling. Claude Knights at Kidscape was also hugely helpful, as was Vanessa Cooper at the Anti-Bullying Alliance. Ivan Lewis, MP, shared his own experience of bullying, and explained how it drove him to do something useful in his ministerial post; thank you. Thanks, too, to Adrienne Katz from YoungMinds, John Stead from the NSPCC, and the various members of staff from the YWCA, the Samaritans, Stonewall and Parentline, who shared their views and time. One of the most helpful individuals was Tim Field, from Bully Online, whose website has grown to become one of the largest anti-bullying organisations in the world. Tim was a huge source of inspiration, advice and information, and it is with great sadness that I report that he died of cancer during the writing of this book. He will be sorely missed, but there is no doubt that his work will be carried on. I'd also like to thank Rob Osbourne from Leicestershire City Council, who gave me insight into how he and his team have tackled bullying problems in the area; Greg Sampson of R Time, whose enthusiasm for his project can't help but inspire the children he works with; Karen Pereira of Carmarthenshire Council in Wales; the various schools who have given me details of the projects that have worked for them – and those that haven't; and Dr Ken Rigby for his expertise and help – his unremitting dedication to the fight against bullying has been inspirational.

There are many, many other individuals and organisations that have helped. One that stands out is Bully Police USA – a website that was the brainchild of

Brenda High, whose son Jared was bullied to such an extent that he took his own life. Brenda has devoted her time and much of her life to fighting for anti-bullying legislation in the US, and has given me advice, guidance and much useful information over the past year. Thank you. A Canadian organisation, Bully Beware, has also been hugely helpful, and I would like to thank Cindi Seddon for her input. In Australia, Philip Slee, researcher and professor, who shared his vision and ideas, deserves many thanks – and also for sending his peace pack many miles at top speed. Thanks, too, to the many researchers who shared their information (even if they were unaware that their colleagues were so helpful!). These include Helen Cowie, Professors Peter Smith and Stephen Joseph, and Sonia Sharp. Their work has had a huge impact on both this book and on anti-bullying legislation and programmes worldwide.

At Rodale, I'd like to thank Anne Lawrance for her supreme patience. For various reasons, this book took precisely a year longer than anticipated to write and she has been a model editor, offering advice, friendship and exhibiting the kind of tolerance this book sets out to achieve! Thanks to Jillian Stewart, my 'hands-on' editor, who has been inspirational and supportive throughout the process. Thanks also to Midas, for undertaking the PR.

Finally, I'd like to thank my family, who have become heartily sick and tired of the subject of bullying, but who have offered a listening ear, useful input and plenty of babysitting, to allow me to sit at my desk for longer than three minutes at a stretch. Thanks to Max, Cole, Luke and wee Marcus. Friends have also been hugely supportive and some have passed on their own experiences of bullying, which has only served to enrich the book. Many, many thanks in particular to Gill Paul, and also to Melanie Woollcoombe, Ann Abrahams, Lisa McGown and Carey Smith. This has been a book worth writing, and I am grateful to all.

Foreword

This book should be helpful for teachers, parents and all those concerned with reducing bullying in school and increasing the happiness and wellbeing of children. It achieves two aims in particular. First, it provides an up-to-date overview of what we know about school bullying. Second, it provides a broad range of detailed guidance for parents, as well as teachers, in terms of spotting when bullying is happening, and dealing with it in practical and helpful ways.

School bullying has become recognised as a very serious issue for schools, teachers, parents, and of course for the children and young people who are involved. Thorough investigation on this topic started some 25 years ago, and it has become studied and acted upon at an international level, most especially in the last 10 years. Much of this effort has focussed on what we can do to 'stop the bullying'. This book also addresses how to 'spot the bullying', which is equally important.

The concern about school bullying stems from the well-established findings of the negative consequences it brings. Victims of bullying often suffer low self-esteem, and may experience psychosomatic symptoms that interfere with their school work. At the extreme, there are cases of suicide due to the distress caused by school bullying. Some of the children who do the bullying may also be psychologically disturbed; others may be relatively confident and popular, but engage in bullying for their own purposes if they can obtain benefits from it (money, status, etc.) in a school and peer group environment that allows this. But as research has shown, persistent bullies at school are at substantially greater risk of delinquent and antisocial behaviour, including domestic violence, in later adult life.

A considerable number of large-scale school-based interventions against bullying have now taken place; their success is variable (Smith, Pepler and Rigby, 2004). Work in Norway by psychologist Dan Olweus has achieved a reduction in bullying of 50 per cent, but after another 15 years of research, this looks like a maximum figure given our present state of knowledge; the more usual outcome figures are reductions in the region of 10–20 per cent. These are still very worthwhile, but they demonstrate that we still have much to learn about effective action and strategies.

What factors are important for success? Probably the most important is the extent to which the school willingly implements anti-bullying interventions on a whole school basis. It is also important to start early; generally, interventions in primary schools seem to have better outcomes than interventions in secondary schools. Interventions need time to take root – one term is not enough – and interventions need to be maintained over time; anti-bullying work is a continual process.

A systemic approach is also helpful. A variety of interventions appear to complement each other. A whole-school policy against bullying is useful and perhaps essential as a coordinating framework. Teacher-inspired efforts such as curriculum work, improved supervision and clear sanctions against bullying, are important. So, too, are efforts to change the climate of the peer group, through peer support systems. Finally, parents have a vital role to play and this book will be especially useful in helping concerned parents understand more about the issues and play a strong role in spotting and stopping bullying. It will also be helpful to teachers, and other concerned adults, and should help significantly in working on this very important social issue.

Peter K. Smith
Goldsmiths College, University of London, UK

Introduction

For 15 years I have written about the emotional and physical health of children, and the issues that surround childhood and bringing up children. Issues tend to change over time, and new concerns arise constantly; however, one thing has become clear over the course of my last few years' work. Bullying is prevalent and is seriously affecting the health of our children on countless levels. As a parent myself, this is something that has personal implications. Do I really want my kids growing up being afraid of going to school? This is a book that had to be written, as bullying touches the lives of so many parents and children – not only here in the UK, but worldwide.

I started by speaking to parents and children who had been bullied, and began what became more than a year of researching studies and anti-bullying approaches. To say I was shocked would be an understatement. Countless lives have been blighted by bullying, and some children's childhoods effectively destroyed. The words of the children I interviewed and the stories I read about children who took their lives – otherwise happy kids who had been pushed that little bit too far – were deeply upsetting. And it wasn't just the bullied kids who were affected – it was the bystanders, too; those children who are witness to regular violence, extortion, threats, verbal abuse and more in their own school halls. They live in fear that they might be next, or that they will fall out of favour if they stand up for a bullied child, or resist coercion to join in.

According to a report by the charity Young Voices, and Oxford University, more than half of all British schoolchildren have been bullied. Previous research from the children's charity the NSPCC, showed that more than half of children aged eight to 15 years sometimes or often worried about being bullied at school and that younger children worried most. According to the NSPCC,

43 per cent of young people have, at some point in their childhood, experienced bullying, discrimination or being made to feel different by other children. Nearly all (94 per cent) of these experiences took place at school. Other studies have shown the problem to be even greater – one study in particular found 82 per cent of children between the ages of five and 18 to be affected to some extent.

Such alarming figures are not uncommon. In 1997, research from New Zealand found that within any particular year at least half and perhaps as many as three-quarters of children are bullied; ten per cent are bullied weekly. And in Australia, one in six children is bullied at school on a weekly basis, according to bullying expert Ken Rigby. About 20 per cent of those bullied frequently stay away from school, and more than 50 per cent consider doing so. Sadly, too, 40 per cent of boys and 25 per cent of girls who are bullied weekly do not tell their friends.

So the problem is pervasive; it's happening everywhere. However, it's not all bad news. Bullying is a problem that has become increasingly recognised, and studies show that many of the bullying initiatives that have been created over the past years, and adopted by schools, local authorities, governments and children's charities, have had at least some impact. Children are now empowered to stand up for themselves, or to find support when they are backed into situations from which they feel they can't escape. There are helplines, nation- and school-wide initiatives adopting a zero tolerance approach to the problem, and many schools are taking it upon themselves to teach the messages of respect, tolerance, understanding and fair play.

Ultimately, however, it is parents who can do the most to counteract bullying. The first step is to try to understand what is undoubtedly a complex problem. What causes children to bully, and is bullying on the increase? What makes a child a victim, and how can parents help children to develop the necessary coping skills to deal with problems at school and on the streets? When does most bullying occur, and what are the triggers? And what actually constitutes bullying and abuse? These questions, and more, will be answered in this book. The amount of research is staggering; the results even more surprising. We know a lot about why kids behave the way they do, and what makes a child a bully and another child a target. An analysis of the facts and statistics will give you a clear picture of what is probably going on in your child's life.

This book addresses the very real worries that parents have regarding the subject of bullying, whether their child is being bullied or has become a bully themselves. It looks at the different types of bullying (including the newest and most insidious forms, such as happy slapping, instant messaging, texting and emails), as well as the different types of bullies, the effects bullying has on a child's emotional and physical health, the methods that work both inside and outside of school, and those that simply exacerbate the problem. I'll lead you through assessments of whether your child is being bullied and trying to hide it, or is bullying other children. You'll also find guidance on raising children who are resilient and emotionally healthy enough to cope with bullying. I'll look at how and when schools can be involved, the legal implications, the different problems associated with different age groups, and the issues of peer pressure and parenting, which underpin a great deal of the bullying that goes on. There's help for carers and teachers as well, with advice on nipping the problem in the bud before it takes hold in the classroom. You'll also find case histories, which illustrate children's experiences of bullying, and a wealth of resources that can offer further help and guidance.

We all want the best for our children and taking a stand against bullying – both in the home and at school – is a vital part of creating a safe and nurturing environment in which our children can thrive and grow into happy, healthy adults.

1

What Makes a Bully?

A recipe for violence is a mean streak combined with an unwarranted sense of self-worth.

Martin Seligman, past president of the American
Psychological Association

I F YOUR CHILD HAS BEEN THE VICTIM OF A BULLY, it may seem strange that this book begins with an investigation into the nature of bullies themselves. However, it's important to remember that bullies are children too. Children are not born to bully; it's something they learn along the road to adulthood. Does this mean that any child has the capacity to become a bully? The simple answer is yes. There is a defined set of characteristics that typify most bullies, and many of these are external – that is to say, they are the product of their upbringing, their experiences, the way they live their lives and how they learn to communicate. Bullies have, for obvious reasons, been given a very bad press – often justifiably so. However, understanding the motivation behind their behaviour, their common features and even their shortcomings can help you to get to grips with a bullying problem – whether your child is the victim, the bully, or just a bystander.

In the Introduction I outlined the scale of the bullying epidemic, and it's clear that many children worldwide are suffering at the hands of bullies. These children need help, and later in this book we'll look at the ways in which we can make a difference and possibly even put a stop to the bullying that occurs in our children's schools, in the playground and on the streets. But there are other issues, too. Bullies themselves face an unhealthy and uncertain future if their actions are not brought to a halt. The statistics make sobering reading.

Students (particularly boys) who bully are more likely to engage in other anti-social and delinquent behaviour, such as vandalism, shoplifting, truancy and drug use. They are four times as likely as non-bullies to be convicted of crimes by the age of 24. Evidence indicates that bullying is not a 'phase' that a child will grow out of. In a long-term study of more than 500 children, researchers at the University of Michigan in the USA discovered that children who were viewed as the most aggressive by their peers at the age of eight grew up to commit more (and more serious) crimes as adults. A five-year UK study found a possible link between bullying behaviour in school and later violent behaviour. From a group of 50 pupils (of both sexes) who were disruptive but not bullies, 17 had criminal convictions (with a total of 33 offences, including 4 which involved violence). However, a group of 50 pupils who were both disruptive and bullies had a much higher number of criminal convictions – 31 had 162 convictions and 36 of these offences involved violence.

In the UK study, the tentacles of bullying spread far and wide. Girl bullies were more than three times as likely as non-bullies to have tried drugs. Boys who

Boys who bully are physically stronger and have a need to dominate others. Girl bullies tend to be physically weaker than other girls in their class.

were bullies were twice as likely as non-bullies to have been in trouble with the police. And the undercurrent of violence at home is never far from the surface. Harsh or negative parenting with high levels of conflict tends to be reported by bullies and over-protective or neglectful parenting often reported by victims. Over half the bullying boys reported that they had experienced adults making violent threats and 42 per cent said they had experienced violence from an adult, with 35 per cent saying they'd been beaten. Thirty-one per cent of bullying girls report an adult using violence against them. These children are more likely to say that they are prepared to use violence to get something they want – the lessons of power have been learned young.

Unless new behaviours are learned and adopted, bullies continue to bully throughout their lives. They bully their friends, their children, and possibly their subordinates in their place of business.

Then there is the effect on schools – a place that should be safe, secure and an important foundation of both their emotional and educational advancement. Research shows that students not only tend to feel less safe, but also less satisfied with school life, in schools where bullying problems occur. And in schools where bullying is ignored, students may start to regard such behaviour as acceptable, which may result in more bullying behaviour.

? Who are the bullies?

We know from research undertaken in 1992 that boys bully and are bullied more often than girls. It's worth remembering, however, that this may have to do with the way in which bullying is defined and/or identified. Boys tend to be 'direct bullies' – more likely to inflict physical assaults – whereas girls tend to be 'indirect bullies', and more commonly use ridicule, teasing and social isolation. Subsequent studies, however, have shown that boys are becoming better at emotional and verbal bullying, and girls are catching up on the physical side (see page 132).

And there's more: we know that boys tend to bully both boys and girls, and that they tend to bully pupils from other classrooms and age groups. Girls tend to bully girls, particularly from their own class, and usually work by spreading malicious gossip or making the victim an outcast from their 'group'. Boys who bully are physically stronger and have a need to dominate others. Girl bullies tend to be physically weaker than other girls in their class.

Bullying by girls is often more subtle and harder to detect than bullying by boys, and girls are also more likely to bully in a group (see page 19).

? What about age differences?

The good news is that bullying does appear to decline as children grow older, though some experts believe that it merely changes shape rather than disappears entirely, and that many of these changed forms of bullying go unreported – the older the child, the more embarrassing the problem and therefore the less likely it is to be reported. Bullies are averagely popular up to the age of 14 or 15. In fact, some children even look up to them because they are powerful and do what they want to, or have to, to get their way with their peers. By late adolescence, however, the bully's popularity has begun to wane. At this stage, his or her peer group will include other bullies, or, more seriously, he or she will have developed or will be developing gang alliances.

Studies show that victimisation decreases across year levels: i.e. more primary school children report bullying compared to children in the later years.

Children in lower school years are more likely to be the victims of older bullies, whereas children in higher years are more likely to be the victims of same-age bullies.

Not surprisingly, in secondary school, bullying behaviour most frequently involves teasing and social exclusion, but it may also include physical violence, threats, theft, sexual and racial harassment, public humiliation and destruction of the targeted student's property. Bullying behaviour in primary years is more likely to involve physical aggression, but is also characterised by teasing, intimidation and social exclusion.

By late secondary school, regular bullying incidents are often a thing of the past, but all victims know who the bullies are, and avoid them. By age 16 or 17, bullies and victims are usually moving in different directions in terms of curricular interests in school, so their paths rarely cross. Social groupings are clearly defined by this time and invisible boundaries have been drawn.

So we know what's happening and when. Girls and boys are both involved. Could it be your child? And if your child is being bullied, can you pinpoint the perpetrator? There is a wealth of research into bullying in all shapes and forms – from toddlerhood right through to corporate manhandling. Experts across the years have come up with many different characteristics of bullies, and have failed to agree on many of them; however, of the many so-called definitive characteristics, there are now 19 that pretty well almost all experts agree on. They are listed on page 20. Some may surprise you.

Characteristics of bullies

Bullies are controlling, hot-tempered and lack empathy. Victims may lack social skills, blame themselves for their problems and be afraid to go to school. These traits are among the most common indicators of bullying and victim behaviours in children, according to a study undertaken at Ohio University in the USA.

In conjunction with a group of 14 international experts on school bullies and victims, researchers developed a list of 19 characteristics common to bullies and 21 characteristics common to victims (see page 58 for the latter). According to the lead author of the study, Richard Hazler, the list could help parents, teachers and child therapists identify which children may become bullies or victims before problems become serious.

Girls who bully

You don't need to look far to find newspaper articles and documentaries charting the rise of increasingly aggressive girls. In the USA, the book *Odd Girl Out*, by Rachel Simmons, which deals with the 'hidden' culture of aggression in girls, was an unprecedented bestseller. In the UK, bullying by girls is a serious problem in many schools and playgrounds. It is said even to have overtaken bullying by boys. There are stories about girl violence, girl gangs, girls who drive their victims to suicide and even girls who murder.

In 2002 the YWCA (Young Women's Christian Association) produced a report entitled 'If Looks Could Kill: Young Women and Bullying', which points to a study that found that half of a random selection of 3,000 schoolgirls had experienced bullying. The study also found that girl-on-girl bullying had increased by 48 per cent in just five years.

Mananda Hendessi, head of policy and campaigns at the YWCA, said that girl bullies themselves were also at risk of going on to lead damaged lives, of becoming involved in girl gangs, criminality and drug and alcohol abuse. 'Girls are now more involved in sustained bullying than boys and they have more fear of going to school,' she said. 'We have been finding that girls who are self-excluding from school or even taking a lot of time off sick have actually been bullied. We find these young women leaving school with no qualifications and going on to become teenage pregnancy statistics or worse. It is an especially grave issue among ethnic minorities where racist bullying goes undetected. These girls leave school with their self-esteem and confidence crushed.'

Indirect bullying and cyberbullying (see page 51) are particularly prevalent among girls, but physical violence has also increased dramatically – perhaps due to the 'ladette' culture (girls simply mimicking boys), but also for some of the same reasons that bullying in general has become more insidious: increased and more accepted violence in society, and alcohol abuse and binge drinking in young teens. Taken from the popular film of the same name, the expression 'mean girls' has become a term used to describe the growing culture of girls who bully – and 'mean' is what many girls, particularly those in gangs, aspire to be. We'll look at the issue of increasing violence and aggression in girls on pages 132–33.

The 19 definitive characteristics of bullies are:

1. Controlling others through verbal threats and physical actions*

2. Quick to anger and resorts to using force quicker than others*

3. Tendency to have little empathy for the problems of the other person in the victim/bully relationship*

4. Frequent exposure to various types of aggressive behaviour*

5. Chronically repeating aggressive behaviours*

6. Inappropriately perceiving hostile intent in the actions of others*

7. Being angry and revengeful

8. Having parents who are poor role models for getting along with others

9. Typically there is some contact with aggressive groups

10. Having parents who are poor role models for constructively solving problems

11. Seeing aggression as the only way to preserve self-image

12. Inconsistent discipline procedures at home

13. A perception that physical image is important for maintaining a feeling of power and control

14. A tendency to focus on angry thoughts

15. Having many more family problems than usual

16. Parents who often do not know the child's whereabouts

17. Suffering physical and emotional abuse at home

18. Creating resentment and frustration in peer group

19. Exhibiting obsessive or rigid actions

* Denotes that all 14 experts collectively agreed on the characteristic.

What does this mean?

If you are the parent of a bully, you may be shocked by the constant references to the home environment. Does the fact that your child is a bully mean that you are a bad parent?

All children are different and respond in their own unique way to various stimuli. One child may go on to bully, while a sibling in exactly the same domestic set-up will be calmer and better adjusted. There is no doubt that some children have a greater sensitivity and susceptibility than others – they respond to their home environment in ways that lead them to develop unacceptable behaviour.

Parenting today is difficult. Childcare has become a 24/7 job; there are few, if any, extended family members around to help or provide advice; many more

WHAT MAKES A BULLY?   21

But I'm a good parent!

Usually bullies come from middle-income families that do not monitor their activities. The parents of bullies are generally either extremely tolerant and permissive or physically aggressive and abusive. However, there are many loving and caring parents who have discovered their child is taking part in bullying. Reasons why kids slip into bullying behaviour might include violence on TV/films, and the influence of 'bully' friends. You can't watch your child while s/he is at school, so there is the possibility of him/her hanging out with a child (or children) who have a negative influence. Sometimes kids admire bullies for their strength, or befriend them so as to stay on their good side! So if you're a wonderful parent knocking yourself for what you did wrong, remember what a strong influence peers can have on your child.

couples work full-time and rely on childcare outside the family unit; and children and adults are all under considerable pressure to perform at optimum level. We'll look at stress in more detail in Chapter 6, but it's important to note that it's a vital factor. Consider, too, the impact of violence from television and other media, and the school environment itself, which is entirely different today from what we may remember from our own childhood.

Many parents today live through their children – fulfilling long-lost dreams vicariously. There is constant pressure on children to be the best, and failing to live up to their parents' expectations can be a heavy cross to bear. Parents work hard, are tired at the end of the day and often discipline erratically, if at all. It's fair to say that the increasing number of 'latch-key' kids has also coincided with the increase in bullying. Why? Because kids who are not parented regularly, and with warmth and guidance, tend to lash out elsewhere and take out their frustration on others. It's difficult to blame parents entirely for this problem, since many families are victims themselves of a relentless society; but if we are to tackle the problem, we need to start by asking ourselves some serious questions.

Let's look at what the research says.

Family influences

Bullies are often victims of bullies. According to recent research, 40 per cent of bullies are themselves bullied at home or at school. It has also been discovered that a victim at home is more likely to be a bully at school. This may be because when a bully sees another child who appears weak and cowering, it disturbs him because it reminds him of his own vulnerability at home.

Many bullies have under-developed social skills and believe other children to be more aggressive than they actually are. An unintentional slight to a bully is perceived as a personal or even physical threat – in fact, in a nutshell, the majority of bullies see threats where there are none, and 'displace' their own hostility and resentment by seeing it in others, even if it's not there. Few bullies have any real social skills, so they do not see events in their true light. How does this pertain to families?

An overview of the research indicates that a bully's parents may be permissive and unable to set limits on their child's behaviour. From early on, the bully can do whatever he wants without clear consequences and discipline. His parents may have been abused themselves as children and may view disciplinary measures as a form of child abuse. While their lax style may have suited an easy-going, older sibling, it will not work with a more aggressive child (again, different children react differently in the same environment). A bully may be allowed to dominate younger siblings and even take over his entire family – in this case everything will revolve around his agenda. Most of us have seen examples of this on some of the recent reality parenting programmes – one little tyrant has the capacity to rule the roost, literally!

A bully's parents often discipline inconsistently. If they are in a good mood, the child gets away with bad behaviour. If they are under stress, they take it out in angry outbursts against the child. The child never learns or fully understands rules of conduct or respect for authority. In essence, s/he never really knows where s/he stands, so interpersonal skills are equally erratic.

Aggressive behaviour develops when parents fail consistently to label, track and provide consequences for negative or unacceptable behaviour. As a result, many children's behaviours go unpunished, while some are punished excessively. Furthermore, parents' use of harsh punishment practices act as a model of aggressive and antisocial methods of problem-solving and relating to others. Harsh and inconsistent punishment practices have now been proved to be related to bullying behaviour.

Childrearing factors

Although we don't know how bullying arises in all cases, some contributing childrearing factors include:

- Authoritarian or punitive parenting. Children brought up in a harsh home environment often become angry and aggressive.
- Coercive parenting. Parents who dominate their children, and use 'power' techniques, especially physical punishment, shouting and name-calling, often generate fear of punishment in their children. These children also tend to identify with, and model, aggressive authority figures.
- Carers showing negative attitudes such as indifference, lack of warmth or involvement.
- A permissive attitude towards aggression, which is often the result of failing to set adequate or age-appropriate limits and boundaries.
- Temperament of the child, e.g., an active or hot-headed child (see page 25).

But bear in mind that just as we do not know the direct cause of bullying, we do not know why some children who grow up in a home that could be expected to foster bullying behaviour manage to avoid this path. It may also be that factors in children's social environment, particularly the classroom, permit bullying to arise and continue.

Self-centred, neglectful parents can create a cold, devious bully. Since his parents do not monitor his activities or take an interest in his life, he learns to abuse others when no authority figure is looking. Such bullying can be carefully planned and sustained, with the bully humiliating his victim through a well thought-out campaign, and coercing other children to join him in his vendetta.

A bully has not learned empathy and compassion. This is not surprising, given that the parents of bullies often have prejudices based on race, sex, wealth and achievement. To some parents, other people are just 'competition', or in the way. Their child must always be the best in sports or academic work, while others are considered inferior or simply irrelevant. A child growing up in this type of environment never learns to care about others, and tends only to look out for 'number one' – other children are an inconvenience or even a threat. As a result, bullying behaviour becomes more likely because these children simply cannot understand another person's feelings, are easily irritated by someone who appears to threaten their own goals, and feel no remorse for actions that would be considered unacceptable in most families and schools.

Family stress has also been related to increased negative and hostile interactions between parents and their children, and to inconsistent and harsh punishment practices. These types of interactions are believed to encourage aggressive behaviour and bullying through several processes. First of all, parents who are aggressive towards their children are teaching them that the use of aggression and power is normal social behaviour. Second, harsh parenting

Research has consistently shown that highly strung, active, hot-headed and hyperactive children are more likely to become bullies.

practices encourage children to develop hostile attitudes to, and relationships with, others in their social environments. The aggressive behaviours may then be modelled at school, where they manifest in the form of bullying. Most bullies are hostile. It's a fact. And it's very often learned behaviour.

A number of child-rearing styles have been found to predict whether children will grow up to be aggressive bullies. A lack of attention and warmth towards the child, together with modelling of aggressive behaviour at home and poor supervision, provide the perfect opportunity for aggressive and bullying behaviour to occur. Modelling of aggressive behaviour may include use of physical and verbal aggression towards the child by parents, or use of physical and verbal aggression by parents towards each other. The connection between children – particularly male children – witnessing their mother being assaulted by their father and bullying behaviour by children towards peers and siblings, has not been well studied, but those studies that do exist indicate that aggressive behaviour of all kinds is much higher in children who witness this kind of violence.

Whatever happens at school, in the playground or on the streets, it must be remembered that children's behaviour patterns are almost always first established at home. And while bullying may be learned by observing high levels of conflict between parents, sibling interaction may also be a training ground for bullying. Aggression between siblings is the most common form of family violence. More importantly, perhaps, parents may inadvertently support bullying by accepting it as just a normal part of growing up and leaving children to solve their own problems.

Although certainly not all bullying stems from family problems, it's a good idea to examine the behaviour and personal interactions your child witnesses at home. If your child lives with taunting or name-calling from a sibling or from you or another parent, it could be prompting aggressive or hurtful behaviour outside the home. What may seem to be innocent teasing at home may actually be at the root of bullying behaviours. Children who are at the receiving end of it learn that bullying can translate into control over children they perceive as weak.

Other influences
Temperament
The most recognised characteristic of bullies is an active and impulsive temperament. Temperament basically refers to personality and the way a child relates to others (his interpersonal skills). Research has consistently shown that highly strung, active, hot-headed and hyperactive children are more likely to become bullies.

School environment
It's been confirmed through numerous studies that school and the school playground are the major settings for bullying behaviour. It should come as no surprise therefore that the social environment at school, supervision, anti-bullying programmes and overall attitude to the problem play a major role in both the frequency and the severity of bullying.

Inadequate supervision has been pinpointed as the chief indicator of bullying. Just as neglectful parenting can lead to individual children bullying, inadequate supervision at school – particularly in the playground, hallways and toilets – is linked to bully problems. There's no doubt, too, that the way teachers or other adults react to bullying when it is discovered is paramount, and in Chapter 8 we'll look at the type of interventions that appear to work best.

For now, however, it's safe to say that when a school has a warm, healthy atmosphere; is welcoming, accepting and respectful of all students; encourages teachers and students towards mutual respect; teaches the importance of empathy; gives children appropriate models for behaviour; and does not tolerate aggression, there are far fewer bullying problems. It is crucial, therefore, that an overall school code of conduct towards everyday behaviour, a set of fair and clearly illustrated rules, and an anti-bullying policy are firmly in place – with consequences clearly defined.

Popularity

It's a long-held myth that bullies are unpopular, but held in high (though grudging) esteem because of the power they exert. Not so, say the experts. According to new research from the University of California, bullies are popular and their classmates think they're cool.

'Many of the existing programmes in schools still operate under the assumption that kids bully their peers because they feel bad about themselves,' said Dr Jaana Juvonen, UCLA professor of psychology and the lead researcher on the study. 'Our findings show quite the contrary. Bullies do not need ego boosters.'

In the study, students were asked to list up to four classmates who fitted descriptions of bullies and up to four who fitted descriptions of victims. Students were also asked to nominate the 'coolest' kids in their class and kids they did not like to 'hang around' with.

The bullies were psychologically strongest and enjoyed high social standing among their classmates, according to the study. Victims were emotionally distressed and socially marginalised by their classmates – they reported the highest levels of depression, social anxiety and loneliness.

However, though bullies were regarded as the highest and victims as the lowest in social status, classmates avoided both bullies and victims, indicating that the social prestige of bullies is motivated in part by fear. Whatever the reason, bullies are popular and seen as 'cool' in many cases – a viewpoint that increases their power and encourages further bullying, including mimicking behaviours in others who look at the bully's 'popularity' with envy.

Stress

Stress is a major factor in many cases of bullying, and it is the catalyst for many bullies. Societal stress, demands at home and at school, competition, poor family relationships and the problems associated with peer pressure are all factors that can tip the scale of a child's emotional health. Children under pressure often respond by becoming violent, and taking out their stress on others. We'll look at this equation in more detail in Chapter 6.

Self-esteem

This is a contentious and interesting subject. As I researched this book, I found countless references to the fact that bullies have low self-esteem. What? Popular children with a gang of followers? It didn't ring true. Further delving uncovered the truth: all recent research points to the fact that bullies have high

Superiority and control

According to Dan Olweus, a leading researcher into bullying and bullying behaviours, children who bully may believe that they are superior to other students, or blame others for being smaller, physically weaker or different; students who bully 'may brag about their actual or imagined superiority over other students'. Olweus also found that bullies frequently fight with others as a way to assert dominance: students who bully often pick fights with those they believe to be weaker, and who do not want to be involved in the conflict. Students who bully may also 'induce some of their followers to do the "dirty work" while they themselves keep in the background'. Most worrying, perhaps, is the fact that students who bully tend to have little empathy, 'derive satisfaction from inflicting injury and suffering', and 'seem to desire power and control'.

So not only do bullies generally feel confident and good about themselves, they also lack the empathy that guides the majority of children to see the harm they may potentially cause, to see their behaviour from another's point of view, and to take responsibility for their actions.

self-esteem. In fact, many have higher than normal self-esteem. Bullies usually have a sense of entitlement and superiority over others, and lack compassion, impulse control and social skills. They enjoy being cruel and sometimes use bullying as an anger management tool – the way a normally angry person would punch a pillow.

All bullies have certain attitudes and behaviours in common. Bullies dominate, blame and use others. They have contempt for the weak and view them as their prey. They lack empathy and foresight, and do not accept responsibility for their actions. They are concerned only about themselves and crave attention. Despite all this, they hold themselves in high esteem and believe that they are superior.

So how can a child who has achieved the holy grail of self-esteem be the perpetrator of violence and problematic behaviour? Have we not been force-fed the idea that children need to be built up to believe they are the best in order to achieve, be happy and fulfil their potential?

Here is where the parenting issue becomes blurred. Many very good parents have adopted the self-esteem mantra, and ensured that their children feel great about themselves. There are even books designed to foster even further the wonder that a child should feel in himself. Take, for example, *365 Positive Activities for Kids*, by Diane Loomans, which has sold hundreds of thousands of copies. Among the book's recommended 'activities' is the daily recitation of self-congratulatory phrases, such as 'I am more amazing than I thought!' and 'Today I will remind myself that I am a marvel.'

There's no debate here. We all think our children are wonderful, and we want them to be happy and confident – and to believe in themselves and their capabilities. But the self-esteem rollercoaster has run out of control. The popular over-focus on self-esteem in the past few years has caused parents to over-nurture, and to allow their children to get away with unacceptable behaviour in the belief that they have the right to express themselves and their unique characteristics. The result of this is, of course, that children become tyrants and expect the world to bow to them. This is unhealthy for many reasons, but in terms of discipline, its impact is significant. Over-pampered children have no respect for anyone else and feel that they have a divine right to have their needs met. This is dangerous not only because such children tend to believe that they are 'above' or 'better than' others, but also because they never actually develop self-respect. It's all too easy. Respect has to be earned. A child who is not invested with self-respect will never fully understand the concept

Are you encouraging bullying?

Any parent who discovers that his or her child has been or is bullying others will understandably be shocked. One parent I interviewed said it was the worst moment of his life when he found out that his son was the ringleader of a gang of boys who preyed on younger kids for their lunch money. 'It's not as though he needed the money,' said the father, 'he had plenty. It was all about control.' He realised that his son had been very strictly parented at home – to the point where he had no say in anything. Angelically behaved with his parents, he vented his frustration over his lack of power by bullying younger children.

Sometimes it's a difficult pill to swallow. You may be a strict disciplinarian and believe that children need to toe the line, or you may, perhaps, let your kids get away with more than they should. Either way, your parenting could be having an impact on your child in ways that you have not considered. Could you be encouraging bullying without meaning to? Do you:

- fail to take bullying seriously or believe it is happening
- tell children to 'stop telling tales' or 'stick up for yourself'
- blame the bullied child
- show favouritism
- join in with teasing or name-calling as a joke
- use sarcasm as the main method of controlling your children
- use unfair or harsh punishments
- go on about a child's problem in front of others
- blame your child for everything
- laugh at or apparently accept racism, violence or bullying in the media
- leave your child to his or her own devices too often

These are all factors that could lead a child to bully others. If any of these ring true, read on. In Chapter 7, Getting it Right at Home, we'll look at ways to redress the balance.

of discipline and accepted codes of behaviour – or, more importantly, inter-action with others.

Bullies have high self-esteem. Victims have lower self-esteem. As parents and teachers, we need to find the middle ground.

Violence

Researchers have found that children are more physically and verbally aggres-sive immediately after watching violent television and films. It is also clear that aggressive children and teenagers watch more violent television than their less aggressive peers. A few studies have discovered that exposure to televi-sion and movie violence in childhood is related to increased aggression years later.

The case is less strong for the link between youth violence and music videos and video games, because only a small amount of research has been conduct-ed. There is some indication that violent music videos can increase aggressive thinking, but their impact on actual physical aggression has not been established. Violent video games do, however, appear to have an effect on levels of physical aggression.

Television is probably the worst environmental culprit. It repeatedly pres-ents kids with athletes, film stars and politicians who achieve success through aggression. And rather than releasing 'pent-up hostility', watching displays of aggression appears to provoke further aggression.Children view an average of 10,000 acts of violence yearly on television alone. They spend 16–20 hours a week playing video games, and 4–8 hours watching films. In general, 57 per cent of all TV programmes include violence, 73 per cent of which goes unpunished, and for 58 per cent of which no pain is registered as a result. Recent research shows that children who have conduct problems display responses to violent movie clips that indicate a type of numbing-out of violence. Sometimes a smile indicates that responses to the violence have been suppressed. Whereas this could be a survival tactic of some value when conscious, if it becomes too much of a habit, it creates an apparent remorselessness and lack of empathy in the child. Overall, the evidence shows that repeated, merciless violence in the media – newspapers, films, television or the internet – may predispose a child to violent thoughts and acts.

Bullying problems may also reflect cultural and societal tolerance of aggres-sion. The consistent message in media representations of violence is that

Risk factors for bullying

There are individual, family, peer and school factors that can place your child at risk of participating in bullying behaviour. Let's look at these:

Individual risk factors
- impulsive, hot-headed, dominant personality lacking empathy
- difficulty conforming to rules and low frustration tolerance
- positive attitudes towards violence
- physically aggressive
- gradually decreasing interest in school (achievement)

Family risk factors
- lack of parental warmth and involvement
- overly permissive or excessively harsh discipline/physical punishment by parents
- lack of parental supervision

Peer risk factors
- friends/peers with positive attitudes towards violence
- exposure to models of bullying

School risk factors
- lack of supervision during breaks (e.g., lunchrooms, playgrounds, hallways, locker rooms and toilets)
- unsupervised interactions between different grade levels during breaks
- indifferent or accepting teacher attitudes towards bullying
- indifferent or accepting student attitudes towards bullying
- inconsistent enforcement of the rules

aggression is an effective solution to social problems. Studies show that aggressive children are more likely than non-aggressive children to be drawn to and imitate media violence. Bullies, therefore, may be predisposed to act out the aggressive behaviours they view in the media.

And it's not surprising. Constant viewing of violence encourages desensitisation. And when violence is used on television as a vehicle for humour, it is difficult for children to fully understand the difference. Teasing, tricks and acts of cruelty might be funny on television, but in real life they can be devastating. When a child is learning the ropes of life, he or she may not understand that this kind of violence is inappropriate in the real world. This is one reason why it is wise to watch television with your children. The fine line between fantasy and reality (particularly with so many reality television shows littering our screens) can be difficult for a child to discern. Hence adult input is crucial.

? Is your child a bully?

Research shows that bullying can be a sign of other serious antisocial and/or violent behaviour. Children who frequently bully their peers are more likely than others to get into serious trouble. If you aren't sure, it's worth considering the possibility that your child is a bully.

Q: Does your child regularly disobey you?
☐ Yes   ☐ No

Q: Does your child have a bad temper or is s/he 'hot-headed'?
☐ Yes   ☐ No

Q: Do your child's teachers complain s/he causes disruptions in class?
☐ Yes   ☐ No

Q: Does your child enjoy violent video games, music or films?
☐ Yes   ☐ No

Q: Does your child show a 'lack of warmth' towards siblings or you?
☐ Yes   ☐ No

Q: Is your child easily frustrated?
☐ Yes   ☐ No

Q: Has your child skipped school?
☐ Yes   ☐ No

Q: Is the authority figure in your child's life overly permissive or extremely harsh?
☐ Yes   ☐ No

Q: Is your child left alone often?
☐ Yes   ☐ No

Q: Has your child been injured in a fight?
☐ Yes   ☐ No

Q: Does your child often disagree or argue with you?
☐ Yes   ☐ No

Q: Has your child been sent home from school for fighting?
☐ Yes   ☐ No

Q: Has your child ever stolen property or money from you or someone else?
☐ Yes   ☐ No

Q: Has your child ever destroyed property belonging to you or someone else?
☐ Yes   ☐ No

Q: Does your child act out violent scenes from films or video games?
☐ Yes   ☐ No

Scoring: It's obvious! All these questions pinpoint a risk factor for bullying so any yes answers may be significant – and obviously the more there are, the greater the likelihood of a problem. It may well be that your child is supremely well-adjusted and your score is zero. But if you answer yes to as few as 2 or 3 questions, it's time to ask yourself some serious questions. Is there bullying going on that you don't know about? Could your child be a bully?

Warning signs

If you see these immediate warning signs, bullying is a serious possibility:
• loss of temper on a daily basis
• frequent physical fighting
• significant vandalism or property damage
• increase in use of drugs or alcohol
• increase in risk-taking behaviour
• detailed plans to commit acts of violence
• announcing threats or plans for hurting others
• enjoying hurting animals
• carrying a weapon

If you notice the following signs over a period of time, the potential for violence and/or bullying exists:

- history of violent or aggressive behaviour
- serious drug or alcohol use
- gang membership or a strong desire to be in a gang
- access to or fascination with weapons, especially guns
- threatening others regularly
- trouble controlling feelings like anger
- withdrawal from friends and usual activities
- feeling rejected or alone
- having been a victim of bullying
- poor school performance
- history of discipline problems or frequent run-ins with authority
- showing constant disrespect
- failing to acknowledge the feelings or rights of others

Does any of this sound familiar?

Drawing the distinction between typical childhood cruelty and bullying may be difficult. Usually you have to rely on others for information and feedback, because it's unlikely that your child will come home and say, 'This is what I did in school today; I beat up a guy who was bugging me and I stole a girl's lunch.' You need to rely on information from teachers and other families.

Even if your child is quiet and placid at home, don't assume that he or she is the same with his or her peer group. You need to ask good, pointed questions and should also be willing at first just to observe, without trying to jump in and change things. The idea is to see if your child's behaviour is not just an isolated incident, but reveals a pattern over time.

The key is to be aware. We all hope that our children are well-adjusted, happy and have normal relationships with their friends. However, this may not be the case. Don't be caught out. One of the keys to good parenting is sensitivity – you need to be vigilant and keep tabs on what your child is doing. And that doesn't mean asking a lot of questions that can be fobbed off or answered inaccurately. It means watching for signs that all is not well. Remember, bullies are usually popular. They have high self-esteem and they often do very well at school. You may (and quite rightly) be sure that your child is on the right track and that all is well, but it's worth considering, in every case, whether you might be wrong.

What motivates the bully?

Research undertaken by Dan Olweus in 1995 suggests three things that motivate bullies. They might:

• have a need for power and dominance
• be hostile towards the environment and feel satisfied when inflicting injury and suffering
• be compelled to acquire things of value that confer prestige

The first motivation is significant. Several researchers have pinpointed 'power struggles' as a cause of bullying. American bullying expert Richard Hazler believes that power is at the crux of bullying and victimisation, and that children begin learning how to deal with power struggles at an early age. For example, toddlers fighting over a toy are learning about issues of being in control or being controlled. 'Most kids learn how not to be a bully and still have personal power. Most learn how not to be a victim. Adults have been in both roles at one time or another, and we've learned how to deal with those issues in productive ways,' Hazler says. 'All kids have abused the power they have over someone at some time. Most learn it doesn't get them all they want in the long run.'

Good research has been done into the idea that power struggles are behind a great deal of today's bullying. One set of researchers compared schools which had bullying problems with those with no discernible issue and found the same things occurring repeatedly. Even in several good schools, where there was high attendance, good or even excellent examination results and a strong ethos, it was discovered that many of the younger children 'didn't like going to school'. Why? Because they were being bullied in the playground by older children. And this is a recurring feature of bullying in large schools – rather than taking younger children under their wings, stressed-out kids often take out their frustrations on them, making the lives of the littler members of the school a complete nightmare.

Case history

Maria, a year 6 girl, dreaded going to school each day. For some reason unknown to her, several girls in her class had turned against her and for weeks had been whispering behind her back, ignoring her when she spoke, moving away from her when she sat down, leaving nasty notes for her and excluding her from all of their activities. Maria tried to talk to them, but it didn't work. She wondered whether she was carrying the wrong rucksack, didn't have the right trainers... However, the more she tried to fit in, the worse the bullying seemed to get. Maria was afraid to tell her teacher or parents – they might think she was being silly or exaggerating, and should try to solve her own problems. If she told the truth, she believed the girls would be angry and become even more cruel. Maria was a victim of the worst type of 'girlish' bullying – social exclusion, which is every bit as painful as physical abuse.

Types of bullies

Just as there are different types of bullying, there are different types of bullies. Researchers and experts have categorised them according to their overwhelming characteristics.

Aggressive bullies: The most common type of bully, these children are usually strong, fearless, manipulative, have high self-esteem, and fail to empathise with other children and/or adults. Dan Olweus's research shows that this type of bully is most popular in early school years, but less so in later years, when teenagers grow tired of the intimidation and 'tough guy' stance. Aggressive bullies actively seek out power and are motivated by a need to dominate other children. They see hostility where there is none, and perceive normal behaviour in others as being aggressive and incendiary.

Passive bullies: A different kettle of fish, and it's worth noting that these bullies may not be obvious. Passive bullies are usually insecure, and may suffer from lower self-esteem than their aggressive bully peers; however, they are not under-confident, because they do believe in their ability to be 'important'. They are less popular than aggressive bullies, and tend to stay on the sidelines until a bullying session is in progress before becoming involved. While aggressive bullies tend to believe in themselves and do quite well at school, passive bullies are less confident, have trouble concentrating and are more prone to violent outbursts or temper tantrums. In fact, they are much less likable, and it's something that probably irks them. Rather than stick their necks out, they become eager participants in any bullying scenario – after the action has started. They stick with bullies and pretend to be one of them. Most of these bullies have an unhappy home life and hope to redress the balance outside the home.

Verbal bullies: Verbal bullies use words to hurt and humiliate their victims. The verbal bully usually resorts to name-calling, insults, racist comments and constant teasing, either publicly or in private. While this type of bullying may not be as obvious or as physically dangerous, it nonetheless causes great distress and even humiliation. Verbal bullying is the easiest form of attack for a bully. It's quick and painless for the bully, but often remarkably harmful for the victim.

Relationship bullies: This type of bully ambushes his or her target by convincing peers to exclude or reject the victim – they play on a victim's insecurity and know how to press all the right buttons to ensure total humiliation and hurt. These bullies often use the same taunts and teasing that a verbal bully uses, but take it further, by including others, thus isolating the victim and making him or her an easier target. This is an extremely harmful form of bullying because it excludes the victim from his or her peer group at a time when children are making their first social connections.

Reactive victims: Reactive victims bully to feel competent, in order to escape the feelings of powerlessness that threaten to overwhelm them. These victims fall somewhere between bully and victim, and they are often difficult to pinpoint because they frequently appear to be targets rather than perpetrators. However, the usual scenario is that they become so fed up with being bullied that they turn on their bullies, often viciously. They may even become highly oversensitive, reacting to even unintentional slights with anger and violence. The usual defence for this type of bully is 'self-defence', though it clearly runs a lot deeper than that.

Bully-victims: This group represents children who have been bullied themselves and then go on to bully others in an attempt to redress the damage. These bullies often have more characteristics of victims than of bullies (see page 59), and may be physically weaker than most bullies. However, they choose weaker children to bully when it's their turn, and are often provocative in an attempt to inflame a situation. In many cases they provoke trouble and then feel sorry for themselves when they are attacked. Research shows that bully-victims are generally unpopular with their peers, and are more likely than other types of bully to be both anxious and depressed.

In many cases, bully-victims come from households where they are rarely supervised, where parenting and discipline are inconsistent, and where parental warmth is low or absent. In other words, they received little or no help when they themselves were victimised. A number of studies have shown that the most common response to victimisation is anger. Without adult help in channelling their anger in positive ways – such as getting their abusers to stop, or expressing their feelings through words or positive actions – bully-victims get rid of their feelings of victimisation by picking on other children. Several researchers consider bully-victims to be the most potentially violent type of bully, largely because their rage is high and their support network weak.

In her bestselling book, *The Bully, the Bullied and the Bystander*, Barbara Coloroso identified seven types of bullies:

- **Confident bully** – swaggers, powerful personality, big ego [not strong ego], feels good when superior over others
- **Social bully** – uses rumour, gossip, shunning and verbal taunts; devious and manipulative; can act caring and compassionate but uses that to get what s/he wants
- **Fully armoured bully** – cool, detached, shows little emotion and strong determination; vicious and vindictive towards the target but may be charming to others; has trouble identifying feelings deep in a place of darkness and angst
- **Hyperactive bully** – struggles with academic work, poor social skills, probably has a learning disability, doesn't pick up social cues well, reads in a hostile intent where none exists, blames others
- **Bullied bully** – both a target and a victim, bullied and abused, perhaps by older adults or kids; feels powerless and bullies for relief; strikes out at those who hurt her or are weaker; least popular of the bullies
- **Bunch of bullies** – a group of friends who collectively do what they wouldn't do individually; 'nice kids', they know its wrong and it hurts but still do it
- **Gang of bullies** – frightening group who depend on control, domination and subjugation to defend their turf and qualify their actions; they act as a family of sorts, and many members support the group's activities in order to achieve respect; members tend to show disregard for themselves as well as others, with little empathy or remorse.

It is crucial that you discover the reasons why your child is bullying, what factors may have led to his bully 'status', and what types of people and situations encourage him to continue. Also important is to pinpoint the type of bullying that is going on, so that you can take steps to stop him in his tracks. The more you know about the type of bullying, the easier it is to help your child understand why it is wrong. We'll look at the various forms of bullying in the next chapter.

For now, however, it's vital to remember that all sorts of children find themselves in the position of being bullies, and that almost all of these children have experienced events in their lives that have led them to become the type of people they are. Bullying can be very serious, as we will see in the next chapter, and causes enormous distress for its many victims – even to the point of being a catalyst for young people taking their own lives. But with insight and support, you can change patterns of behaviour in even the most hardened bully.

Whether you are the parent of a suspected or confirmed bully, of a bystander, or even of a victim, understanding the psyche of bullies can help you to find the most effective ways to nip the problem in the bud.

2

They Will Find You: The Different Types of Bullying

UK SCHOOLGIRL GAIL JONES WAS 15 YEARS OLD when she took a fatal over-dose in May 2000. She had been bombarded with silent calls and text messages to her mobile phone, sometimes receiving up to 20 in half an hour. Gail's father had suggested that she get rid of the phone, just days before her death, but police required a diary of the nuisance calls in order to track the perpetrators. Before she died, Gail left a suicide text on her phone. She was the victim of one of the newest types of bullying – cyberbullying – and it drove her to take her own life.

Bullying is not a new phenomenon. What is new, however, is that it has become a 24-hour problem. With the advent of the internet, instant messaging and mobile phones, kids are no longer safe even inside their own homes. They can be at the mercy of a well-constructed bullying campaign day and night, no matter where they are or whom they are with. Perhaps that's one of the most frightening aspects of modern-day bullying – that it's potentially non-stop. And this may be one of the reasons why more and more children are driven to take their own lives.

There are many, many types of bullying, some more serious than others. Some cases are even disputable, though it's important to remember that being a victim is all about perception. If a child feels that he is being bullied, that is his reality, no matter how minor an adult may perceive the problem to be. He is being bullied. Having an apple taken from a lunchbox every day can be as disruptive and distressing for some children as being taunted or even beaten up in the play-ground; being sidelined or 'sent to Coventry' by a gang of girls you once considered friends can be as destructive as being called 'fatty' or 'gayboy'. The single most important element of bullying is that a bully takes a well-aimed swipe and finds a victim's Achilles heel. In other words, bullies learn exactly what but-tons to push in order to cause the most offence and hurt; and hurt they do.

Childhood and adolescence represent the most important periods of devel-opment in our lives. Self-image is defined, and the foundations for emotion-al development and interaction are laid down. If this foundation is constantly undermined, it can lead to problems that are carried well into adulthood and sometimes never shifted. Negative self-image is a destructive condition, and is the precursor to later relationship problems, to depression, eating disorders, poor communication skills, weight problems and substance abuse, even sui-cide. In their formative years, kids believe what others tell them – they are pro-grammed to do so. Abuse on any level is unsettling and causes children to question themselves and their identities. For this reason, among many others, bullying should never be ignored, no matter how innocuous it may seem.

The difference between play and bullying

Children are very good at differentiating play fighting from bullying. However, many studies indicate that teachers find this difficult and often misinterpret play fighting or 'rough and tumble' as bullying. This misinterpretation can lead to teachers stopping play fighting or rough-and-tumble play. It's important to make the distinction. Kids who are playing take turns being 'victims' and 'ruffians', or 'chasers' and 'fleers'. No one child is singled out as a victim, and no one child or gang is always in control.

Research indicates that rough-and-tumble play accounts for approximate-ly 17 per cent of school-age children's play, and has developmental value for young children. It can help to develop the skills needed to participate in other types of play, such as games with rules. It may involve a great deal of physical contact between players, such as wrestling, but it is appropriate in that all players are agreeing to it. Children involved in bullying situations, however, do not agree to the physical contact. This is an important difference between play and physical bullying.

Verbal bullying can also be difficult to pinpoint. Some adults confuse bul-lying with teasing, and believe that kids should be left to get on with things. After

Bullying hotspots

Three different studies report students as saying that most bullying occurs in the school playground. Researchers' observations of children in playgrounds and in classrooms confirm that it occurs frequently: once every seven minutes in the playground and once every 25 minutes in class.

Bullying tends to occur in crowded conditions, which are difficult to supervise, and where bullies are likely to attract some peer attention to their handiwork. One study found that teachers are often unaware of playground bullying, and that they intervened to stop only 4 per cent of the bullying episodes.

Bus stops, hallways, locker rooms, changing rooms and school lavatories also provide easy opportunities for bullies to isolate and intimidate their victims. Most incidents last only a few seconds, but in an unstructured setting this is long enough to cause serious harm and distress. Bullying is two to three times more likely to occur at school as on the way to and from school.

The newest type of bullying – cyberbullying, or 'digital bullying' (see page 51) – is on the increase and can take place at any time and virtually anywhere. With so many youngsters instant-messaging one another, sharing email addresses and mobile telephone numbers, the scope for this type of bullying is overwhelming. So the extent to which a child can be bullied, and the fact that the possibilities for these occurrences are virtually limitless, has taken bullying to new heights. You have to be a very aware parent, carer or teacher to keep tabs on the potential hotspots – and a very good detective to find the perpetrators of increasingly anonymous attacks.

all, teasing can be done in a friendly way, with some humour, and can teach children to take themselves less seriously – and to laugh at themselves. But if it leads to embarrassment, anger or distress, it's no longer teasing: it's bullying. All children need to learn the fine line between poking fun and causing pain, even if the victim is perceived to be oversensitive.

Kids can and do tease one another as a form of familiarity and affection. Nicknames can be part of social bonding. Malicious intent is, however, something different. Picking on a child's personal appearance is considered by children to be the most hurtful, though some consider it to be acceptable in the context of friendship. Girls more than boys find this type of ribbing the most distressing, and it has been associated with a higher occurrence of body image problems and eating disorders. It's important to note that most children who are victims of verbal abuse do not report the incidents – partly because they are embarrassed and unsure themselves about whether they are being oversensitive, or whether the aggressors were 'playing', but also because it is much less easy to claim hurt for something that is blatantly emotional, rather than physical. Teachers and parents should always take a child aside if bullying is suspected, and ask for an interpretation. It is, in many cases, the only way to tell the difference between play, social banter and bonding activities – and bullying.

Types of bullying

Bullying can be catalogued into many different types, which is useful in analysing the particular type of bullying that your child or a child in your care may be experiencing. Some are more subversive than others and more difficult to pinpoint. None can be considered any more or less serious. Bullying involves using power to hurt or reject, and the sheer breadth of ways in which this can be done is fairly mind-boggling. The personal experiences noted in the following pages do more than any statistics to explain the distress that bullying can cause.

Physical bullying

This is the most common type of bullying, and the easiest to spot. After all, a black eye or a broken limb is fairly clear evidence that all is not well. However, though young children tend to bully physically, they do not usually cause serious bodily harm – most physical bullying is intended only to embarrass and humiliate the victim. This type of bullying is considered to be 'direct', in that it is directed obviously and with intent to the victim. It can include any type of physical harm, such as pinching, hair pulling, punching, beating, kicking, tripping, or more serious assault. It also includes the threat of physical harm.

There is no clear research suggesting that this type of abuse is any more damaging than less direct types, but boys in particular find it mortifying to be targeted and physically hurt by others. It's often the humiliation rather than the physical pain or injury that causes most distress – and, of course, the way the event is perceived by the peer group and dealt with by school or other authorities.

Case history

Greg, 11, called ChildLine in the UK and explained that he was terrified of going back to school on Monday. 'This group of boys come and find me every playtime. They hit me, punch me, drag me around the playground and tear up my work. I'm always getting into trouble with the teachers for looking scruffy and not handing in my homework.'
Greg told the counsellor that he had horrible nightmares every Sunday. 'I feel as if I can't ever get away from them – they wait for me after school. Last Friday I was hiding in the changing rooms and they found me and blocked the door. One of them had a knife.' The boys had threatened to 'batter him on Monday'.

Direct verbal bullying

Verbal bullying can take two forms – direct and indirect. Both forms can be called emotional bullying as they are designed to affect a victim psychologically rather than physically. The direct form involves taunts, name-calling, verbal threats, incessant mocking or laughing at a victim's expense, and intimidation or insults – to the victim's face. It can accompany physical bullying or take place on its own. There are obviously many ways in which a bully can verbally abuse a victim, including drawing attention to physical abnormalities, race, religion, sexuality, or even gender. We'll look at these in detail below.

Indirect verbal bullying

This type of bullying includes cruel comments behind a victim's back, intended for him or her to overhear, unfair or unkind notes or letters, graffiti and spreading rumours. Girls in particular tend to use this tactic.

An interesting study was performed in the UK in 1998, looking at teachers' attitudes and actions towards bullying between boys and girls. Researchers Sue Birkinshaw and Mike Eslea found that physical and direct verbal acts were significantly more likely to be considered bullying by teachers than were indirect acts. Physical acts were rated by teachers as significantly more distressing than verbal acts, and verbal acts significantly more distressing than indirect acts.

Teachers said they were significantly more likely to punish physical bullying than verbal bullying, and verbal more than indirect.

However, previous research has shown that those children who had experienced bullying felt that social exclusion was the worst form, followed by verbal, then physical. It could be that teachers simply do not recognise indirect acts as bullying, and are not aware of the consequences to the victims.

Case history

Marcus, 11, had this to say: 'I have to pretend that I don't notice that they say my name in a stupid voice, and that they put my name on the wall with the name of the fattest girl in my class. And I have to pretend that I don't notice that they put a note right in front of my face that says Marcus is gay and say really loudly that Marcus is gay when I walk past. And they told the new boy in the class who I was really hoping to be friends with that I was a skunk. And I don't even know what they mean. And so I don't want to go to school any more because I can't even tell because the teachers will say they never saw it. I guess nobody could see it because it's sneaky.'

Exclusion or isolation bullying

Exclusion bullying is considered to be the most painful type of bullying, and has dramatic long-term psychological effects as well as marked short-term behavioural effects. It involves deliberate exclusion from playground activities and friendship groups, or total ignoring of the victim. Girls tend to inflict pain on this type of psychological level. For example, they might ostracise victims by freezing them out of lunchroom seating arrangements, ignoring them in the playground, or shunning them when party invitations are handed out. In extreme cases, victims are ostracised completely by whole year groups – for some perceived fault – and spend their time completely alone. But even short-term exclusion by groups of friends (and this type of bullying also includes pressure to conform) can have devastating effects. Girls are excluded from cliques of so-called friends; they become anorexic or bulimic because they fear being excluded from a group of thinner, more popular girls. Boys reluctantly bully others because they are frightened of not fitting in with a gang at school, or they turn to substance abuse for the same reason. Unfortunately, adults often use exclusion bullying with their own children and with others, so this type of bullying is frequently accepted as a normal and certainly a learned behaviour.

Racial bullying

Ethnic minority children are at risk of racial bullying. Often, rather than being a part of the student body as a whole, they cluster together in smaller groups. Name-calling is one of the common techniques used in racial bullying. Individual taunts are directed towards the child and his or her family as well as towards his or her ethnic group. This type of bullying generally begins in the preschool years. Most racial bullies pick up prejudices and racism from their parents and/or communities. Events such as 9/11 and the London bombings create a climate of fear in which people associated with a 'suspect' religion, faith or ethnic background are ostracised.

In a US study combining data about bullying at and outside of school, 25 per cent of students victimised by bullying reported that they were belittled about their race or religion (8 per cent of these victims were bullied frequently about it). Racial bullying is also a problem in Canada and the UK. In Toronto, one in eight children overall, and one in three of those in inner-city schools, said that racial bullying often occurred in their schools. In four schools – two primary, two secondary – in Liverpool and London, researchers found that Bengali and black students were disproportionately victimised.

Case history

Shamila, 15, called the ChildLine charity in tears saying that she dreaded going to school. She told her counsellor how she used to be outgoing but she 'didn't like talking much now'. For the past month Shamila had been bullied by a gang of girls in her class because, she said: 'I'm about the only Asian girl in my school.' Shamila explained that she couldn't talk to her parents about how she was feeling because her mum and dad were not getting on very well and she didn't want to add to their worries.

Sexual bullying

This type of bullying includes any unwelcome sexual behaviour that interferes with a child's life, including unwelcome sexual advances, demands for sexual favours, sexual rumours, sexual touching and accusations of homosexuality and lesbianism. There can be repeated exhibitionism, voyeurism, propositioning and sexual abuse – frequently undertaken via the internet or mobile phone, thus allowing the bully anonymity. The intention of this type of bullying is to harm, degrade, violate and control, but many adults (teachers included) tend to see it as 'flirting' or put it down to some adolescent mating ritual.

In a UK study involving 25 schools and nearly 3,500 students, 9 per cent of the students admitted to having bullied others by sexual touching. A 2003 study found that the use of sexual put-downs, such as 'faggot', is so common that parents do not think of telling their children that it could be hurtful. Four out of 5 students say they hear and reject expressions of anti-gay bias; less than 5 per cent speak up for the target.

One study found that 51 per cent of schools reported at least one incident of homophobic bullying in the last term, but only 6 per cent of schools had bullying policies that specifically mentioned homophobic bullying. Research also shows that up to 40 per cent of young lesbian, gay or bisexual people have attempted suicide because of bullying at school. Three-quarters of those being bullied have a history of truancy.

Case history

Azmi, *a student at a Canadian secondary school, filed a complaint with the British Columbia Human Rights Commission in June 1996. Year after year, he had been incessantly taunted and teased by his peers, bombarded with homophobic slurs like 'gay', 'faggot' and 'queer', punched, pushed and spat upon, and had various objects thrown at him. Azmi wasn't actually gay, but was harassed as though he was. The school took disciplinary action following each incident, but failed to address the problem in a systemic or proactive fashion. The Tribunal initially sided with Jubran, awarding him damages and ruling against the School Board. That decision was appealed and overturned by the BC Supreme Court. On 6 April 2005, the Court of Appeal reversed the Supreme Court's decision and restored the initial decision by the Tribunal. In its decision, the BCCA confirmed that it's not good enough for school boards to wait for bullying to occur and then discipline the bullies afterwards.*

Sexual harassment in schools

A new report from the US indicates that sexual harassment (words and actions) occurs much more frequently than originally believed, and forms a part of everyday life for schoolchildren.

The report *Hostile Hallways: Bullying, Teasing, and Sexual Harassment in School*, by the American Association of University Women Educational Foundation, was based on a national survey of 2,064 public school students in 8th through 11th grades. Students surveyed were provided with the common definition of sexual harassment as 'unwanted and unwelcome sexual behaviour that interferes with your life. Sexual harassment is not behaviours that you like or want (for example wanted kissing, touching, or flirting).'

According to the report:
- 83 per cent of girls and 79 per cent of boys report having experienced harassment.
- For many students sexual harassment is an ongoing experience: over 1 in 4 students experience it 'often'.
- 76 per cent of students have experienced non-physical harassment while 58 per cent have experienced physical harassment.
- When given 14 examples of non-physical and physical harassment, students say they would be very upset if someone did the following:
  - spread sexual rumours about them (75 per cent)
  - pulled their clothing off or down, in a sexual way (74 per cent)
  - said that they were gay or lesbian (73 per cent)
  - forced them to do something sexual other than kissing (72 per cent)
  - spied on them as they dressed or showered at school (69 per cent)
- Although large groups of both boys and girls report experiencing harassment, girls are more likely to report being negatively affected by it.
- Girls are far more likely than boys to feel 'self-conscious' (44 per cent to 19 per cent), 'embarrassed' (53 per cent to 32 per cent), and 'less confident' (32 per cent to 16 per cent) because of an incident of sexual harassment.

Material bullying

This type of bullying, also known as 'extortion bullying', involves having possessions stolen, belongings damaged and money taken. In some cases, the victim may also be forced to complete homework for the victim, or do other tasks. This type of bullying may sometimes be a further consequence to physical bullying and usually has a prolonged history attached to it, as the bully is rarely satisfied with isolated incidences of extortion. Young children are particularly vulnerable to extortion bullying. Demands for money, possessions or equipment, lunch vouchers and money or food may be made, often accompanied by threats. Children may also be dared or forced to steal from the school, leaving them (at the mercy of the bully) open to further intimidation. It's worth noting that extortion, blackmail and destruction of property are criminal offences, and reporting the crime may be one way to stop a bully in his or her tracks.

Case history

Kyla, 14, said: 'It sounds really oik and stupid but every single day someone opened up my lunch and took my drink. And so maybe I was thirsty and could just have water from the fountain, but it really bugged me. And sometimes I hid my drink in my schoolbag and it was still always stolen. And then my sandwiches were opened up and half of them were eaten. I told my teacher and she said I could put my lunch in her drawer instead of my desk but I felt really stupid doing that. But one day my whole lunch was gone and just crusts and wrappers left, and so I put it in the teacher's desk. They got it anyway. And that day they were really crazy because they also took my pencil case and when I left the school there were three boys there saying that I had to give them my bus fare or they would tell the whole school that my lunch was in the teacher's desk. I don't want to go to school any more. And I told my mum that I don't want lunch.'

Hazing and fagging

Hazing tends to be more common in North America than anywhere else, and involves embarrassing (even humiliating) initiation rituals in secondary schools, universities or colleges, clubs, sports teams, and fraternities and sororities. Although it is considered to be an established method of initiating new students (or testing their worth for entrance into an institution or club), and is accepted by some authorities as being undertaken in a spirit of fun, there is no doubt that this type of behaviour comprises bullying – and can be very serious for the victims. Many US and Canadian schools have taken a stand against hazing, and for the purposes of eliminating it have defined it as 'any act committed against a student, or coercing a student into committing an act that creates emotional, physical or psychological harm to a person, in order for the student to be initiated into or affiliated with a student organisation for any other purpose.' Even more than bullying, hazing often leads to serious injury or death. Under the guise of it being a ritual that everyone has had to undergo, limits are pushed to the extreme. However, because it peaks later than bullying (at its worst in mid-secondary-school years), it often involves alcohol or other substances, takes place off school premises, and can run riot. It's also aimed at the youngest, and most sensitive and vulnerable, members of a school or institution. One victim called it 'institutionalised terrorism'. Common features include binge drinking (even for those who are underage); tattooing; piercing; headshaving; branding; sleep deprivation; physical punishment; kidnapping; consuming unreasonable or unacceptable foods; and inappropriate sexual behaviour.

Fagging is something different again, and has mostly been eradicated from mainly private boarding schools in the UK, where its practice was once considered fundamental to school life. The fagging system allowed older boys to treat younger boys as personal servants, and was used in many cases as an opportunity for gross cruelty. In some institutions, older boys were, until very recently, permitted to use physical punishment against younger boys.

Cyberbullying

There is no doubt that this is one of the most prominent and potentially dangerous types of bullying – mainly because it allows bullies a certain anonymity, but also because it is so invasive and pervasive. Cyberbullying began surfacing as modern communication technologies advanced. Through email, instant messaging, internet chat rooms, text messages and electronic gadgets such as camera phones, cyberbullies forward and spread hurtful images and/or messages. Bullies use this technology to harass victims at all hours, in wide circles, at warp speed. Websites are set up to judge, rate or insult classmates, and then dissolved in an instant – but not before hurt has been achieved. Pay-as-you-go phones are purchased, SIM cards changed frequently and caller details invented, to allow anonymous use. Phones can be set as 'private', so no details appear on a receiver's screen, and instant messaging and emailing allow for screen names that do not betray the bully's identity.

According to a recent survey by UK children's charity NCH, 'Putting U in the Picture', one in five kids has been bullied via a digital phone or computer. Bullying by text message was the most common form of abuse reported, with 14 per cent of children interviewed saying they had received upsetting messages on their mobile phones, a figure that was echoed in a recent Australian study. The interactions run the gamut from disconcerting to downright terrifying. Insults, silent calls and threats target hapless victims, and because so many kids own mobile phones, there is a ready market for this type of bullying.

The NCH survey collated responses from 770 youngsters aged 11 to 19. One in 10 said someone had used a camera phone to snap their picture in a way that made them feel uncomfortable, embarrassed or threatened. Of those, 17 per cent believed the images had been forwarded to others. The report cited instances of 'happy slapping', an extreme form of techno-bullying where physical assaults are recorded on mobile phones and distributed to websites and other phones via video messaging.

According to police and anti-bullying organisations, the happy slapper fad, which began as a craze on the UK garage music scene before catching on in school playgrounds across London, is now a nationwide phenomenon. What makes the attacks all the more bewildering is that many victims do not realise they have been happy slapped until after the event. For this reason, many cases go unreported – egos are bruised and the victim is shocked, but there is often no real physical damage of which to complain.

However, in a number of cases the damage – both physical and emotional – is far more severe. Recently, British police announced that they had arrested three 14-year-old boys in connection with the alleged rape of an 11-year-old girl whose attack was videotaped and sent to peers at her London school.

Bullying by teachers

Bullying at school does not always take place outside the classroom. There are also many cases of bullying by teachers. Possibly the worst aspect of this type of bullying is the fact that parents are often reluctant to believe it, and children reluctant to report it. Furthermore, it's often difficult to pinpoint. Harmless teasing? Or abuse?

While the vast majority of teachers are hardworking people doing a difficult job, there are some who bear resentment and/or have an attitude problem. In the same way that children bully children, teachers can and do use the same tools to harass students – using verbal abuse, public humiliation and even threats of physical harm. The problem is that this type of bullying can be even more subtle and sophisticated than playground bullying, as teachers not only have the forum of a classroom full of children (a willing audience who will usually respond with laughter to overt sarcasm and humiliation), but can roll eyes, make offensive jokes and use body language to make a child feel stupid and worthless without actually or obviously doing anything wrong. Children are brought up to believe that teachers are authority figures and should be respected, which makes this type of bullying extremely confusing. What's more, when a child is threatened by an adult, he is often genuinely afraid to report the incident for fear of having to face the bullying teacher again.

A new study from the USA, undertaken by Dr Stuart Twemlow and entitled 'Teachers Who Bully Students: A Hidden Trauma', found that 25 per cent of teachers surveyed admitted to occasional bullying. Two per cent stated they did it frequently. This can add up to a lot of kids, over the years.

Case history

Clarissa, 15, tells of a bullying campaign by one of her teachers: 'I think it was because my mum is on the board of governors or something. She did things like say: "Oh Clarissa, we know you have your hand up and we know you want to talk – you always want to talk. Oh Clarissa, shall we ask mummy to come in and make sure everyone hears you?" She would always roll her eyes and shrug her shoulders in front of the whole class. She never chose me to do any of the assembly things, and even though all of my grades were As, I only got Cs in her class. I thought I was going mad, but a few people said that they noticed she was really mean to me. So we did a test. I wrote my friend's geography essay for her class and also did my own. My friend got an A star, and I got a C. My friend's essay said: "well reasoned argument and excellent use of the material." I did the same argument and used the material in the same way, and she wrote that I had not thought things out. So then I knew. But I can't tell my mum because she's a governor and she will make a fuss and it will get way worse.'

Bullying at home

Siblings and parents can also bully, using the same techniques and with the same results. As with bullying by teachers, children can be bewildered and doubt their own sanity – accepting the abuse because it comes from a respected member of a family. Few children will admit to being bullied at home – and sometimes it's the only thing that they know, so they assume that it's normal.

There's no doubt that many children will 'cry' bullying or abuse when they are being disciplined in an acceptable fashion. Normal teasing and rough-and-tumble between siblings can also be misconstrued – and there's no doubt that siblings have an uncanny ability to hit hard where it hurts. This is not necessarily abuse or bullying; it's part of learning to live with others and to nego-tiate situations that may not always be favourable. Parents, too, can be tired and frustrated, and can pick on a child, draw attention to weaknesses in the throes of a disagreement, and even be unkind. It can be very upsetting for the child involved, but it can also be difficult for a parent, who may then apologise and feel guilty for having given in to fighting at a child's level.

What constitutes bullying, however, is something different. It becomes abuse if it is persistent. If the hurting, whether it is emotional or physical, continues for a long period.

? Is your child being bullied

In the next chapter we'll look at how to spot the signs of bullying, and how to work out if your child is a victim. It's not as easy as you might think. Scan the types of bullying outlined in this chapter. It can often be difficult to work out the *type* of bullying that is going on because many children employ a multitude of different techniques at one time.

The key is to watch for changes in behaviour and notice the little things – coming home hungry after a good lunch has been packed is a sure sign that something is going wrong. 'Losing' money or clothing, or suffering suddenly from accidents, can also indicate a problem. You may need to use stealth to work out what is going on but there is no doubt that a child in need will eventually feel relief and gratitude that the problem is being addressed and he or she no longer needs to live in fear or shame.

Remember, too, that bullying can take many forms – and, for unlucky kids, virtually every form. The final case history in this chapter is an appalling example of this. The simple message is: act before it's too late.

Case history

Vijay, *a 13-year-old schoolboy, hanged himself only days after being given top marks for a poem he had written about his suffering at the hands of bullies. Vijay's body was found hanging from a banister at his home in Manchester. His family later found a pad in which he had written a diary of his experiences of bullying.*

'I shall remember this for eternity and will never forget,' he wrote.
'Monday: My money was taken.
Tuesday: Names called.
Wednesday: My uniform torn.
Thursday: My body pouring with blood.
Friday: It's ended.
Saturday: Freedom.'

Days before his death Vijay, the eldest of six children, had been given a merit award for a poem he had written about bullying for an English lesson at school – one of the first schools to appoint a full-time counsellor to deal with pupils' problems. The school said it had no idea how Vijay had slipped through the safety net.

In the poem, Vijay wrote:
'I'm frightened and scared, my body has been shaking, my mouth open wide and frozen. The tears drop as they destroy my face. Take my money and flee to where they can go. Bullies I call out. They have no feelings at all.
'Bullies are the people who have no feelings or emotions. They are people who are not so clever at things that others are. They do this because they have no skill for anything else. . .
'Bullies are bad and selfish people. They are also cowardly people, cruel and evil people. They are more than all this but they're also guilty. They hurt us with words, hurt us with body contact, but not clever.
'I'm scared and worried. I feel shaky and cold. My whole body has frozen solid. The beat of my heart goes faster as they come towards me.'

His teacher marked the poem: 'Excellent work, Vijay.'

Schoolfriends said Vijay, who wore a turban, had been subjected to racial taunts on the football pitch and had been bullied by pupils from other schools, too.

3

What Makes a Victim?

One man scorned and covered with scars still strove with his last ounce of courage to reach the unreachable stars; and the world was better for this.

Cervantes, *Don Quixote*

THE IMPACT OF BULLYING ON VICTIMS cannot be underestimated. A wealth of research has confirmed both long- and short-term effects that can undermine the quality of a child's life: his development, self-image, academic prowess, health and ability to form relationships long into the future. Despite this, however, far less is known about victims than about the bullies themselves because the majority of research has centred on the psychology and motivating factors of children who bully. Part of the problem we have in understanding victims is that many children are afraid or embarrassed to admit the extent of the bullying they are experiencing, or to elaborate on the way it makes them feel. Many suffer in silence, and parents become aware of the problem only when much of the damage has been done. Until recently, too, there has been a fairly cavalier approach to victims – 'It's part of growing up' and 'You need to learn to stand up for yourself' were common responses to complaints about bullying – and this has had an impact on the way victims have been treated. Many parents are also uncomfortable with the thought that their child is perhaps not as forthcoming, brave or popular as they would like him or her to be. For this reason, too, many cases of bullying have been swept under the carpet.

However, the growth of anti-bullying initiatives is making it easier for victims to confide in people, including teachers and parents, which means we are getting a better insight into what leads children to become victims, and the effect it has on their lives.

There are several characteristics common to victims, some of which involve what appear to be weaknesses or insecurities. For many parents it can seem a huge injustice to have an already bullied child labelled with such negative qualities, and having our parenting skills questioned can add insult to injury. The word 'victim' is also emotive, suggesting that a child is in some way inferior or pathetic. No loving parent will happily accept that their child is in some way different, or worthy of poor treatment. And there is no doubt that whatever the situation, the personality, or the perceived limitations of your child, he does not ever deserve to be the target of bullying.

It's important to remember that not all of the characteristics below may apply to your child, or reflect on the way you've brought him up, but it's worth considering what researchers have pinpointed as being common to the majority of victims.

Characteristics of victims

Children who are victimised tend to be perceived as being physically weaker and have fewer friends than those who are not victimised. Gay, lesbian or bisexual adolescents are more likely to be victimised than their heterosexual peers, and overweight and obese children suffer more harassment than normal-weight children, particularly among girls. Children are victimised for their physical appearance, mannerisms, or just because they don't 'fit in'. In fact, one survey shows that 'not fitting in' is the most common reason why children are abused by peers.

Myths that sustain bullying

One study into bullying found that in order to justify it, many adults resort to some of the following myths, all of which help to sustain the problem:
- Boys will be boys.
- You should never 'tattle' (tell tales).
- She asked for it.
- If attacked, stand up for yourself.
- He will always be a victim.
- Bullies suffer from a lack of self-esteem.

Another 1996 study found that victims are not only bullied for gender, appearance or race, but because of the way they behave. Research shows that children who are repeatedly victimised are more likely to reward bullies by giving up their lunch money, by crying or showing humility, and are less likely to present a threat by fighting back.

According to Peter Sheras, PhD, an expert in adolescent development, the essential quality that a bully looks for in a victim is not difference, but vulnerability. This quality allows a bully to abuse without fear of retaliation. Sheras believes, for example, that a child who wears less fashionable clothes, but has good social skills and friends is not vulnerable to attack, whereas a child who is less fashionable, has poor social skills and is isolated, is an excellent target. He also claims that shyness, a lack of friends and the absence of adult support will make a child a particularly likely mark.

The same US researchers who developed a list of 19 characteristics common to bullies also came up with a list of 21 qualities shared by most victims. Richard Hazler, lead author of the study, says, 'The experts clearly saw the home environment as providing strong indicators of negative factors in the environment of bullies and victims. For victims, the experts agreed that fear of going to school and having families that may be over-involved in the students' decisions and actions were other important characteristics that differentiated the victims from others.'

These experts agreed that victims:
• believe that they cannot control their environment*
• have ineffective social skills*
• have poor interpersonal skills*
• are less popular than others
• have underlying fears of personal inadequacy
• blame themselves for their problems
• are given labels suggesting inadequacy
• are isolated socially
• are afraid of going to school
• are physically younger, smaller and weaker than peers
• have limited skills for gaining success and acceptance
• run out of communication capabilities during high stress incidents
• have a poor self-concept

- show physical mannerisms associated with depression
- have frequent feelings of personal inadequacy
- perform self-destructive actions
- believe others are more capable of handling various situations
- have difficulty relating to peers
- have family members who are over-involved in the student's decisions and activities
- believe that perceived progressive failures cause this person to put forth less effort with each presenting opportunity
- feel external factors have more of an impact on them than internal control

* denotes characteristics which all 14 experts agree are common to victims.

Other researchers have found that victims tend to score higher on internalising and psychosomatic behaviours, meaning that instead of aggressively acting out they are prone to anxious and depressed feelings, perhaps to the point of displaying physical symptoms. There are also several types of victims (see page 62–4), some of whom are slightly less 'innocent' in that they can stir up trouble. Some children, in particular proactive victims, seem actively to draw bullying responses to themselves by pestering, insulting, baiting or invading another child's space. They may be irritating (hyperactive, for example) and even unintentionally exasperate their peers by being socially awkward or chronically annoying. Many victims also lack humour and positive social skills, meaning that they may crumble or display signs of distress with even very minor teasing. Social skills are particularly important (see pages 98–101). If a child uses 'inappropriate' group entry tactics, he may set himself up as a target for other children. And without peer protection and good friends, kids are more likely to be rejected and subject to victimisation.

Perceived weakness

Children become victimised for many different reasons and there is not a single victim type. Your child may have one or more of the above characteristics, as well as what bullies perceive to be a weakness. For some children, these characteristics are present before bullying occurs. For others, they may develop as a result of bullying.

Both boys and girls report being victimised because of their gender. And, as discussed in Chapter 1, age also plays a part, with younger children being more likely to be bullied then older ones. Temperament, too, plays a role. Some victimised children tend to be anxious and withdrawn – there is more evidence of this among preschool children than among school-aged children. Physical appearance is another issue, though it tends to be because victims look 'different', rather than unattractive.

Self-esteem is an issue also (see page 72). Victims often report low self-esteem, again as a result of their upbringing or personal environment, but also because of repeated exposure to bullying. And another chicken-and-egg scenario is depression. Both boys and girls who are victimised report symptoms of depression, such as sadness and loss of interest in activities. This may, however, be caused by bullying rather than being present before bullying begins. Remember, it takes only one bullying episode to undermine a child's self-esteem and emotional wellbeing. A perfectly happy, innocent child who is bullied can develop serious problems with self-image and self-belief, which has the added effect of making him more vulnerable and therefore more susceptible to bullies. Similarly, both boys and girls who are victims report symptoms

... children who are repeatedly victimised are more likely to reward bullies by giving up their lunch money, by crying or showing humility, and are less likely to present a threat by fighting back.

of anxiety, such as tension, fears and worries. These may be present before the bullying begins, or they may be the direct result of being systematically picked on. Either way, when children are damaged by bullying, they set themselves up for further abuse by developing a 'victim mentality'. This is one reason why parental or school intervention at an early stage is essential.

A 1997 study found that victims are often targeted for being either too 'clever' or below average intelligence, or for being of a lower socio-economic background. Victim characteristics often differ by gender as male victims are often not 'tough' and tend to have a close relationship with their mother. Girls, on the other hand, are bullied for being unattractive, not being dressed fashionably and being physically overdeveloped. Other research has concluded that victims, regardless of gender, tend to have over-protective mothers and emotionally negative fathers. Victims tend to have poorer family functioning and poorer relationships with parents, with female victims reporting negative feelings towards their mothers and male victims reporting negative feelings towards absent fathers in single-mother families. Female victims are also more likely to come from dysfunctional families than male victims.

Types of victims

Victims are generally divided into passive and provocative victims, a classification devised by researcher D. Ross in 1996. Other researchers have gone on to break down these groups even further. If your child is being bullied, it is worth trying to work out which group s/he fits into. Only then can the situation be appropriately and successfully addressed.

Passive victims

Passive or submissive victims do not directly provoke bullies but signal to others through attitudes and behaviours that they are insecure individuals who will not retaliate if victimised. These represent the largest group of victimised children. They tend to be socially withdrawn; often seem anxious, depressed and fearful; and have a poor self-image. They have fewer friends than most children (some seem to have none at all), and appear lonely, sad and nervous about new situations – all of which can act as a red flag to a potential bully, who has an uncanny ability to detect vulnerability in other children.

In the primary-school years, passive victims tend to respond to bullies by crying, withdrawing and presenting 'futile anger', which has the effect of making them the butt of jokes and further humiliation. In later years, passive victims tend to take steps to avoid bullying encounters, which often translates into absenteeism from school (often unknown to parents) and even attempts to run away from home.

While it is clear that some passive victims have characteristics that contribute to their victimisation, it is also apparent that many of their personal attributes are the direct result of being bullied. It's a self-perpetuating cycle in which the victim becomes increasingly fragile and susceptible to bullying.

Common characteristics of passive victims include:
• Being physically weaker than their peers (particularly boys).
• Displaying 'body anxiety'. They are afraid of being hurt, have poor physical coordination, and are less skilled in physical play or sports. Boys especially rate physical prowess as important, and hold gifted sportsmen in high regard; a

failure to be a useful team member or exhibiting amusing attempts to perform are all features that attract bullying.

- Having poor social skills and difficulty making friends.
- Being cautious, sensitive, quiet, withdrawn and shy.
- Crying or becoming upset easily.
- Being anxious, insecure and suffering from poor self-esteem.
- Having difficulty standing up for or defending themselves in peer groups.
- Relating better to adults than to peers (which may also be the product of suffocating or overly close parenting – see page 66).

Subgroups

Passive victims have also been broken into smaller groups; these include:

Vicarious or surrogate victims, who either witness or hear about bullying incidents at school. These children are victims of the school's climate of fear. They worry about their own potential to become targets of bullying. They choose not to help victims of bullying or report bullying incidents, even though they often feel sympathetic, because they are frightened of direct retribution from bullies. This often leads to feelings of guilt. Their anxiety makes them more vulnerable, and thus a target for bullying themselves.

False victims tend to be a small group of children who frequently complain without justification that they are being bullied. False victims have a need for attention and sympathy. Unfortunately, it has the opposite effect in most cases, as teachers and parents become immune to their complaints, and, if genuine bullying does occur, fail to believe or recognise it. What's more, other children suffer, as all complaints about bullying may be ignored.

Perpetual victims are those victims who are bullied all of their lives. Some children may develop a victim mentality, in which the victim role becomes a permanent part of their psyches. This not only makes them more vulnerable to bullying, but makes them less likely to get support and sympathy.

Provocative victims

According to Dan Olweus, provocative victims are characterised as 'hot-tempered, restless, anxious, and ones who will retaliate when attacked'. These victims tend to be less common than passive victims, and their behaviour may make them hugely unpopular with peers. Not surprisingly, they also receive far less support and sympathy from adults and other children because there is an overwhelming (and often accurate) belief that they encourage the bullying, and bring it on themselves.

Provocative victims tend to possess a series of characteristics that are likely to disrupt a classroom and lead to social rejection by peers. These include irritability, restlessness, messing around when others are trying to concentrate, overt silliness and hostility. They may share characteristics with some bullies, in that they can be dominant and aggressive, act antisocially and have low levels of tolerance for others, as well as sharing with passive victims social insecurity, a perception that others dislike them and low self-esteem.

In 1997, researcher Peter Randall presented a good example of this type of victim in Nathan, aged ten: 'He was described by his class teacher as a child who lived "on the edge of his nerves", never still, and with "his brain disconnected from his mouth". The latter trait made it likely that he would make loud remarks about other children's appearance or their work that would make them angry. He would then say to them, "What are you going to do about it then?", whereupon two or three of them might show him, violently. Nathan was described as the most unpopular child in the school, as the one "everybody loves to hate". '

Many children who fall into this category suffer from disabilities, such as attention disorder problems, learning disabilities and even conditions such as Tourette's. In such cases, they unintentionally annoy their peers and as a result are more likely to be abused by them. In other words, not all provocative victims are aware that their behaviour is aggressive, disruptive, challenging or inflammatory.

Common characteristics of provocative victims include:
- Exhibiting some or all of the characteristics of passive or submissive victims.
- Being hot-tempered and attempting to fight back when victimised – usually not very effectively.
- Being hyperactive, restless, having difficulty concentrating and creating tension.
- Being clumsy, immature and exhibiting irritating habits.
- Being disliked by adults, including teachers.
- Trying to bully students weaker than themselves.

Annoyed by vulnerability

Bullies choose their victims not only because they are vulnerable and less likely to retaliate, but also because they unintentionally wind up the bully by reminding them of aspects of themselves that they would rather not address. Psychologist Nathanial Floyd believes that the defenceless children who end up as victims remind bullies of their own defencelessness against abuse at home and the shame and humiliation it causes them. Bullies, he believes, feel threatened by their victims' vulnerability. 'In every bully, there is the shadow of the little kid who was once abused himself,' Floyd says. They bully 'as if to say, "You're the victim, not me". '

Factors that contribute to victimisation

Earlier we looked at characteristics that many bullied children share, and some of these should be elaborated upon to present a clear picture of why some children are more susceptible to bullying than others, and to offer insight into areas that parents or teachers can address to help rectify the problems. Some of these factors include parenting styles; emotional influences, such as insecure attachment; poor problem-solving skills; low self-esteem; and poor social skills and social cognition.

The influence of parenting styles

Parental warmth and some degree of parental control over children's behaviour are thought to be crucial in the development of social competence. Just as particular parenting practices have been associated with the development of bullies, so too have certain parenting techniques been linked to the development of victim behaviour in children. Various researchers have identified factors such as insecure attachment to the primary caregiver as being associated with victimisation (see page 71). Others have focused on gender differences, looking at how different behaviours by mothers and fathers relate to different victim behaviour in girls and boys.

Research on bullying published by the British charity Young Voice claims that parenting styles can influence whether children will become the victims or the perpetrators of bullying. They found, for example, that 42 per cent of severely bullied boys were victims of some form of violence at home, and 35 per cent of severely bullied boys were beaten at home. The charity's executive director, Adrienne Katz, said that, 'children need to learn to fight their own corner – and if children are deprived of the experience of fighting back in the safety of their own home, it can make them more likely to become victims.'

Further Young Voice research found the over-protective or neglectful parents increased the risk of their children being bullied. Young people who were victims of bullying were more likely to complain of over-protective parents who 'treat me like a baby', parents who 'take no notice of me' or who 'try to control everything I do'.

Other research has also shown that parents who dominate their children, or who do not allow them to make their own decisions, leaving them without the self-confidence necessary to resist bullying, are also more likely to produce children who are victims. Parents who are overly involved in their children's activities, and give them little autonomy, raise kids who feel that they have no control over their own environments, resulting in an inability to deal with social situations or problems.

According to a 1989 Scottish study of bullying, it appears that children living with their father only, or with someone other than their parents, are more likely to be victims of bullying. Only children are slightly less likely to be bullied and children with two siblings are least likely. According to Scandinavian research, being a bully or a victim is unrelated to the socio-economic conditions of student's family, such as parental education or income; however, the Scottish study found that children of parents with professional and managerial jobs were less likely and those with parents who were skilled manual workers were more likely.

Could you be contributing to the problem?

It's hard for parents to admit that their actions or parenting methods may be at the root of their child's problem, but because so many aspects of the victim status, such as self-esteem, self-belief, self-image, social skills and resilience, have their roots in childhood and upbringing, it is important at least to consider whether or not there are ways that you can change how you relate to your child. The following questions may help you to see areas that need attention.

1. Do you regularly make decisions for your child?

Yes could mean overdominant parenting. Children learn by making their own decisions.

2. When your child makes his own decisions, do you challenge them and suggest another way?

Yes could mean overdominant parenting. Children need to be confident enough to make decisions, learn the consequences of mistakes, and then go on to rectify them.

3. Do you allow your child to make his own mistakes?

No could mean overdominant parenting. Children learn through mistakes.

4. Does your child have regular responsibilities around the house, for which he is praised?

Without responsibility, children do not learn self-respect or initiative, and they do not develop a sense of pride in their achievements. Responsibility is empowering and raises self-esteem. The correct answer is yes.

5. Do you offer praise for effort?

Praise encourages children to feel good about themselves, and to repeat the action that garnered that praise. In other words, they will learn not to give up and to give their very best.

6. Do you reward good results?

Good results, whether it is a bedroom cleaned to expectations, good grades at school, good behaviour or an achievement of any nature deserves to be rewarded – in line with the theory of 'learned behaviour'. When a child is rewarded, he continues this behaviour. It encourages confidence and self-esteem, and a feeling of self-respect, all of which 'bullyproof' a child.

7. Do you respect your child's privacy?

All children need privacy, and respect for your child will help him to develop self-respect as well as respect for others.

8. Do you respect your child's opinion?

Whether you share it or not, all children should be given the opportunity to express an opinion and to defend or debate it without fear of recrimination or punishment. Self-confident children are those who can communicate freely, and they are also more likely to develop the social skills necessary to defend themselves against bullies.

9. Do you criticise the way your child looks or the way he acts?

If you appreciate your child as an individual, he will become more confident and self-assured.

10. Do you offer to take over or 'do it yourself' when your child experiences difficulties?

Parents who take over do not give their children the opportunity to test out their own problem-solving skills, and a lack of these underpins many cases of bullying. Again, children need to make their own mistakes and, with your guidance rather than an 'I'll do it for you' approach to parenting, your child will learn to take pride in his abilities and have the confidence to deal with new situations and problems.

11. Do you organise your child's life, in particular his activities and free time, so that he has little say about what he does?

All children need freedom to choose, and deserve to be empowered enough to make their own decisions. Free time is essential for children of all ages, and the way children spend it should (within reason) be dictated by their own interests. Children who have quality time alone or with their peers, should they choose, are more confident about their abilities and themselves.

12. Do you have very high aspirations for your child, which may not be age appropriate or even feasible?

Overly high aspirations can dent a child's confidence and be a source of stress. Regularly failing to meet your expectations will result in poor self-image, poor self-esteem and a negative attitude.

13. Do you spend regular time with your child, and just listen rather than offering advice?

All children, no matter what their age or situation, want their parents to know how they are, and would love to be able to rely on them in times of trouble. Children who are offered a listening ear rather than constant advice also learn more problem-solving skills, which helps to deflect the bullies.

14. Do you criticise your child's friends?

Children need the space to make their own choice of friends, whether you approve or not. Criticism is about control, not acceptance.

15. Do you know who your children's friends are?

Understanding your child and opening the door to communication means showing an interest in the little things in their lives, including friendships. In times of trouble, it helps to know who his friends are.

16. Do you have a clear idea of what your child does in his spare time?

Again, an interest in your child's activities is important for communication. If a parent-child relationship is strong and open, a child is much more likely to have the strength to defend himself against bullying.

17. Do you allow your child age-appropriate freedom?

All children need freedom to be themselves, to take on new responsibilities, to test their problem-solving skills, and to make their own decisions. Check with other parents you trust to ensure that your child is doing things that other children are allowed to do. Children who are overparented and allowed little freedom tend to withdraw.

18. Does your household have more rules than most?

Rules are important, but so is personal freedom and the empowerment of all members. If you rob a child of all power, he will feel frustrated, lose the ability to self-regulate, and develop low self-esteem, all of which contribute to a victim status.

19. Do you discipline consistently and with warmth, taking the time to explain rules and expectations rather than taking the 'do it because I said so' approach?

Parenting is not an easy job, but if you bully rather than explain, you miss the opportunity to teach your child something of the world around him. He'll learn to believe that his feelings and opinions are valueless, and that his actions are controlled externally rather than internally. He will then be more susceptible to outside hostility and influences.

20. Did you have any trouble bonding with your child when he was an infant?

Poor attachment with a baby can lead to problems in later life (see page 71).

21. Did you suffer from post-natal depression or extended baby blues?

Insecure attachment, which is now known to be a precursor to becoming a victim, may have been the result.

22. Did you return to work before your baby was six months old?

Your child may suffer from insecure attachment.

23. Are you comfortable with physical affection, including hugs, kisses and other signs of a warm relationship?

The power of touch has been widely documented. A child who is offered physical affection is much more likely to feel good about themselves and their bodies, and to develop self-respect and self-esteem.

24. Do you get involved in arguments between your children?

Parents who overly involve themselves in the arguments of their children do not allow them to develop negotiating skills, learn self-defence, or understand the way people operate together. Children who are reliant on their parents to fight their battles are not resilient.

25. Do you offer plenty of opportunities for your child to interact on his own with other children?

The development of social skills from a young age is crucial to a child's ability to engage with peers, and to avoid becoming a victim.

26. Do you encourage self-expression, even if you don't like what you hear?

Self-expression is crucial. A child who believes his opinions are valueless will not be confident enough to stand up to a bully, and may avoid situations where he is challenged in any way, or put on the spot.

27. Does your child have a reasonable number of material goods that are considered 'must-haves' at his school?

Although love and a stable upbringing are far more important than material goods, there is, unfortunately, a great deal of emphasis placed upon having the 'right' clothing or possessions. While it is important to teach children that personality and attitude are the keys to making friends, it is also important that your child does not draw undue attention to himself by being different – particularly if he does not want to. A social leper will never develop confidence. Teach your child the difference between wants and needs, but be sure to listen to what he considers to be needs!

28. Do you allow your child to choose the way he dresses without comment?

Empowering a child leads to greater self-esteem. Individuality is a trait to be celebrated in children, and when children are allowed to make choices, they develop a strong sense of self-worth and self-image.

29. Do your children know that it is OK to express anger or dissatisfaction?

Children who are never given the opportunity to express negative emotions may internalise them, and either take them out on others, or internalise them, making it difficult for them to communicate effectively, or to develop a strong sense of self-worth.

30. Do you use humour when you discipline or relate to your children?

Laughter is important to good health and wellbeing, and all children deserve the opportunity to find happiness in their home. Children who are used to laughter are much more resilient, are less prickly when others laugh, and learn to laugh at themselves – one of the most important traits there is.

31. Do you become involved in your children's homework?

All children need guidance, but when a parent takes over a child's domain, the child is disempowered, and learns nothing but frustration and resentment

– as well as developing a low sense of self-worth and a lack of trust in his own abilities.

32. If your child tells the truth, are you likely to punish or blame?
Children need the safety net of unconditional love that only a parent can offer. If your child is honest with you, or reports a problem, he should not be blamed. Children who develop a strong line of communication with their parents are more confident and experience higher self-esteem. They will also be more likely to report bullying incidents if and when they arise, which is crucial to the success of dealing with them.

33. Is there someone at home when your child arrives back from school?
Latch-key kids often experience a sense of neglect, which can make them feel less worthy and more susceptible to bullying.

Insecure attachment

Several studies, including one undertaken in South-East London by Rowan Myron-Wilson and Peter K. Smith, show that early insecure attachment has been found to predict increased aggression with peers and difficulties with conflict resolution. The association between insecurity and aggression difficulties indicates that an insecure child is more likely to become involved in bullying (ironically, both as a bully and/or victim), implying that bullying behaviour is influenced by early attachment relationships.

Attachment usually develops during the first year of life. As we get older we are able to reattach to different people: our partners, children and friends. Generally speaking, attachment occurs when the child feels that the parent is not interchangeable with any other adult, and the parent feels the child occupies an essential place in his life. Attachment is important, because an attached child is a secure child. A secure child has healthy self-esteem and as she grows up will be able to face life's challenges in an effective and mature way.

For attachment to work, a parent must react to the child's helplessness and respond to the child's needs. This way the child knows he can rely on his or her primary caregiver in times of danger; he or she feels secure. The first person with whom the baby attaches takes on an exaggerated importance as the child relies on the caregiver for everything. Feeding, smiling, eye contact and movement are all ways that infants and their parents interact, and the child learns to feel secure.

Insecure attachment can lead to a poor image of self and an inability to relate to others (the precursor to poor social skills), all of which set up a child for victimisation.

It seems, then, that both overprotective parents and those who fail to bond sufficiently with their children as babies are more likely to produce children who become victims of bullying.

Self-esteem

A child's self-esteem is crucial to his victim status. In other words, if he has low self-esteem, he is much more likely to be chosen as a bullying target – largely because he does not have the confidence to defend himself or to retaliate when confronted. Being bullied compounds self-esteem issues; at least nine different studies show that being bullied leads to depression and low self-esteem, problems that can carry on into adulthood. With a loss of self-esteem comes a loss of self-confidence and self-belief, and several researchers have shown that many victims begin to believe they deserve to be bullied. They've also found that the victims of bullying see themselves in a more negative light than students who have not been bullied.

Signs of low self-esteem include:
- social withdrawal
- anxiety and emotional turmoil
- lack of social skills and self-confidence
- depression and/or bouts of sadness
- less social conformity
- eating disorders
- inability to accept compliments
- inability to see yourself accurately, or to be fair to yourself
- accentuating the negative
- exaggerated concern over what you imagine other people think
- self-neglect
- treating yourself badly but not other people
- worrying whether you have treated others badly
- reluctance to take on challenges
- reluctance to trust your own opinion
- expect little out of life for yourself

Social skills and social cognition

Bullied children, or those who are rejected by their peers, often display social skills that make them undesirable playmates and friends. Children who act in an aggressive or disruptive manner (provocative victims, for example), account for about one third of all bullied children. Furthermore, children who withdraw from peer interactions also limit their ability to fit into their peer group, while socially isolated children have a more difficult time adequately developing the skills needed to be accepted among peers.

Because they often lack social skills, victims of bullying frequently misinterpret ambiguous statements, resulting in negative feelings. Children who are teased often perceive the teaser as wanting to fight or teasing them because they enjoy the reaction they get. Emotions play an important part when children 'process social cues'. If a child experiences negative feelings, she may interpret another person's intent as hostile.

Not surprisingly, many children with social skills deficits find themselves ostracised due to their inability to handle the back-and-forth of conversation, and difficulty reading common social cues. They often irritate others, unaware of the negative impact they are having and not knowing when to quit. They are often surprised and unprepared for the negative responses they receive. And they are prime targets of bullying.

Stress

Just as stress may cause children to bully, it is also the byproduct of bullying. Almost all victims report feeling overwhelming stress. When emotional and physical health suffer as a result, a child's self-esteem dips and he or she loses confidence and feelings of capability. As a result, children can develop something of a victim mentality – through factors that are completely out of their control. Stress is examined in more detail in Chapter 6.

The impact of bullying

This is an area that has been increasingly studied around the world, and one that all parents and teachers should note. Most children do not 'grow out' of the feelings they experience when they are bullied; many carry them into adult life and suffer from long-term social problems and feelings of inadequacy. Moreover, an Australian study found that victimisation in middle adolescence predicted poorer physical health in later adolescence. The psychosocial

Friendships

Most research points to the fact that the majority of bullied children do not have many (if any) close friends and do not, therefore, have a support group within their peer environment.

In general, children who are bullied may perceive themselves negatively (particularly after repeated harassment and victim-isation), and shy away from confrontation and conflict – traits that other students may pick up on. As a result of the bullying, they may often appear distressed, unhappy, depressed and tearful, and their performance and interest in school may begin to deteriorate. These qualities and behaviours are not precursors to healthy and useful friendships.

Further, bullied children may frequently be chosen last for teams or other group activities, which isolates them, and lowers self-esteem even further. If bullied repeatedly, they may also try to stay close to the teacher or other adults during breaks, avoid lavatories and other isolated areas, and/or make excuses to stay home from school as much as possible, none of which is conducive to building all-important friendships.

Furthermore, victims of bullying often lose their friends both directly and indirectly as a result of their bullying experiences. Some friends confuse a victim's efforts to avoid the bully with attempts to avoid them; others are afraid of becoming victims themselves; and still others come to dislike the victim due to his inability to deal more effectively with the bully.

A 1993 Australian study by P. T. Slee and Ken Rigby, involving 87 boys from primary school, found that personality played a large part in being bullied. In particular, a strong link was found between being bullied and being quiet and shy (introverted). It was pointed out that an introverted child might well feel uncomfortable in a group and as a result might prefer to spend time alone. This 'staying apart' might also increase the chances of being bullied. In addition to the link between being bullied and introversion, this study also found a strong link with low self-esteem.

consequences of bullying are also significant: victims of bullying have reported increased rates of depression, suicidal intentions and loneliness. One study in particular showed that young people who had been bullied repeatedly throughout middle adolescence had lower self-esteem and higher depressive symptoms as young adults, compared to those who had not been bullied. Victimisation has implications for academic success as well. Experiencing peer harassment has been associated with lower grades, disliking school and absenteeism. In addition, people who were victimised as children or adolescents have increased rates of violence-related behaviours.

In 1998, the UK charity Kidscape conducted a retrospective survey of over 1,000 adults to find out if bullying in school affects people in later life. It showed that bullying not only affects self-esteem in adulthood but also the ability to make friends and to succeed in education, work and social relationships. A follow-up study, 'Bullying at School', by psychologist Dan Olweus found that by the time former male victims of bullying were in their early twenties, they had generally made a positive social adjustment, as they had more freedom to choose their social and work milieu. However, they were more likely to be depressed, and had lower self-esteem than a comparison group who had not been bullied.

A 1987 study also revealed that adult males who were bullied as children were more likely to be 'love-shy' than non-victims, suggesting that the social withdrawal experienced by bullied children appeared to lead to later problems in forming adult relationships. Research presented in 1994 reported that adults who were bullied as children had recurring memories of these events and that there is evidence of psychological distress in their adult lives.

And, in the short term, there are both physical and psychological factors to consider. Physical abuse can cause serious injury, such as broken bones and internal injuries, but even minor injuries, such as bruising and lacerations, can undermine a child's overall health and wellbeing.

Psychological injuries include anxiety, embarrassment, guilt, loneliness, loss of self-esteem and depression, as well as psychosomatic, sleep, speech, obsessive-compulsive and dissociative disorders, panic attacks, paranoia, self-mutilation, plus delays in physical, mental and emotional development. The most severely bullied students develop post-traumatic stress disorder, as do many domestic violence and child abuse victims.

Research also indicates a strong correlation between bullying and suicide.

Three studies by Ken Rigby and associates in Australia between 1993 and 1996 found that suicidal thoughts and self-harm were significantly associated with bullying. Rigby points to the 'growing number of accounts of children committing suicide following a history of peer victimisation. It is difficult not to conclude that severe bullying for some children can be devastating.'

The psychological harm continues into adulthood. The 1998 Kidscape study found that in later life 46 per cent of those who were bullied contemplated suicide compared to 7 per cent who were not. The results of Olweus's study showed that former bullying victims have higher levels of depression and poorer self-esteem at the age of 23 years, despite the fact that they may no longer be harassed or socially isolated. 'Those who have been bullied may view such treatment as evidence that they are inadequate and worthless and may internalise these perceptions.' Bullying victims are also more likely to become victims as adults.

The problem is serious, and its effects often underestimated. The sooner the bullying is stopped, the better the long-term outcome for victims. And the earlier you can achieve a resolution and take steps to improve your child's self-image, self-esteem, social skills and status with his peers, the less likely it is that the damage will be long-standing.

? Is my child being bullied?

Do not assume that you will be the first to know. Even children who are very close to their parents are often embarrassed to admit that they are being bullied, for fear of letting them down, or being over-emotional. Many children may also be unaware of what exactly constitutes bullying, and believe that extortion or verbal abuse, which do not leave physical scars, may not be worth reporting. Adolescents in particular are notorious for withdrawing from parental communication, and many parents may not have a clear idea about what is going on in school – or on the streets after classes.

Don't beat yourself up if you've missed the signs. A 2002 paper stated that teachers – who are in close contact with bullies and victims for the entire school year – could accurately identify 50 per cent of the bullies, but were able to pick out only 10 per cent of the victims.

According to researcher Peter Sheras, exhibiting the following warning signs may indicate that your child is being victimised at school, at home, in the neighbourhood, or elsewhere:

- reluctance to go to school
- complains of feeling sick; frequent visits to the nurse at school
- sudden drop in grades
- coming home hungry (because bullies have stolen lunch or lunch money)
- frequently arriving home with clothing or possessions destroyed or missing
- experiencing nightmares, bedwetting, difficulty sleeping
- appearing afraid of meeting new people, trying new things, or exploring new places
- refusing to leave the house
- waiting to get home to use the lavatory
- acting nervous when another child approaches
- showing increased anger or resentment with no obvious cause
- making remarks about feeling lonely
- having difficulty making friends
- reluctance to defend himself when teased or criticised by others
- showing a dramatic change in style of dressing
- having physical marks – bruises, cuts, etc. – which may have been inflicted by others or by himself

You may want to consider some of these other warning signs, which are appropriate to age:

Primary school
- regressive behaviour, such as thumb-sucking, talking in a baby voice, clinginess, temper tantrums or bedwetting
- leaving school with torn or disordered clothing and/or damaged books
- having bruises, injuries, cuts and scratches that are not easily explained
- saying they 'hate' a particular person, but won't elaborate on why
- fewer playdates or invitations
- embarrassment about things, such as clothing, appearance or material possessions, which have never been a feature before
- using words that are age-inappropriate, and often with intent to hurt
- becoming more violent towards siblings, parents or friends, without real reason

Secondary school

- not bringing classmates or other peers home after school and seldom spending time in the homes of classmates
- may not have a single good friend to share free time with (play, shopping, sports and musical events, chatting on the phone, etc.)
- is seldom or never invited to parties and may not be interested in arranging parties (because they suspect nobody wants to come)
- does not participate in extracurricular activities such as school clubs
- chooses an illogical route to and from school
- loses interest in school work
- appears unhappy, sad, depressed, or shows unexpected mood shifts with irritability and sudden outbursts of temper
- requests or steals extra money from family (to accommodate the demands of bullies)
- becomes obsessed with a mobile phone and reluctant to explain persistent calls or texts
- becomes increasingly sensitive about or obsessed with physical features, weight, clothing, etc.
- begins to bully other family members for no obvious reason
- becomes highly critical of activities and people s/he used to enjoy

If your child exhibits any of these symptoms, s/he needs your help. Be prepared to investigate further whether your child provides an explanation or not, and take the role of listener and detective rather than allowing your frustration, anger and concern to overwhelm your child.

In the next chapter we'll look at how to tackle the problem, from the bottom up – dealing with the various types of bullying, and working on all the aspects that may be contributing to your child adopting the role of victim. It's not easy to turn things around, but it is possible with insight, determination and, of course, love.

Who do children talk to?

Research commissioned in 2003 by the UK's leading children's charity, ChildLine, uncovered some interesting facts about who children turn to when they are bullied. The research found that:

- More than two-thirds of secondary-school pupils said they would not feel comfortable talking to a teacher about being bullied because they were concerned that they wouldn't be taken seriously or would suffer reprisals as a result. Children believe that some teachers are better at dealing with bullying than others – those they would be likely to speak to were 'firm but fair', better at listening, and more likely to take them seriously.
- Friends topped the poll of people children said they would talk to if they were being bullied. Seventy per cent of pupils said that friends were crucial in preventing bullying and helping them to cope with its effects. Unlike teachers and other adults, friends were said to be in a position to witness bullying in and outside school, and to provide support when needed.
- Primary-school pupils were far more likely than older children to talk to a parent about being bullied but overall children were divided on the question of whether parents were helpful. While parents were valued for offering emotional support and for raising children's concerns with teachers, there was a fear that they might over-react and make matters worse. Mothers were felt to be more approachable than fathers.
- On the whole, siblings were unlikely to be the first point of contact for children to talk to about bullying – fewer than four in ten pupils said they would find it easy to talk to a brother or sister. However, almost half of black and Asian secondary-school pupils said they would approach a sibling to talk about bullying.
- Some children pinpointed confidential counselling services as a valuable source of help, a means of reducing emotional tension, and enhancing self-confidence and self-esteem. While children were concerned about parents and teachers breaking confidentiality, they perceive counselling services as allowing them to deal with the bullying at their own pace.

4

Tackling Bullying

I swore never to be silent whenever and wherever human beings endure suffering and humiliation. We must always take sides. Neutrality helps the oppressor, never the victim. Silence encourages the tormentor, never the tormented.

Elie Wiesel, *Night*

LEARNING THAT YOUR CHILD IS BEING BULLIED is possibly one of the worst things a parent may have to face. Many parents do not realise the extent of the problem until well after the bullying has begun. This leads to feelings of guilt, and a sense of powerlessness, as parents may, for the first time, realise that they do not have the capacity to protect their child. A whole host of emotions may be brought to the fore: frustration that a child appears to be unable to stick up for himself; anger that he is being picked on for no obvious reason; a sense of hurt pride – that you have somehow failed in your responsibility to produce a happy, confident child; and, of course, distress that your child has suffered. Dealing with these conflicting emotions can be stressful, and can cause you to 'leap before you look' – to rush in to resolve matters without thinking it through. Whatever you do, don't panic. No matter how upset, hurt or angry you may be, a reasoned, careful approach to bullying is much more likely to reap rewards.

You will need to adopt a carefully constructed plan – and this starts at home. There may be reasons why your child has been targeted – factors to do with his character or confidence, the way he interacts with others, his choice of activities and friends, or, of course, an inability to 'fit in'. These must be addressed every bit as much as the bully himself, because without working out which aspects of your child label him as a victim, the chances are that the bullying will recur. Some children are not naturally resilient, and you may find that your parenting methods or your family dynamic play a role in creating the conditions for victim status. In Chapter 7 we look at how the family can be organised to best achieve happy conditions for all, and we examine the concepts of self-respect, self-esteem and disciplining with conviction. Again, these are equally important in righting any problems that might be affecting your child's confidence, self-image or self-belief.

Lashing out at the bully, blaming teachers or other parents, or blasting the school system will not help. The first, and most important, thing you have to do is to develop a clear channel of communication with your child in order to find out all the details, no matter how hurtful, distressing or humiliating they may be. Different types of bullying require different responses, and going in with all guns blazing may mean that you miss the opportunity to find the most obvious and successful method of dealing with a particular problem. What's more, you may actually escalate the bullying, since there is nothing more embarrassing or isolating for a child than having a parent fight his battle for him.

There is plenty you can do by way of contacting schools, education authorities, and even, in some cases, the bully's parents, but it must be done calmly and systematically, or it is likely to be dismissed as the action of yet another 'angry' parent. If you have all the facts in front of you, and do things 'by the book', you are much more likely to get the results you want. Prepare yourself for hostility, too. Just as no parent wants to discover that his child is being bullied,

Different types of bullying require different responses, and going in with all guns blazing may mean that you miss the opportunity to find the most obvious and successful method of dealing with a particular problem.

parents of bullies are equally distressed and probably reluctant to admit that there is a problem. Go in lightly, and you will avoid getting people's backs up. Similarly, teachers and educators will be unlikely to take your concerns seriously if you do not approach them in the right frame of mind. No school wants to admit a bullying problem, and you may find your concerns dismissed out of hand if you are not systematic in your approach.

Most important of all, remember your child. Bullying is distressing, and for some children it can tip the balance between happiness and serious emotional and mental problems. It is not unknown for children to find things so difficult that they contemplate, and even commit, suicide. Offering support, encouragement, love and a willingness to help in a positive, practical way is much more important than taking over and trying to resolve things on your child's behalf. A child who has been battered, either emotionally or physically, does not need more power stripped away; she needs to be given realistic techniques to have her power restored, to learn to deal with problematic situations herself, to negotiate and communicate effectively, and, ultimately, with your encouragement, to find the wherewithal to sort out the situation herself. Some children require more help than others, and some will just need to know that they have your moral support and a listening ear into which they can pour their concerns. Play it carefully, and assess what your child most needs in order to become resilient enough to deal with bullying in whatever form it takes. One of our roles as a parent is to ensure that our children have the tools and techniques, not to mention the confidence, to deal with such situations as they arise throughout their lives. We can't change the world around us, but we can make our children strong enough to cope.

The last to know

Many parents are disturbed to discover that they are often the last people their children turn to when they are bullied (see page 79 on Who do children talk to?). Research has found that students feel that 'talking to their parents' does little to ease the stress of bullying. Authors of the 2001 survey 'Talking with Kids about Tough Issues', by the Kaiser Family Foundation and Nickelodeon in the USA, asked 1,249 parents of children aged 8 to 15 and 823 children aged 8 to 15 about their problems and whether they sort them out by talking to each other.

Seventy-four per cent of 8- to 11-year-olds say teasing and bullying occur at their school, more often than smoking, drinking, drugs or sex. As kids get older – 12- to 15-year-olds were a separate group in the survey – the number rises to 86 per cent, still higher than substance abuse or sex. And both age groups referred to teasing and bullying as 'big problems', ranking higher than racism, AIDS, or the pressure to have sex or try alcohol or drugs.

Yet kids who say they have discussed these problems with their parents state that these conversations were infrequent and not very memorable. One in two 8- to 11-year-olds whose parents say they discussed their troubles with them don't even remember the conversations.

One of the most important things you can do for your child, regardless of his age, is to *listen*. Active listening is an art, and is one of the techniques used in schools to reduce bullying problems (see page 277); but it is a technique rarely used by parents. Children need to be heard – not just treated as the source of background noise. If they think something is important, it is crucial that you give them the airtime they need. Some very vocal children will recite their entire day down to the last detail, so that parents tend to tune out, and possibly miss the message hidden within the outline. Other children are more reticent and require probing to uncover any real information at all. But in either case, if your child confides in you – expresses worries about teasing, bullying, the behaviour of peers or even of teachers – it is crucial that you listen, and listen carefully. As we noted earlier, many children feel humiliated about problems and are too embarrassed to report them. Others may try to dress them up as something else and hide the issue in a story. The best thing you can do, in all cases, is to listen. Draw a child out on anything she may be worrying about, and ask questions. Open up the channels of communication so that she can elaborate when and if she feels the need, and so that she knows that her parent or parents are there for her, and will hear her out. Never assume that fears are unfounded – perception is what matters here. If a child perceives that she is being bullied, then she is. No matter what.

Improving problem-solving skills

One of the key facts that research has picked up regarding victims (and, in many cases, bullies) is that problem-solving appears to be insufficient or even non-existent. How well does your child deal with problems? Perhaps more importantly, do you ever give him the opportunity to solve them himself? Many parents are quick to intervene when something goes wrong in their children's lives, and even quicker to suggest or create a solution. In a word, this type of behaviour is 'overparenting'. Children need to make their own mistakes and to learn to negotiate themselves out of difficult situations. All children leave home at some point, and without the skills of self-management, problem-solving, negotiation and successfully communicating needs, they will get nowhere. Life is *not* easy, and all children must learn to use the tools at their disposal to negotiate its minefields. Stepping in and taking over may put an end to a problem, but it will teach your child nothing at all. What's more, you will probably undermine his confidence and self-belief along the way.

In the early 1980s, developmental psychologists Myrna Shure and George Spivack developed the theory that children behave violently because they lack interpersonal cognitive problem-solving (ICPS) skills, such as how to brainstorm a variety of solutions to a problem, how to predict the consequences of one's own actions, and how to link causes to effects in interpersonal interactions. Without these skills, the researchers reasoned, children are more likely to have frustrating social encounters. This frustration, in turn, leads children to misbehave, therefore feeding into the cycle of unpleasant social interactions, hurt feelings, frustration, bad behaviour and, of course, bullying. As we know from previous research, a lack of problem-solving skills can be a predictor for both bullying and victim status.

Shure and Spivack conducted a two-year-long study with nursery school and kindergarten children. For the first three months, half the children would play games and practise dialogues about solving problems and expressing their feelings. The researchers did not tell the children exactly how to solve their problems, but rather taught them how to generate possible solutions and how to consider their consequences. The other half were not taught these problem-solving skills.

It was found that teaching ICPS skills improved children's impulsive behaviour and social adjustment, relative to children in the control condition. They saw these improvements in both nursery school and kindergarten children for one full year after the intervention. Moreover, well-adjusted children who learned the ICPS skills in nursery school were less likely to develop behavioural difficulties over the two-year period than were well-adjusted children who did not learn these skills.

In addition, a five-year longitudinal study showed that children trained by teachers in kindergarten and first grade (reception) showed these same improvements compared to children in the control condition at the end of year 4. What's more, children of parents who best learned to apply the problem-solving approach when real problems came up had children whose cognitive and behavioural gains were strongest.

What can you do?

Fortunately, research shows that it is never too late to encourage problem-solving in children, and that adolescents will also benefit. Try the following:

• Actively ask for their advice on household matters or problems that arise, from time management, to plotting a journey, organising the rota of household chores and even baking a cake. Your child needs to become used to being faced with tasks and coming up with plans and solutions when necessary.

- Offer choices, which helps to encourage children to make their own decisions. Offering choices is a good tool for consistent, effective discipline. This is examined in more detail in Chapter 7. So, for example, if you want some help in the evening with the washing-up, say: Do you want to wash or dry? (Make it clear that not doing the dishes is *not* an option!) Or, do you want to do your homework before dinner, or get some help from Dad after dinner? Do you want a lift to the library to get that book, or can you plot your own journey?

- Make a big effort to encourage problem-solving by listening when your child has a problem, and helping your child to define it. Ask questions such as 'What would happen if you tried to...?' or 'Let's think of three strategies, and see which one works best.' Together, come up with some solutions and choose the best one. Afterwards, talk about what worked and what you could try next time.

- Always avoid leaping in with your own solutions, or offering to 'do it for you'. Children learn nothing unless they are given the opportunity to make choices and decisions.

- Older children, such as teenagers, must be given some scope for negotiation. Clear limits (see pages 216–19) are still very important during these years, but children need to have the power to make a point, even if it seems that they are 'talking back'. When children start thinking for themselves, they will come up with reasons why your methods/choices/ideas are not appropriate or acceptable, and it is very important that you listen to what they have to say. Clamping down and taking away their voice will limit their own ability to think for themselves, to make decisions, put forward a reasoned argument, and solve problems.

- Let your child fail. No child learns from having his life handed to him on a plate. He needs to learn to solve problems through failure. By all means help your child to evaluate what went wrong and how s/he can prevent it from occurring again – and ask for your child's insight into a problem – but let him or her do the thinking and the acting.

- Through trying and failing, then trying again and succeeding, our kids learn about patience, perseverance and experience the feeling of pride in their accomplishments. Not only is this important in terms of problem-solving (one success will spark a whole new interest in trying again), it will also teach self-respect (see page 203).

- Give your child an opportunity to talk about why s/he thinks things didn't go the way s/he wanted or expected them to go. Even youngsters can express their feelings, and one of the best things a parent can do is listen. Your child might even provide some insight into what happened of which you were not aware.

- Remember that your child watches how you respond to failures in your own life. It's OK to share your disappointment and important to show them how you learn from the experience. Equally important is modelling the behaviour you want to see. If something goes wrong – say, you are passed over for a promotion, or the bank has refused an all-important loan – don't stamp your feet and blame others, or simply lose your temper. Show that you will face a problem head on and come up with a solution.

- When reading to or with young children, ask them to imagine what will happen next in the story. This teaches children to think ahead, which is a very important part of solving problems.

- Actively listen to your children's conversation, responding seriously and non-judgmentally to the questions they raise.

- When your children express feelings, ask why they feel that way.

- Suggest that your children find facts to support their opinions, and then encourage them to locate information relevant to their opinions.

- Use TV programmes or films as the basis of family discussions.

- Use daily activities as occasions for learning. For example, instead of sending a child to the shops with a simple shopping list, talk to the child first about how much each item might cost, how much all the items might add up to, and estimate how much change s/he should receive.

- Offer opportunities for children to take full responsibility – giving a teenager the regular job of getting the rubbish out on time (and if he misses the collection date, what should he do?), emptying the dishwasher (what happens if the dishes aren't as clean as they should be?), looking after the family pet (from grooming to feeding and walking), or giving a younger child the role of tidying the toys, sorting socks, carrying folded, clean laundry to the appropriate rooms, or whatever. Kids will have to plan their time, work out solutions when things don't go according to plan, and deal with their own mistakes. Responsibility also teaches self-respect.

• Don't be tempted to step in when they find themselves out of their depth – running out of time or ideas for a big school project, or having trouble with peers. Encourage them to come up with some solutions, and to see them through.

Teaching resilience

A significant part of a parent's job is to help children develop skills or tactics to manage challenging situations. But children simply do not have the tools, insight, experience or confidence to face every problem on their own. Part of life is learning how to deal with different people and situations, and parents need to be involved along the way, to ensure that the little things don't become insurmountable issues. Give examples of similar experiences you had when you were a child. Ensure that your child feels that his situation and his response are absolutely normal. Never demand 'a brave face', or suggest that he deal with it on his own. Offering a variety of suggestions, from which he can choose, will help him feel in control. He will be much more likely to ask your advice in future, and feel more confident about his coping skills in general.

Children who are given no power, and who are stifled by over-dominant parenting, are more likely to rebel once they've left the nest. They are also less likely to cope with independence when they finally get it. Over-controlled children have little sense of self and even less sense of the outside world. Giving a child some freedom, at an appropriate age, teaches decision-making and encourages self-esteem and confidence. Children will no doubt make some dubious decisions at times, but they will learn from their mistakes.

It is most important for a parent to acknowledge a child's feelings and to provide the child with an emotional vocabulary. No child feels confident and well all the time, and they need to know that it's normal and acceptable to feel angry, frightened, lonely, jealous, sad and alone. Help your child to put into words how he is feeling: for example, express it yourself first ('You must be feeling very sad not to have been invited to that birthday party', 'You must be very angry that your teacher treated you like that', or 'I can understand why you feel jealous that your brother has made the team and you haven't.'). You may get it wrong, but you will be providing words for them to express their feelings without fear of rancour or embarrassment.

Express your own emotions regularly, so that your child learns that this is acceptable. Keep the channels of communication open. If a child becomes used to opening up, he'll be much less likely to allow problems to build up to an unhealthy level. Get into the habit of having regular conversations, and develop a good rapport. Share his interests so that you can use these subjects as ice-breakers. If you seem genuinely interested in your child, he will feel loved, important and respected and he will be more likely to confide in you.

Some children may be naturally more inhibited when it comes to express-ing themselves. Boys in particular may find it harder to communicate; in fact, studies show that girls are more likely to report positive and supportive peer relationships than boys. Furthermore, boys define themselves as being more competitive and achievement-oriented than girls; given the overly competitive and achievement-oriented nature of the average child's life today, this is an enor-mous disadvantage.

Be positive without belittling your child's perception of events. If your daughter is anxious, upset and stressed after falling out with a friend, it may be tempting to trivialise it. But, if she *perceives* it to be stressful, then it is. Parents

Giving a child some freedom, at an appropriate age, teaches decision-making and encourages self-esteem and confidence.

need to ensure that their children see the positive in every situation, and that they feel good about themselves. If they feel positive and self-assured, they'll be more likely to take things in their stride.

Similarly, suggest that your child focuses on the particular problem or issue and thinks it through. Ask him what worries him most, and what the worst pos-sible outcome could be if his fears are realised. By preparing him for the worst-case scenario, he'll know what to expect. Discuss some coping strategies that he might use if the worst comes to the worst. Events probably won't turn out as badly as he fears, but if he's prepared, he'll feel more confident about facing the challenge.

Learn to identify future potential problems. While this may seem an alarmist strategy, it genuinely helps children to anticipate and plan for unhappy events. Find out what could cause stress, and plan ways to avoid it or deal with it. If you know that exams are coming up, and your child always responds badly to this type of pressure, talk it through well in advance. Develop some coping skills, practise exam and stress reduction techniques and make sure they get plenty

(continued on page 92)

Being assertive

Children who are assertive are able stand up for themselves. Bullies always choose easy prey, so if your son or daughter is prepared to make things a little more difficult, they will be that much less likely to be chosen.

Teach your children to express themselves clearly and firmly, but with diplomacy and courtesy. One of the best means of showing assertiveness is using the word 'I' in statements. This works for two main reasons. Firstly, it makes a child's position completely clear and does not involve others. 'I don't like this game' or 'I don't like being sworn at' are not judgemental, but firm pronouncements that should not put anyone else on the defensive. Secondly, 'I' statements are indisputable: there is no scope for argument. A child who can express himself clearly and stand his ground will not appear to be a victim. And when children learn to express themselves without offending others, without using blame or judgement, they will be more popular with their peers. As we have seen throughout this book, having good friends is crucial to keeping bullies away.

Ensure that your children understand that self-expression is absolutely acceptable. It is OK to feel angry or upset, or frustrated, and it is OK to make your feelings known. If you fail to give children an outlet, they will learn to internalise feelings rather than express them, which causes all sorts of problems with self-esteem and self-image, and makes them feel unworthy in communication with friends. They have never had their feelings validated, so they don't bother to express them. Self-expression is very important. Children need to explain how they are feeling, and to blow off steam. This can all be done respectfully, of course, but a child who is confident about expressing his opinions is far more likely to stand up to a bully than one who is not.

Body language is crucial to assertiveness. There is no point in teaching a child to stand up for himself verbally, if he's looking at the ground, and slouched over in embarrassment. Assertive children will stand up straight, look the other person in the eyes, relax their bodies, and keep their hands steady. Once again, bullies look out for kids who are unsure of themselves, so even if they are feeling nervous or out of their depth, they can appear to be confident and assertive by modelling the appropriate body language.

Some children will need help with self-belief, and one way to do this is to practise self-affirmation. You can teach your child to 'talk themselves' into anything, with an internal monologue, when they feel underconfident or pressure. For example, 'I can do this; I am stronger and much cleverer than these bullies; I will stand up straight, look them in the eye, and then leave without losing my temper or crying; I can do this.' This technique also works to reassure a child that they are OK. It can be soul-destroying to have their appearance or any other aspect of themselves criticised, and by choosing to believe in themselves rather than the bully's words, they can avoid a lot of the damage.

One cautionary note here. Although standing up for yourself is a good lesson and a sign of assertiveness, it's important to remember that some bullies will bait a child in order to get a response (any response). And if your child 'fights back' verbally, the bullying may well continue. So if it doesn't work the first time, leave it, to prevent bullying from escalating. This may be time for parental involvement (see page 110).

Children need to learn that they have the right to say 'no', not only when they are threatened but in a wide variety of day-to-day situations. This type of 'training' begins at home, so it is essential that parents learn to give in occasionally, to listen to a respectful argu-ment, to allow a child to say 'no' and explain her position. Offer choices within boundaries, and show interest and respect in your child's feelings. Very young children can learn assertiveness through role-playing with puppets or dolls, saying 'no' to unacceptable demands. Show a child the difference between being *submissive* and being *assertive*. But teach the difference, too, between assertiveness and aggression. Standing up for yourself should be undertaken with respect for the feelings of others; aggression is never respectful.

of rest. Your child's ability to cope with such pressure will be much improved. This is important. Many victims feel overwhelmed by stress in their lives and may need more help in preparing to deal with it than other, more resilient children. And with every success, your child will become more resilient.

You can't always prevent negative events from occurring in your children's lives, but you can help them manage these events better. Show faith in your children and their ability to cope. Remind them of times when they found a solution to a problem. Suggest they use the same strategies, or help them to come up with different ones. Encourage independence and interdependence. There is a time for each, and a well-rounded child will develop skills from both that will stand him in good stead in the outside world. Show solidarity, as a team or as a family. If your child knows that he has the unconditional support of his family or parents, he will feel more confident, take more risks and exercise his own judgement. Above all, celebrate good coping skills. When a child handles things well, praise his efforts and achievement.

Resist being overprotective. Support your child's efforts to be more independent. If the bullying is happening on the way to and from school, arrange for the child to go to school with older, supportive children, or take him or her until other interventions can take place. Teach your child the social skills s/he needs to make friends. A confident child who has friends is less likely to be bullied (see page 101).

The key behavioural ingredient for being a victim is submissiveness. A bully quickly picks small, shy, frail or whiny children who are loners. A bully needs to feel in control and requires the victim to provide the bystanders with a show of shame or humiliation. Victims are made to feel like fools and often try to submit to the bully in an attempt to stop the bullying. The net effect is that the victim's submission fuels the bully and increases the entertainment for the bystanders.

So one major thing you need to do to encourage resilience in your child is to work on his self-image and self-esteem (see page 94), so that he develops the necessary confidence and self-respect to ward off the bullies. Teach your child to stand up straight, hold his head high, and walk confidently. And consider assertiveness skills (see page 90–91), in addition to teaching a child how to stand up for himself verbally.

In a 2003 study, both primary and secondary school pupils identified 'standing up for yourself' as a helpful strategy for dealing with bullying but the

Emotional environment factors

According to the *Journal of Instructional Psychology*, a family's emotional environment is critical to a child's development of self-esteem and self-image. In an emotionally healthy family, a child feels loved and wanted, as parental approval and acceptance encourages a child to bond and form a secure attachment with each parent. As a result of parents' loving and positive interactions with a child, they convey their belief to the child that s/he is a 'good' and 'valued' member of the family. Consequently, the child develops positive self-esteem, as one who has 'worth', and a positive self-image, as one who is 'good'.

In an emotionally abusive family, a child feels unloved and unwanted. Parents consistently reject a child and a child's behaviour. Emotionally abusive parents will also encourage others to reject and ridicule the child. The emotional family environment is 'cold', as the parents do not express nor show any affection, support or guidance towards the child. A child is deprived of the psychological nurturing necessary for psychological growth and development. Emotional abuse is not just a single event, but a systematic diminishment of the victim. It is a continuous behaviour by the abuser that reduces a child's self-concept to the point where s/he feels unworthy of respect, friendship, love and affection.

Studies show that parental abuses consist of: unrealistic expectations of the child's behaviour, repeated name calling (no good, rotten, ugly, stupid, crazy), and deliberate humiliation in front of others (teachers, siblings, relatives, friends). All children inherently trust and love their parents and seldom complain directly about emotional abuse. They lack the reasoning ability to challenge their parents' attacks upon their self-esteem. They may think that this is normal, and accept the demeaning statements of the parents as 'true' and 'accurate' reflections of their own self-worth. As a result of this abuse, the child develops profoundly low self-esteem and a negative self-image as one who is 'bad'.

means by which they would do this differed. Around a quarter of primary school pupils thought that assertively communicating with the bully would 'always' or 'usually' work, whereas older children pinpointed physical retaliation as having a better chance of success – almost a third (31 per cent) said that learning a martial art might help reduce the risk of bullying.

Counteracting a negative self-image

A comprehensive year-long study, led by researchers at the University of Illinois in the USA, found that adolescents who have a low opinion of themselves tend to shy away from interactions with peers. This uncertainty and withdrawal then draws negative feedback from other students, prompting even more withdrawal and leaving them with few chances to have close friends and as targets for teasing or bullying. The study looked closely at three time periods in the lives of 605 fifth and sixth grade students, particularly at how the youth and their peer groups mutually influenced each other.

The adolescents were asked about their self-views and experiences of stress in peer relationships. Teachers were queried about the adolescents' display of helpless, withdrawn and pro-social behaviours with peers. The researchers focused on how the youths' beliefs about their social self-worth and self-efficacy affected their behaviour and experiences in the peer group, and how these experiences then influenced the youths' future behaviour and beliefs.

The results confirmed the researchers' expectations about downward social cycles, suggesting that early intervention is needed to improve peer interactions in schools. As researcher Karen Rudolph said, 'Understanding why some youth experience chronic difficulties in their peer relationships is critically important for learning how to prevent some of the negative consequences associated with isolation, rejection, and victimisation by peers.'

A negative self-image may be the result of bullying, or it may be one of the catalysts for it, as bullies are drawn to obviously weaker targets. Either way, the long-term effects of a poor self-image have been well studied, and, if the bullying persists, these effects may have serious repercussions for your child's emotional health.

There are many signs of negative self-image in children. Ask yourself if your child fits the descriptions below. Does your child:

1. Have difficulty in forming relationships?

2. Have trouble relating to and bonding with other children?

3. Lack self-confidence?

4. Have trouble expressing emotion?

5. Exhibit extreme shyness?

6. Find that he is victimised or exploited by other children?

7. Suffer from fatigue or listlessness?

8. Experience feelings of helplessness and hopelessness?

9. Feel inadequate?

10. Feel pessimistic and often preoccupied?

11. Have difficulty in concentrating on school activities?

12. Have trouble engaging in or enjoying pleasurable activities?

13. Have a tendency to self-injury – nail-biting, being accident prone, pulling or twisting hair, or other self-harm, such as cutting the skin

14. Make self-deprecating remarks, such as 'stupid', 'no good', etc.

15. Sometimes become bullying and hostile to others?

Experiencing several of these characteristics is indicative of a poor self-image. And in this situation, not only will your child 'up' his potential for becoming a victim, but his grades will suffer and his social skills will probably be damaged. He will also become increasingly isolated and more likely to take part in high-risk or damaging activities, such as drugs and alcohol, running away and even criminal activities – all of which are considered to be 'self-abusive'. Kids with poor self-image are also prone to suffer from depression and anxiety disorders, and to engage in abusive relationships with others, well in adulthood.

? What can you do?

• Make sure that your family life is emotionally healthy, and that your child's home is both a sanctuary and a place where his self-esteem and self-respect are enhanced (see page 93). Remember, the family forms the bedrock of a child's self-image, so ensure that yours is strong and healthy.

• Avoid labels. Quiet children are often labelled early on in life, and develop a self-image based on how others perceive them. So calling your child shy, timid, weak – or, indeed, anything else negative, such as skinny, fat, big, useless, spotty, ugly, silly, stupid, jealous, spiteful, selfish, etc., – will leave a mark. By labelling a child you undermine her confidence and create a self-fulfilling prophecy.

- Encourage your child in what he does well, and let him know that you love, value and approve of him – unconditionally. In other words, don't base all praise or approval on success. Let your child know that he's OK just as he is.
- Make sure your child has attractive and fashionable clothes. For one thing it will help her to take pride in her appearance, which can spark an interest in looking after herself and raise her confidence. But it's also important that kids don't feel different from their peers, and that you avoid giving some of those nastier peers further grounds for teasing. Helping them to look good is one way of encouraging kids to feel good about themselves, which can help to shift unhealthy patterns and raise self-image. This is important, too, for the concept of 'fitting in' (see below).
- Work on helping your child to create healthy friendships and to achieve a circle of close, good friends (see page 101). Children who are reinforced by a healthy peer group are less likely to experience poor self-image.
- Encourage your child to undertake activities that make them feel good, and at which they have the opportunity to shine. These may not be the 'run-of-the-mill' activities that other kids are doing, but don't hesitate to let them explore anything that interests them. Children who perceive themselves to be good at something develop a stronger and healthier self-image.
- Talk to your child. A child who is able to express herself develops self-respect and, with that, a healthier self-image. She feels valued and important.
- Encourage social involvement in community, church and school activities, which build social skills and confidence.
- Finally, work on bully-proofing your child (see page 102), which will help build the confidence necessary to lose the victim status.

The importance of 'fitting in'

As discussed earlier, one of the most important and most common reasons why children are targeted by bullies is because they don't 'fit in'. It's a sad state of affairs that being the 'same' as peers is the only way to be socially acceptable, but unfortunately it seems to be true. That's not to say that being 'different' is wrong, but a child must have the confidence and self-belief to carry it off, and many victims simply do not have the wherewithal to defend their own views and to stand up for themselves.

So, helping your child to fit in is essential. This can mean any one of a number of things, from encouraging him to find a group of like-minded friends who will support him and offer much-needed 'group' protection, as well as giving him the sense that he does 'fit in' somewhere, to making sure that he has at least some of the 'right' clothes and material possessions.

In no way am I encouraging materialism; indeed, this can backfire shamefully, and leave a child with an even poorer self-image, when he learns to equate popularity with what he has rather than what he is. Seek out kids who are popular without all the 'gear', and point out some of the reasons why this is so – confidence, sense of humour, kindness and generosity, self-belief, etc. All children need to learn that fitting into a peer group involves a lot more than having the right trainers or the newest iPod.

Having said that, there is nothing worse than feeling like a social leper. Don't be the one parent who refuses to let his child watch TV, play on the Playstation, go to the cinema on his own, or have a mobile telephone. Don't be the one parent who insists that your child wears only hand-me-downs or 'sensible' shoes. If your child stands out in a negative fashion, it will create scope for bullying and undermine his confidence. All kids want to feel that they are part of the social fabric of their environment, and, like it or not, things like TV and mobile phones are tools with which kids bond – a point of discussion and a shared interest. If your child has nothing to 'share' with his peers, and is the only one who can't make his arrangements by text, for example, he's going to feel left out. And for a victim, that can be a large part of the problem.

So open your eyes a little. Look at how other kids are dressing, what freedoms they are allowed, what gadgets form a big part of their social life, and what seems to be an important aspect of your child's school culture. If you aren't sure, ask other parents. It doesn't have to cost a great deal to achieve this, and you can teach some valuable lessons along the way. Then negotiate a compromise. Agree on one or two new things during a specific time space – this will help him focus on what he really does want, rather than what he 'must' have. If he wants more, he'll have to earn the money to get it – a paper round, for example, or babysitting, or helping around the house – and this will start to teach him the value of money, and make his possessions more valuable because he has earned them. One or two small 'in' things will help him to feel normal, and he will learn to take pride in what he has. The same goes for freedom. Find out what is the acceptable norm and try not to let your child be the only one with unreasonable rules and expectations.

You may find that you have a natural rebel, who enjoys being 'different' and actively dislikes what the majority of other kids like and do. In this case, there is nothing wrong with encouraging independent thought and action. However, if your child is viewed negatively by his peers and bullied as a result of his beliefs or actions, there may be more to it than you think. Confident, friendly children can, as studies have shown, be very popular, even if they are less attractive, overweight, or without the material possessions of their friends. But they add something to a group, and are popular for a reason – they are good company, probably nice people, and good friends. If your child's attempts to be different are simply making him feel isolated, try to work out why. And also try to work out why your child has a need to be different, if it is making him unhappy and the target for bullies.

Improving a child's social skills

It's not easy to 'teach' social skills, particularly in the teenage years when many kids withdraw and become fairly monosyllabic. However, according to recent research, children who lack social skills are much more likely to experience anxiety, depression, somatic complaints and withdrawal. They are less likely to fit in with a peer group, and more likely to become victims. So something clearly must be done.

Research by R. L. Selman has found that social cognition involves a person thinking about other people. Studies of social cognition usually fall into one of three categories:

• Impression formation – making judgements of people
• Social perspective-taking – how people 'accurately make assessments about the thoughts and feelings of others'
• Morality and social conventions – a person's understanding of the rules and norms for social interaction

Socially isolated children have a more difficult time adequately developing the skills needed to be accepted among peers. Selman says that 'Perspective-taking does not develop magically in a vacuum devoid of social experience.' So, in other words, if social cognition involves being able to put oneself in 'someone else's shoes', social interactions are necessary for this to occur.

It has been shown that victims of bullying and teasing often misinterpret ambiguous statements, resulting in negative feelings. Children who are teased often perceive the teaser as wanting to fight or teasing them because they enjoy the reaction that they get from their targets. One researcher also notes that emotions play an important part when children 'process social cues'. If a child is having negative feelings, he or she may interpret another person's intent as hostile.

So social cognition is an essential part not only of 'fitting in' to a peer group and establishing friendships with healthy social interaction, but also of losing the 'victim' mentality. Children without social cognition find it difficult to understand others, their intent and their interaction; what's more, they may fail to understand normal friendships, rules and norms of behaviour.

According to researcher Pamela Tanguay, parents have good reason to be uneasy when their children have trouble getting on with other children, as this is very important from an early age. Peers afford preschoolers some of their most exciting, fun experiences. Not having friends can be frustrating, even painful, for young children. In addition, a growing body of research supports the belief, held by many early childhood professionals, that young children's peer relationships are important for their development and adjustment to school. Preschool children who have positive peer relationships are likely to maintain positive peer interactions in school, while children who have a hard time getting along with 'age-mates' in the preschool years are more likely to experience later academic difficulties and rejection or neglect by their primary school peers. Without the skills to play constructively and develop friendships with children of the same age, kids become excluded from opportunities to develop additional and more complex skills important for future peer interaction.

? What can you do?

- Encourage friendships from a very young age. The more isolated a child is, the less likely he will be to develop important skills (see page 101).
- Talk to your child. Communication is essential to the development of social skills. Explain why you do things, and teach manners and respect for others. Listen to your child and show respect for his views; discourage rudeness and bad behaviour, and do not tolerate sulky silences. Encourage your child to express himself and his feelings and views appropriately, and make sure you do the same yourself. A 1994 study found that children who have more frequent conversations with a parent about peer relationships are better liked by other children in their classrooms and are rated by teachers as more socially competent.

- Take time to teach problem-solving, which will make your child more socially adept (see page 84).
- Model behaviour for your child – allow him to see you interacting with friends and family, with people in the neighbourhood, on the telephone, in shops or garages, anywhere, in fact. Much of what children learn takes place around them, and they absorb it as a matter of course.
- Encourage your children to be self-sufficient – asking for sweets in the shop, running errands on their own where they will be required to ask for things, making phone calls, asking friends round to your home, and asking other children to play in the park. Children who are accustomed to using social skills on a regular basis find it much easier to interact with others.
- The best things you can do is to set strict rules about behaviour. Ensure your children know how they're supposed to behave. If you see them behaving in a way that you don't approve of, set limits. Be sure to say 'no' immediately after you witness the bad behaviour, and take time to explain exactly why it is unacceptable.
- Children have a natural unwillingness to share. This can be one of the most difficult character traits to teach a child. You want to begin teaching your child to share at an early age. Encourage your child to share whenever she's playing with a sibling, with you, or with another child. Whenever it's playtime, make it share time as well. If your child is used to playing not just in the room with other children, but actually with other children, that will make it easier to learn sharing.
- Organise opportunities to play with other children. One of the best ways to do this is to play board games. This encourages a child to ask for help on understanding rules, to wait her turn, and to ask other children politely in order to get permission to do things.
- Talk to your child's school; there is much that can be done. I've read of many useful interventions, such as a 'friendship cushion' for younger children – the idea being that anyone alone, feeling left out, or having no one to play with in the playground sits on the cushion and can then be sought out by playmates to join in. It isn't as isolating as you might think! In some schools, kids fight to sit on the cushion in the hope of being the next one asked to join a new game. No child needs to be left out, and there are measures to ensure that this doesn't happen. Some schools have a policy where there must be at least three people playing any game – so a third party is actively sought out.

- Encourage children to learn empathy for and understanding of others by explaining how you feel in certain situations, giving them the words to explain how they feel, and watching others to gain an understanding of what may motivate certain behaviours. Watch television or films together, and talk about how people are feeling and what their behaviour might reflect.
- Teach your children to be resilient when things go wrong with their friends. Exclusion by peers will occur at many stages of life, and it's important that they develop the right attitude. Several studies show that children who become angry and believe that others are 'out to get them' will go on to react with aggression and hostility to even mild slights by peers, which will make them even less likely to fit in socially. Or a child who takes the pessimistic view and thinks he's useless will withdraw from further peer interaction, setting the stage for bullying. Socially competent children, by contrast, tend to explain these rejections as temporary or in ways that recognise that a social situation can be improved by changing their own behaviour. And an ability to be self-aware and to modify our own behaviour in social situations is an important skill.
- Let children sort out problems with peers themselves. By all means offer guidance, but let them work things through, problem solve, and come up with solutions that work. They will learn to negotiate, to alter their own behaviour when required, and to find a way to get on rather than relying on external cues.

Encouraging friendships and interests

This may sound obvious, but it is very important. Friends raise self-esteem, they develop a child's social skills, and can help to prevent bullying from occurring by providing a supportive peer group and a 'buffer'. Remember, it's children who spend too much time alone and are isolated who often become victims.

So arrange dates with other children or encourage your children to join groups and clubs or to take lessons. All children should be doing some sport – not only to relieve stress, but also to encourage better physical coordination, which raises self-esteem. It's a great way to meet other children and to teach teamwork.

You may have a child who is reluctant to meet others, and you may need to exert a little pressure in order to get him involved. But the younger you start, the easier it will be. Actively seek out groups – drama, music, art, sports, magic, Warhammer, model-making, kite-flying, anything that interests your child – and get him out there. Make sure he has the tools and clothing he needs to join in properly. You may have to force the issue at the outset, but even shy, intro-verted children can find a point of contact with other like-minded children. Make an effort.

Invite families round for a game of rounders or football in the park, to an impromptu tennis match or barbecue. Suggest having a party or an outing for your child with friends. Get him used to having lots of people around, and try to arrange for children of his age to be present.

Try not to pick holes in peers or criticise your child's activities. Whether you like his friends or not, they provide a valuable support network for him. If he withdraws in order to please you, he may end up with nothing. If your child has problems fitting in, encourage him to seek out another youngster who's alone a lot, rather than try to break into a group of two or more children. It's easier to participate in unstructured activities, such as playing on the jungle gym, than to join an organised game in progress.

Bully-proofing your child

One of the greatest preventative measures that you can take is to give your child the tools and skills to deal with bullying situations when they arise. You may have a child who has never been bullied, and has been affected only as a wit-ness, but all children need to know how to deal with bullies. The problem is so pervasive that everyone is bound to be affected at some stage of their lives. So as well as working on self-respect, resilience and your home life, and encour-aging social skills, problem-solving and friendships, you will need to teach your child the practical skills needed in dealing with bullies.

Here are some ideas of what you can teach them:

- Learn to control your anger. No child will fail to become upset and angry when they are victimised, but a response is exactly what a bully wants and expects. Becoming angry will never solve the problem, and resorting to violence will only feed the situation. If you become cool and calm, and fail to rise to the bait, the bully has effectively lost, because he cannot 'control' you or your emotions.
- Never use physical force, no matter how often or directly it has been used against you. A bully is dangerous and you may end up in serious trouble or physical threat. Furthermore, violence is an 'anger' response and, once again, it's important never to show anger.

Case history

Tristyn, *nine, says this: 'The thing is that I have some really cool brothers who are older than me and I really used to like them all and just be like them. But my next biggest brother who is nearly 11 is making me really sad. He just calls me names all the time and when I walk near him he punches me really hard. And then he says that if I tell my mum or dad he will kill me. And so I told my dad anyway, and he said that brothers do that and I just need to say stop it because it hurts my feelings. And so I did that. And he stole my pocket money and ate my special sweets that I was saving up for. And now he always just takes my pocket money the minute that I get it and my mum says I am bad with money and she won't give me more and I can't tell her the real truth because she has a stressy work job and she will cry. And so I just have to look at that mean brother and I have to just give in. And my other brothers won't help because they laugh and say well done to him. Like nobody likes me or anything. So I don't want to live at my house any more. I just feel so sad all the time and even stealing Fluffy [Tristyn's stuffed dog] was the meanest thing so I have nothing any more. I think that my brother is sad too because he is crying a lot but I can't be his friend because he hurts me.'*

- Stand up tall; act brave even when you don't feel it; and walk away. Ignoring a bully is difficult, particularly when they push all the buttons to upset you; it may also wind up a bully to the point of fury, because he fails to get a response. But if you walk away with your head held high, you are sending the message that you won't be messed with. Your body language says that you are not vulnerable. By ignoring the bully, you are saying you don't really care and he hasn't affected you. It's tough, but it works. Soon enough a bully will go in search of a more satisfying target.

- It sounds crazy, but try to make the bully your friend. This technique will obviously work better for younger kids (and parents take note: if your child is being bullied by one person, invite him round to play, but keep close supervision). This is a difficult one, especially when you are dealing with negative feelings such as anger and mistrust. However, when you make an attempt to empathise and understand the reasons behind the bullying, you gain empowerment and no longer feel so threatened by the bully's behaviour.

- If you want to talk back, keep your voice level and calm and look the bully right in the eye when you speak. Use 'I' statements, which are indisputable:

'I want you to stop that right now.' Or 'I do not like being treated that way.' Don't wait for a response. Walk away and ignore further efforts to hurt you.

- Employ some humour. Sometimes the best way to defuse an upsetting or dangerous situation is to be funny. Not only will it be something the bully isn't expecting, but it will help you to look clever and in control – and unconcerned. So, make a joke about something irrelevant. Don't laugh or become sarcastic or make fun of the bully – that's not the intention. An audience is important to bullies, and if you can make a clever retort, you may find the 'audience' sides with you, which means the bully loses her support.

- Always tell an adult. Many victims are terrified of confiding for fear of being ignored, belittled or even blamed. There is a certain loss of face and pride that accompanies being bullied. But no child should have to deal with bullies on his own, and keeping quiet will not ease the situation. In fact, if the bully finds he can get away with it, he'll probably continue the behaviour. The message, again, is, tell an adult – someone you trust, whether it is a parent, a teacher or someone on lunchtime duty. It's not 'telling tales' to protect yourself (and possibly others) from dangerous children.

- Don't keep it to yourself. Dealing with bullying on your own can be soul-destroying and can undermine all your confidence. Choose a teacher, a friend, a sibling or counsellor – anyone who can give you the support you need. There is no shame in being bullied. It is never your fault. Talking is a good outlet for fears and frustrations and can give you the confidence you need to stop the bully in his tracks.

- Always support your peers against bullying. You may be relieved that it's not you who has been targeted and simply want to keep your head down, but if children support one another, bullying will be eradicated. No doubt about it. A bully wants to feel recognised and powerful – particularly in front of his peers. If those peers stand up to him and say: 'Hey, that's not fair,' or 'I don't like what you are doing,' or even just leave him alone, he loses his audience and his adulation. Remember that when one person is courageous enough to stand up to a bully, others will too.

- Create a buddy system, which involves choosing one or more friends to accompany you in areas where bullying is likely to occur – for example, on the way to school, in the lunchroom or toilets, in the playground or even at the bus-stop, and offer the same in return. Bullies are less likely to target kids who are in a group.

- Consider some self-defence training or taking up a martial art. Though you will not ever want to respond with violence, knowing that you can protect yourself will make you more confident and less likely to become a target.
- Avoid isolated places whenever possible.
- Don't automatically comply with a bully's requests (for money or anything else). If you give in, you'll set yourself up for the situation to recur. Better to walk (or even run) away.
- Keep a detailed record or diary of any bullying that occurs. If the time comes that you need to report the incidents, you will need all the key facts to hand.
- Try not to cry. Although many types of bullying can be enormously painful, including name-calling and social exclusion, all bullies want a reaction, and if you give them one they will continue. Stay calm and ignore them, while maintaining confident body language.
- Remember that choosing a different route to school, or avoiding bullies in the halls or the playground is only a short-term measure. If they want to get you, they will. What you need to do is to work on being more confident, making supportive friends, and finding ways to deal with the bullies themselves. By all means leave the problem situation, in order to defuse it. But remember that standing up for yourself is ultimately your long-term goal.

Talking to your child

Kids are good at hiding their feelings and even their situation. They may have gone without lunch for months, for example, because their money has been stolen, but failed to tell anyone. So watch out for signs that your child has been bullied (see page 76).

Encourage your child to talk to you and to share problems. Make it clear that it is not telling tales to express concerns or to point out a problem. Be very aware that your child will probably be upset and embarrassed, and respond with reassurance. Listen carefully.

Many children, teens in particular, are reluctant to share problems with parents, and you may have to ask directly to keep tabs on what is going on or, alternatively, beat around the bush a little to get some answers. For example, you might say: Are kids nice to each other at the bus-stop or is there bullying? Does that new anti-bullying plan in your school really work? Which kids are the bullies in your class? Do you know anyone who has been threatened? When does the bullying happen? What happens in the playground after school? Do

Does ignoring it make it worse?

Your child will need to ignore the bullying in order to prevent things from escalating and to get away unharmed. However, there is no doubt that bullies will seek another target. The idea is not to deflect the violence or intimidation, but to reduce the damage in the short term. All bullying should be reported – even if your child has managed to save face or to escape harm. If it's not your child, it will be someone else's.

you know anyone who gets their money stolen? Do you know anyone who gets nasty texts? What would you do if it was you?

This way might make it easier for your child to talk about bullies because it is not so personal, and also helps your child to see that other kids are victims as well. Listen carefully to the answers. If your child seems to be hiding something or reluctant to talk, your response is even more important. And when you do respond to your child, make sure you do not, under any circumstances, intimate that they may have been to blame. They'll clam up and you won't get anywhere. Adding guilt to the indignity of being attacked, threatened, or emotionally abused may be one step too far for many kids.

So don't say: What did you say to those boys?, or Why were you hanging around with the big boys?, or Why didn't you stick to your own friends/playground?, or What were you doing in that area alone?, or Why did you let them see your phone?, or Why did you wear your new trainers when you knew they would attract attention? It won't help. It will make things worse.

Be open and sympathetic. Get as many details as you can with general questions, and listen to the answers instead of leaping in with anger or blind-panic solutions or plots for revenge. It's not easy hearing that a child has been bullied, but your response is paramount. Your child's overwhelming need is for protection. It is essential that children who have been victimised by a bully are not re-victimised by the adults they approach for help.

You should also reassure your child that he or she isn't to blame. Explain that bullies are often confused or unhappy people who don't feel good about themselves, or, alternatively, have an inflated sense of their own worth. Being a victim is not a crime, and your child must be reminded that he has done nothing wrong (though in the case of a provocative victim, you may need to work on what your child did to egg on the bullies). Ask thoughtful questions, and show unconditional support – whether or not you think your child acted in an inappropriate way, or could have done things differently. Criticism will make things worse.

Every day, parents must ask children how their school day went and how they felt about the day's happenings – on the way to school, on the way home, and in the playground. Show genuine interest rather than interrogating, which will be particularly ineffective in the case of teenagers! The more interest you show, the more able you are to keep tabs on what is happening. Remember to encourage independent thought and expression – don't tell them what to do and expect them to follow your lead. If your child can develop a healthy sense of self and an enhanced ability to resist peer pressure and to deal with problems, bullying will be a thing of the past.

Bystanders

Neither overt bully or victim, the bystander represents the third group involved in a bullying episode. Bystanders form the audience, and can wittingly or unwittingly encourage the proceedings. Some bystanders actively support the bully; few come to the aid of the victim; the majority keep quiet or keep their heads down for fear of the bully turning on them as well. A study performed by bullying expert Barbara Coloroso and supported by psychologist Dan Olweus found that peers were involved in 85 per cent of bullying episodes, and reinforced the bullying in 81 per cent of cases. They found that peers tended to be friendlier and more supportive of the bullies than the victims, and intervened in only 13 per cent of episodes at which they were present.

The rationale for this is simple, and was summarised as being 'afraid to get hurt', 'afraid of being the next target', 'afraid to make the situation worse', or 'not knowing what to do'. Quite clearly, too, there are some bystanders who enjoy the vicarious pleasure of being involved in a bullying episode without having to bully themselves. Also, because they tend to side with the bully rather than the victim, they employ a variety of methods to justify their lack of intervention, including blaming the victim, saying, 'They deserved it', or 'They aren't my friend'. 'I don't want to tell tales,' 'It has nothing to do with me,' 'The bully is my friend,' or 'Everyone else did the same as me'.

Bystanders clearly have a moral responsibility to become involved, but in a culture of fear – the classic scenario for a school or neighbourhood with bullying problems – who can be blamed for wanting to keep a low profile? However, there are moral issues here which cannot be discounted. Many parents suggest that their children should stay out of it, or keep their heads down and mind their own business – on the premise that they then won't be involved in any trouble themselves. But the majority of kids who witness bullying and do nothing about it suffer from enormous guilt, distress, fear and helplessness, or they find themselves drawn into the bully's network or gang through peer pressure. It takes a brave child to stand up for a victim, particularly if they are not even friends, but in order to eradicate the problem of bullying, accountability must occur.

Experts have labelled bystanders in four main groups. First, there are the victim-bystanders, who identify with the victim and become afraid of the bully, or, alternatively, who support the bully so that they do not become the next victim. Second, there are the avoidant-bystanders, who may be genuinely confused and not know how they can help or what to do; they may even deny that there is a problem. The third type of bystander gets a vicarious pleasure from watching without being involved – finding it exciting and stimulating. The fourth type are the set-up masters, who arrange the conflict and encourage the bully. Again, they like to be involved, but not directly. The latter two types of bystanders share many more characteristics with bullies than they do with victims, while the former two are more likely to have a potential victim status. And it's worth remembering that in many ways bystanders can be victims just as much as they can be bullies. Children who are witness to violence are prone to developing psychological problems merely from watching – either that, or they become desensitised to the violence, which makes for real problems both in a child's moral fibre and in society.

❓ What can you do?

You can work out what type of bystander your child may be by asking a few simple questions. If he says he likes the bully, or it was the victim's fault, chances are he's the type of bystander who eggs on the bully, or responds in the way he does because of peer pressure. If your child says he didn't see anything, avoids the issue or says he doesn't know what to do, you can bet that he's more a victim-bystander, and he will be affected by what he's seen and by his own powerlessness. Either way, all children need to learn to take responsibility for bullying, and to report problems as they occur. It's not easy, but once someone has done it – and when a school makes it possible for reports to be anonymous – more and more will take part.

Whether your child has bullying tendencies (even if he's not bullying) or is bordering on becoming a victim, you need to take note: the former have the potential to go on and bully themselves, either through peer pressure or because they like the buzz; the latter may well become victims. Look through this and the following chapter to address the characteristics of bullies and victims, and find ways to get your child back on even ground.

There are many other things you can do, including:

- Teach empathy. A good question is: 'How would you feel?' In order to become healthy adults, children need to know what it's like to be in someone else's shoes, and to feel empathy with people in trouble.
- Reinforce the idea that telling someone is merely reporting a problem that affects a great proportion of the school community, and ruins the atmosphere for everyone. Remind them that there are terrible long-term effects on victims as a result of bullying, and that they will have that on their conscience. Reporting a problem is a mature action that protects others.
- There is safety in numbers, and if your child can encourage his own peer group or close group of friends to support him against bullying, and to protect a victim, there is much less likelihood of repercussions. Bullies are afraid of groups, and tend to stick to isolated victims. One kid standing up for another opens himself to be bullied, while a group of kids may well be all it takes to defuse a situation.
- If your child is in a group of children who enjoy bullying or who are supportive of bullying, you may need to suggest (gently) that they are not the kind of people he wants to associate with. Remind him of the damage that bullying can do, and ask him if he wants that on his conscience. If he's afraid to stand up to his bullying friends, then it's probably time to find friends who share his values and who will like him for the person he is.
- Avoid using the word 'victim' and use 'target' instead. Once again, the word 'victim' is emotive and seems to suggest someone who is weak and useless. Children need to learn that kind, sensitive, honest and respectful children are 'targeted' in many, many cases, and they need protection.

- Teach responsibility for behaviour. Not doing anything is, in many ways, as dangerous as bullying because the victim is still harmed, the bully is encouraged by having the support of his peers and an audience, and so the cycle will continue. A responsible child will take charge of the situation, and quietly do what he can to help.

Dealing with different types of bullying

There are certain situations which require special measures, and we'll look at these below in relation to some of the main types of bullying. Furthermore, if your child is being bullied regularly, you will need to intervene to protect him, and this can take many forms, from writing a letter to the school, paying a visit, campaigning for changes to bullying policies, contacting the police and even, in dire circumstances, considering moving your child to another school or even undertaking home learning. You'll need to know the legal implications of much of this, too, to ensure that you deal with the problem correctly and within the confines of the law. First, though, let's look at how to deal with specific types of bullying.

Extortion

- Teach your child not to give in immediately by handing over money or property. Instead, leave the scene with head held high. The more easily he or she gives in, the more likely they are to be targeted again.
- Label everything your child owns – every pencil, crayon and felt-tip pen. If his things are taken, you will then not only have proof that the incident happened, but you may also dissuade a bully from taking things that are so clearly someone else's.
- Encourage your child to leave his important belongings at home. Going without an iPod or a pair of nice trainers during the day is a far sight better than having to give them up to thugs.
- All extortion should be reported to an adult. If your child is afraid or unwilling to do this, then you may have to step in and let the school know what is happening. You can ask that your child's anonymity be protected if necessary – chances are he won't have been the only target of the victim.
- Use all of the 'bully-proof' techniques listed on pages 102–105, including modelling the appropriate body language, saying 'no' firmly while looking the bully in the eye, and using 'I' statements: 'I will not hand over my money or goods.'

- Get clever. I've heard of a few good tricks played on unsuspecting bullies, including carrying a 'dummy' wallet with Monopoly money in it and a note saying 'You've been rumbled', to covering bank notes with dye so that the bully is unable to deny his role, to planting something disgusting – or a note from a parent – in the sandwich of a child whose lunch is regularly taken. Anything that unsettles the bully is likely to stop the bullying in its tracks. Bullying is never a joke, and should not be considered so; however, having some fun with your child 'righting wrongs' in an undamaging fashion may well be therapeutic and put things in perspective.
- Like many other forms of bullying – including damage to property, physical assault and stealing – extortion is a criminal offence. You will be very unlikely to want to travel down the route of having your child enter a courtroom or even press charges against the bully, but where extortion continues over time, you may want to report the incidents to the police so that they are recorded.

Physical bullying

- Assault is always serious and can be very dangerous. This is one type of bullying that must be stopped in its tracks immediately, before your child becomes badly hurt. That's not to say that it is more painful than emotional bullying, which can be disastrous in both the short and the long term, but that there is a short-term risk to health which must be taken seriously.
- Children who are physically bullied are often smaller or shorter than their peers, and are therefore at a physical disadvantage, so consider offering your child self-defence or martial art lessons. The idea is not to encourage the violence to spiral by fighting, but to give him the confidence to protect himself if things get out of control. And, if necessary, to prevent serious damage.
- Take photographs of every injury, no matter how minor, and log them with a time and date. You may get to the point where you need evidence and facts at your disposal.
- All physical violence should be reported to the police. You do not necessarily need to press charges, but it must be recorded and documented.
- The school should be informed in writing (see page 122).
- If necessary, you may need to apply for a restraining order – particularly if there has been serious physical damage.

Emotional bullying

- All children need to learn to stand up for themselves within their peer group, and it is important that all parents of victims take steps to work on self-respect, body language, coping skills, assertiveness and so on. This is one situation where a child must appear confident, must be able to look the bullies in the eye or ignore them, and must show no weakness.

- Ask your child to keep any notes that have been written to or about her, and to keep a diary of any bullying. Even if the evidence is not required later on, it can be therapeutic for some kids to get their emotions down on paper.

- It's also very important in this case to encourage your child to develop a circle of supportive and like-minded friends. There is not only safety in numbers, but your child's confidence will be restored if he knows he is valued.

- Again, teach your child some witty retorts or comebacks – both to 'unseat' the bullies – to show them that they aren't having the expected or planned effect – and to save face. Role-playing will help with this and will teach your child the skills she needs. Actually walk through situations and have her practise different responses.

- If your child becomes withdrawn or depressed, if his grades slip, or if he no longer enjoys activities or friends, you may need to consider some counselling. Isolation-bullying techniques, name-calling and other emotional bullying can be enormously undermining for kids who are just establishing their self-image, and they may not have the emotional maturity to cope. Getting extra help is not a cop-out; in some cases it is a necessity in the interests of self-preservation.

- Many happy, healthy children are emotionally bullied for no other reason than that the bully is jealous, or knows that he has found a target with a low propensity for violence. It may also be because he feels like picking on someone, and a child – perhaps at a low emotional ebb, or unwilling to show the emotional dysfunction of some of her peer group – looks like a good target. Your child needs to be aware of this. Children, particularly those who are the recipient of emotional bullying, tend to blame themselves, or look inward rather than seeing the situation for what it is – a dysfunctional child causing possibly deep emotional harm. Every victim of emotional bullying will need that reassurance.

- According to bullying expert Tim Field, 'Bullies control those they target by using disempowerment and by stimulating artificially high levels of fear, shame, embarrassment and guilt.' Your child will need emotional support to get over this type of negative targeting, and the negative feelings that ensue. Offer it wherever possible.

Racial bullying

In this equation, it's worth including bullying that is undertaken on the basis of a child's religion, sexuality, appearance or race. The underlying and, indeed, overwhelming feature of this type of bullying is that a child cannot control or change his status, and, as dreadful as it may seem, must learn to live with it. There will always be people who judge and who hate on the basis of what a person stands for, the group they belong to, their class, their appearance, their race or their sexual inclination. This type of bullying boils down to fear and ignorance on the part of the bully, and nothing else.

- In the UK, the Race Relations Act 1976 makes it illegal to treat someone less favourably because of the colour of their skin, their race, their nationality or their ethnic or national origin. The Crime and Disorder Act 1998 also created new criminal offences in relation to race, such as racially aggravated criminal damage, assault and public order offences. Another law, the Public Order Act 1986, makes it illegal to incite racial hatred, whether through the language used or through actions, such as distributing racist leaflets. Penalties are severe for anyone convicted of a racially motivated crime. Many other countries have similar bills and acts, so seek out the one most relevant to your child. Don't hesitate to take this further. You can contact the police, who will be obliged to treat even minor incidents seriously. Your child needs protection.
- Your child will need facts on which to rely, and with which to develop self-pride. Different religions and races are less frightening when they are understood, and though your child can never be the 'messenger' or 'representative' for his faith or colour, he can show pride and be willing to explain where that pride comes from. Bullies tend not to be emotionally clever, so if your child can blind them with facts and science, they may well back off. It's certainly worth a try.
- Staying away from problem kids is never really a long-term solution, but in the interests of safety and sanity, your child will do much better if he avoids the bullies at all costs.
- Ensure he has a good support network of like-minded friends who will stand up for him. As we have noted already, there is safety in numbers.

• Make sure your child feels confident about standing strong and being proud to be different or, indeed, just what he is – a unique and worthy individual. It's particularly important to raise the self-esteem of a child who has been racially bullied. They can't change what or who they are, and nor should they try. They need to find happiness within their own skins, and be proud of themselves, no matter what.

Cyberbullying

The full extent of this type of bullying is still unknown, but there can be no doubt that it is insidious and on the increase. Mobile phones are one of the key social mechanisms used by today's children, and much of their social life is undertaken by text. Computer technology, too, forms a strong bond, especially between teenagers, with instant messaging considered to be 'the easiest way to talk to people' (particularly of the other sex) and 'the way we know what's going on' (comments taken from interviews with 121 teenagers in the UK and Canada).

However, this new and 'easy' form of communication also means that children can render themselves anonymous at the click of the button, thus opening up a whole new arena for potential bullying. Young people can not only disguise themselves, they can also distance themselves from their own actions. Because they are not in physical contact with the victim, they can put it all down to yet another 'prank'.

As with other forms of bullying, parents may not be aware of what is going on. Mobile phone bullying doesn't leave bruises or scratches, or torn clothes and books. The culture of secrecy that often prevents parents knowing about bullying is harder to crack when young people are in any case often reluctant to tell parents whom they are texting or calling. Mobile phone bullying frequently takes place when a child or young person is alone, perhaps at night in their bedroom. It may feel even harder than usual to work out what's happening.

But parents may be able to pick up on other signs. Is your child upset after particular phone calls or texts? Is she reluctant to go to school? Is he disinclined to text or phone when you're around?

With this type of bullying the most tempting solution is to remove a child's mobile phone, change the number, or set up a new email account or supplier. But there are two important reasons why you should avoid doing this. The first is that children are amazingly resourceful, and new numbers and email

Mobile bullying

A recent survey by the UK charity NCH found that mobile bullying included:

- Anonymous texts of a generally threatening nature. These were seen as the least threatening, except when an anonymous caller or texter kept getting in touch and/or knew names and personal details. Then it became scary.
- Persistent personal threats by text and phone, where the caller knew the young person.
- Happy slapping (see page 117).
- Taking photos of violent, embarrassing or ridiculous situations, for example, of people kissing, or opening car doors when cyclists are riding by, or doing dangerous dares. These photos then get circulated, sometimes to friends, sometimes as widely as to whole year groups at school.
- Being part of a chain text, with implied threats if the person doesn't pass it on, for example, 'If you don't send this picture on in the next five minutes, your love life will die, or you will die in the next five years.'

addresses can be accessed speedily when required. There is a slick network out there, and numbers and addresses change hands quickly. If your child engages in MSN or another instant messaging service, it won't be long before a new screen name or address is identified.

The second reason not to bother with instant changes is that evidence is crucial. If you change your number, any problems associated with the old number cannot be linked. You and your child need to be scrupulous about noting down bullying phone calls, texts or email messages. Keep a diary of the time of every problematic call, even if it comes up as 'number unknown'. Police and other specialists can trace calls even from 'withheld' numbers. Similarly, if your email account or instant message screen name is targeted, save everything into a separate file.

There is absolutely no need for children to read texts or to listen to messages; set phones to 'divert to message' and let the messages provide the authorities

Happy slapping

Unlike computers, where hard drives usually retain deleted images, mobile phones are relatively basic devices, and criminals can usually cover their backs simply by getting rid of stills or video footage which might be used against them by the police. Police believe that if offenders knew that they could be caught even after they had deleted the images, it might put an end to the craze. One British company is working on ways of recovering deleted images.

One way offenders can be caught is if they send pictures or footage to a friend's mobile phone. This is important.

For happy slapping to be curtailed or eradicated, it is crucial that everyone who receives a video, or any footage, of a happy slapping event passes on those details to an adult they trust – a teacher, a parent or even the authorities. Statistics show that most children feel uncomfortable with the happy slapping trend and are aware that it is morally wrong to film acts of violence on unsuspecting and innocent people – particularly when so many of these acts have ended in horrendous beatings. So do not hesitate to use these feelings and point out the seriousness of the crime. Images can also be sent anonymously to the police or other authorities without fear of retribution, though offenders will never be caught or charged without vital evidence.

Moreover, even witnessing this type of violence may be enough to stop the perpetrators. If images can be downloaded before they are erased, the authorities will have the evidence they need to convict, or at least to caution. So encourage your child to report any evidence of happy slapping, no matter how innocuous. It may seem bizarre to consider encouraging a bullied child to involve himself in catching bullies, but once again, it can be done anonymously, and unless everyone takes responsibility, the trend will continue.

You may also consider lobbying your child's school to ban camera phones. Most schools have some policy about mobile phones, and some do not allow them at all; however, those that do can set restrictions.

The surprise element of happy slapping means that your child will probably be unaware of an attack until it occurs. However, it's worth reminding your child to avoid gangs of any description, to avoid being alone in playgrounds or any quiet public places where help cannot easily be sought, and to develop a more confident persona in public.

with the appropriate details. Encourage your child not to open texts or emails, but simply to save them (or forward them to your computer or phone) in order to keep a record.

It's important to realise that a child's phone may be a lifeline to her, an essential part of her social life, so tread with care when suggesting a replacement or its removal.

If your child is very distressed, you may wish to purchase a second phone – continuing to operate his or her SIM card in the first phone to keep an all-important record – thus allowing your child to continue his or her social life on a new number. A determined bully will probably obtain this number, but there's no harm in trying. A similar ruse can be used with screen names.

There are a number of other tips that are worth considering:

Phones

- Always encourage your child to talk about how they use their mobile phone. If they seem distressed after a phone call, discuss the topic of malicious calls and messages. Don't let them fester in the belief that they have done something wrong and feel that they have no one to talk to. Be supportive.
- If your child knows the sender and they attend the same school, contact your child's class teacher or school head as soon as possible – even if the phone calls and text messages happen outside school hours.
- Keep a record of the calls and text messages to show to the school.
- Change your child's mobile number as soon as possible, but keep the old number (SIM card) in order to provide a trail of evidence if there is doubt about the perpetrators.
- Talk to your mobile phone service provider. They usually operate a 'malicious calls' helpdesk as part of their customer service.

Encourage your child to:
- Avoid giving out any information about himself, such as phone number and address, unless he knows and trusts the caller.
- Avoid leaving alternative contact details as part of a voicemail greeting.
- Avoid replying to any text messages unless he knows the caller.
- Show any messages that are wrong, worrying, from strangers, or simply malicious, to a trusted person, such as a parent or other family member, or a teacher.

- Always check the caller ID. If the number is unfamiliar or comes up as unknown or withheld – don't answer!
- Leave their phone near loud background noise if they do answer a malicious call. If children appear to be alone, it may prompt a further bullying incident.
- Divert their calls to a mailbox, where they can be used as evidence of bullying.
- Make a note of the sender's details at the end of the message.
- Be careful and selective about who they give their mobile phone number to.
- Ensure that friends do not pass the number on to other people that they don't know – no matter how tempting!
- Never reply to an abusive text – it will just encourage the bullies.
- Avoid replying to a missed call if they don't know the number. If it's genuine, they can leave a message or call back.
- Keep abusive texts or pictures. These provide an important record in case it is necessary to call the police.
- Switch off the phone if they are being bullied when they feel particularly vulnerable, for example, late at night.

Internet

Experts on bullying believe that many bullies tend to lack good communication skills and therefore the impersonal nature of email makes it an ideal tool for them to use to victimise others. Unfortunately it is not immediately possible to check where an email has come from – you have to trust that the named writer is genuine. It is not always wise, however, to make this assumption. The best advice is:

- If a name is not familiar, it may be safer not to open the email.
- If the bullying happens through a personal email account, report it to the sender's email account provider – you can find this address after the @ sign.
- Most ISPs allow you to block any given email address from your account or have it redirected to a separate file or account as 'spam'. This can be your 'clearing house' for evidence, should it be required.
- If it is not obvious who the sender is and there is continual bullying using email, then there are tools to trace senders. To find out more about this email tracking, go to one of the search engines, (Google, Yahoo, etc.) and type in 'email tracking software' – this software can then be downloaded. Once you know

the identity of the bully, get in touch with your Internet Service Provider (ISP), who can then block the sender from your email.

- If the email bullying is occurring in school, this should be dealt with through the school's anti-bullying policy (see page 117).
- Keep a record of all bullying incidents either by saving or printing emails.
- If an email message is disturbing or breaks the law, do not hesitate to contact the police.
- You may be aware of recent episodes where people have been victimised via websites – one incident involved pupils setting up an offensive website about their teachers. Of course, the victim may not always be aware that these sites exist. However, if your child realises that s/he has been bullied in this way, the first course of action is to contact your ISP. They can find out who runs the site and can request that it be removed. If the person responsible is at school with your child, let the headteacher know. Any false accusations or anything on the website which you feel is breaking the law should be reported to the police.

There are many types of bullying, but the premise for dealing with them remains the same – give your children the strength, the emotional power, the pride and the confidence to believe in themselves and what they stand for. Help them to make friends if they are having trouble. Teach them appropriate body language and techniques for dealing with criticism and the negative actions of others. Help them to maintain a strong self-image and to deflect the attentions of bullies by whatever means necessary.

There will undoubtedly come a time, however, when you need to become involved, and the way you deal with the situation is crucial to eradicating the problem and protecting your child. What follows are the basics; the subject is dealt with in more depth in Chapter 9.

Helping a bullied child

Most children cannot deal on their own with being bullied, and the simple truth is that they need protection. Parents must be able to offer that without blame, rancour, anger or even disbelief. No matter how seriously you take the situation, a bullied child will be suffering on many levels, and attempts to 'toughen him' or make him 'stand up to the bullies' will undoubtedly fail. Children do not have the emotional wherewithal to cope with many

Avoid confrontation

Do not, under any circumstance, try to sort things out with the bullies themselves, or with their parents. You may undermine your own position by losing your temper or doing something that would not be considered appropriate. In most countries there are hundreds of laws protecting children, and even talking to them in what they consider to be the wrong way may be construed as harassment. What's more, few parents are going to be happy to learn that their child is a bully, and you may end up having real problems of your own, or, indeed, undermining the process. Leave it to the experts.

of the demands on their young lives, and bullying can push them over the line. Don't underestimate the impact that it can have on your child's life, and be prepared to help in whatever way possible.

Establishing the facts

The most important step you can take is to put together a log or diary of incidents. This should include the names of the perpetrators and witnesses, the place and time, and any action undertaken. Without bullying your child yourself, you must get as much information as you can. This is crucial not only to establishing the truth about the encounters, but also to providing the necessary evidence. You need your facts to hand. Some children may be reluctant to blame others, or to give details of who witnessed the incident, for fear of retaliation or further loss of face. Reassure your child that you are working on a report, not telling tales. Further reassure him that he did nothing wrong and that he is entitled to live his life without fear of bullies. Be supportive, and whatever you do, don't say: Right, leave this with me; I'll sort it out. It is a mutual problem and you need to work on problem-solving together. Your child may have strong ideas about the best way to deal with it, and it is important to listen.

Making contact with the school

In the first instance, and if the bullying has not reached danger point, contact your child's teacher and explain your concerns. A phone call will suffice at this point. Get her reaction and suggestions, and make the salient points. Ask her to contact you in a week or so to report any feedback.

In the meantime, encourage your child to keep a diary of every single encounter, in order to provide the best possible picture of what is happening. Work on raising your child's self-esteem and take steps towards 'bully-proofing' her. The idea here is to prevent the situation from escalating until it has been appropriately dealt with.

If you feel that you have not received an acceptable response, or that nothing is being done to protect your child, it's time for a face-to-face visit.

Making an appointment to see your child's teacher

Try to ensure that the head of the school is also present at the meeting, as well as anyone who has responsibility for the emotional health and wellbeing of the students, or who is responsible for dealing with bullying. Your child may wish to come along, and it's a good idea if they do so, because they will be able to answer questions and elaborate where you cannot. But if your child is worried or overly daunted, don't push it. As long as you have a full log of the facts to hand, you should be able to deal with questions.

Go in with a calm attitude and express your concerns. Do not attempt to blame anyone, including the school or the teacher, as you will only put their backs up and ultimately get nowhere. Succinctly state the problem and the salient details. Ask what they suggest you do, and ask how you can help. Expect some resistance. Many schools will deny a bullying problem (and if this happens, you can be sure there is one!), while others may even suggest that your child was at the root of the problem. Some may be bewildered, having genuinely missed the problem, and will need reassurance from you that you are not blaming them, but that you expect results.

Take notes of everything they say. This is important, as it will form part of the basis of a follow-up letter. Agree to meet in a week, or to have regular phone calls made to check the progress of any investigation or of any measures that should be put in place to deal with the bully.

Don't be afraid to ask for plenty of information, such as how previous bullying cases have been dealt with, how children are normally penalised (for example, are they excluded or suspended?), and what measures are in place to prevent the problem. Ask about supervision at break time, and in the school halls and playground.

If you don't get anywhere, there are further options (see below).

Writing a letter

It is better to follow up a personal meeting at the school with a letter than to start off by sending a letter out of the blue. Letters are easily discarded, misread or ignored. See them in person and then, after the meeting, write a letter detailing everything you have said to them (including all of the key information: facts, times, people involved, etc.), everything that was discussed, and everything that was agreed. Arrange a date for a further meeting or telephone call, and provide all your contact details.

Make your letter clear, concise and non-judgemental. You may have to rely on it as evidence in the worst possible case scenario. It's also a good idea, depending on the severity of the problem, to send a copy to your local education authority. Ask that your letter be placed on your child's file. Mark it as 'personal and confidential' and make it clear that the information within it should not be divulged without your permission.

Schools have a duty of care, and allowing a child to be continually bullied when the school has been alerted to the problem could be seen as a breach of that duty.

Going further

If your child is seriously distressed and suffering physical symptoms, see your family doctor and make sure that the problem is documented in his or her medical notes. You may also ask your doctor to write a letter to the school confirming the physical or emotional symptoms that your child presents.

In many Western countries, there must, by law, be a bullying policy in place at the school. It's worth asking to see documentation of this, and asking the appropriate questions. There should be something there that pertains to your child, and you will be able to deal more effectively with any authorities if you know what should have been done.

If you find, following an appropriate number of visits and follow-up letters to the school, that your child's case has not been addressed, you are well within your rights to contact the education authority or school board, or to seek a meeting or comments from the governors of the school. Send a letter with details of all correspondence, copies of letters, a summary of the facts, and the steps you have taken to address the problem.

Ask around. If your child is being bullied, the chances are that other children are too. Work together with parents of other bullied children to compile a document that portrays a picture of what is actually going on, and what you have done to try to get some help.

In the extreme, you may have to consider moving your child, taking legal action, or even educating your child at home. We'll look at these options in Chapter 9.

But remember...

A good deal of this chapter focuses on what research perceives to be shortcomings or overwhelming characteristics of victims. Do remember that many children who become targets are honest, respectful, intelligent children who have been in the wrong place at the wrong time, have incited feelings of jealousy in the bullies, seem like an easy target because they won't become violent and therefore present no threat, have somehow rubbed a bully up the wrong way by being what he wants to be or, alternatively, everything he despises, or have simply showed vulnerability.

A victim of bullying is nothing more than a target for someone else's wrath, rage and problems. Remember that. What your child needs is support and protection, and a place where his unique characteristics will be celebrated. Do your best to offer that.

In the next chapter we'll look at how to deal with bullies. They are, it must be said, children too.

5

When Your Child Is the Bully

There are only two forces in the world, the sword and the spirit. In the long run the sword will always be conquered by the spirit.

Napoleon

THERE CAN BE LITTLE WORSE FOR PARENTS than to discover that their child is a bully. Not only is there an implied suggestion that you have failed as a parent, and that your child lacks the social skills and values necessary to sustain normal and healthy interactions with other children, but the idea that your child could be capable of hurting others is desperately worrying.

There is no doubt that much bullying has its roots in the home, and in Chapter 7 we examine ways to make your home a healthier, happier place, where issues such as violence, sibling bullying, parental violence or even arguments, discipline and self-respect are all given the attention they require in order to combat bullying tendencies. But remember, too, that your child's temperament, the way he sees the world around him, and his ability to empathise can also influence his ability to bully. Peers also encourage and abet bullying, and many normal kids find themselves trapped in a situation they feel helpless to change. What's more, in an unhealthy school climate, where bullying is rife and bystanders are drawn into the proceedings in order to protect themselves, or to maintain peer relations, nice kids can become bullies out of fear, through persuasion, and because they feel powerless.

I am firmly of the belief, however, that even bullies must be treated with compassion. After all, children are blank slates upon which their environment and upbringing are imprinted. No child comes into the world wilfully setting out to damage property or hurt other children. A culture of aggression, a problem with power, a temperamental issue, or an inability to find the confidence to withstand peer pressure may be at the root of bullying. So the question we must ask ourselves is: What drives a child to become a bully?

Children learn what they live. Parents who express anger physically are much more likely to produce children who express anger physically. Children from homes where there is domestic violence tend to over- or underestimate violence, thus strongly affecting their later relationships with others and with their own children. Also, many parents – and indeed society as a whole – find 'different' customs, practices, patterns of behaviour, appearance and beliefs frightening or threatening, and therefore children learn, through role models, to ostracise people who stand out or appear to endanger the premises upon which we build our lives.

All children need protection, including those who have suffered at the hands of parents or siblings, or through an unjust system, or a societal acceptance of violence. If we ignore the needs and causative issues of bullies, we are in effect suggesting that it's OK to raise a generation of misfits who will live unhappy lives and threaten the world around us. Unless we deal with the causative factors of bullying – both on a personal level with the bullies themselves, and in the context of the school environment – we will never eradicate the problem, and we will never do the children involved – both bully and victim – any justice.

As already stated, many bullies have high self-esteem and are popular with their peers. They appear to be well-adjusted, they get reasonable or very good grades at school, and they manage to persuade anyone looking that they are model citizens. So what cunning lies beneath this treachery, and what drives a child who seems to have everything to want to harm the lives of his peers? What makes a nice kid from a good, well-off family want to extort money from younger boys, or steal phones, or send nasty messages, or insult, beat or taunt kids who get in his way? Unless we find an answer to these questions, we will never get any further in the fight to lay bullying to rest.

In this chapter we'll look at what you as parents can do to address the problems. There is no point in being proud or denying a potential problem. It's essential that you look carefully at all the research and work out if there is any element that may be relevant to your child. Many studies show that parents are blind to their children's shortcomings, and actively avoid seeing anything they don't want to see. A clever bully will hide things from his parents as well as he does from teachers and other authority figures. Look carefully for the signs before deciding that your child is blameless. But, more importantly, look for the causative factors. It may be that your child is under a great deal of stress in some areas of his life (see Chapter 6) and acting uncharacteristically. It may be that she has been bullied herself, and has become the quintessential 'bully-victim', channelling her anger and powerlessness into abusing other people. It may be that your child is being taunted by siblings, or overwhelmed by violence in the media or at school. Perhaps you've created a little monster by raising her self-esteem to the point where she thinks she is invincible, better than others, and therefore 'in charge' of the playground or classroom. There could be many causes, but without the willingness to identify and address them, the problems won't go away.

Before you decide that your child is not a bully, but the innocent recipient of a 'mad' victim's wrath, ask yourself a few questions.

Clues that your child may be bullying

1. Does your child become easily frustrated when she doesn't get her own way?

2. Do you know who your child's friends are? If you don't, is there a reason?

3. Have you seen your child interact with others? Is she dominant or aggressive? Think about how her peers relate to her – is she always the 'boss' and in control, without negotiating or compromising anything?

4. What does your child do in her spare time? Do you know where she is and what interests her? The sad truth is that parents who are unaware of their children's leisure activities may be in for a shock, as 'hiding' the truth from parents obviously suggests activities that children are aware will not impress. A reluctance to talk about anything she does is also a danger signal.

5. Does your child use negative words to describe other children, such as 'She's stupid', or 'She's useless'?

6. Does your child talk about some children 'deserving' bad things?

7. Does your child show empathy for children who have been victimised or bullied, or even hurt, or does she find reasons why the victim 'deserved it'.

8. Does your child seem to have a lot of anger that is expressed in unsuitable ways? In other words, does she explode for no obvious reason?

9. Does your child have a good, non-violent role model at home?

10. How does your child perceive violence or other people's reactions to violence? Does he laugh or applaud, or seem sensitised?

11. Is there any violence in your home?

12. Is you child impulsive and quick to judge?

13. What is your family approach to bullying and violence, and to other races, religions or classes? Is anyone racist or happy to accept violence? Does anyone believe that bullies are only balancing the social system, and that victims need to be taught a lesson?

14. Has anyone ever told your child that victims 'need to toughen up', or that victims are 'wimps' or that 'bullying is a part of life'?

15. Does your child seem excited by violence? Is he the first on the scene to witness a fight, and instantly take sides? Does he become agitated and flustered by violence in the home or on television?

16. Can he express his emotions, or is he overly calm and controlled?

17. Does your child have trouble interpreting other people's behaviour? In other words, does he see violence where they may not be any, or hostile intent when there is none?

18. Is your child a seasoned liar, and can he normally charm you to get his way?

19. Does your child appear to have 'henchmen' who look up to him and obey his every wish?

20. Has your child ever been abused at home?

21. Has your child ever fallen in with the 'wrong' crowd?

22. Has your child ever been diagnosed with a conduct disorder?

23. Have there been periods in your child's life where he has been neglected (and this includes emotional neglect, such as having little or no time with parents) due to external circumstances?

24. Has your child been bullied himself, and taken on a cavalier, tough-guy approach to the problem?

25. Does your child ever mention getting revenge?

26. Does your child ever appear to think that he is superior to his peers, or blame others for being physically weaker, different or smaller?

27. Is your child aggressive or manipulative with her siblings?

28. Is your child aggressive or manipulative with you?

29. Is your child unable to play cooperatively? Do most encounters end up in a row or with violence?

30. Does your child boast about her exploits?

31. Does your child equate being popular with being the best or being in charge?

32. Does your child defend or spend time with other aggressive children?

A 'yes' answer to any one of these questions could indicate a proclivity to violence and bullying. If you have several 'yes' answers, there is a very good chance that your child is bullying.

You can also probably tell that your child is bullying by these clues:

1. Has your child ever been accused of bullying at school or anywhere else?

2. Has your child been in trouble for fighting (physical or emotional/verbal fighting is equally relevant)?

3. Does your child have an excuse or 'reason' for any reports of bullying (such as, denial, playing it down: 'I was just messing around,'; or blame: 'He started it'; or defence: 'He was looking for trouble,' or 'He went completely mad on us')?

4. Does your child turn the tables and say that someone else has been bullying her, when there is clear evidence to the contrary?

5. Does your child rely on the evidence of his friends or other witnesses to defend himself? In other words, could it be that his henchmen are doing their job?

6. Does your child seem to have more money than he should?

7. Does your child come home with items that do not belong to her?

8. Does your child claim she doesn't need a lunch because she'll 'get something at school'?

Think carefully. Many of these signs are indications that all is not well, and that your child is undertaking activities that may harm others.

The parenting question

Chapter 7 examines the type of home environment and discipline policies that are necessary to raise emotionally healthy children. Many studies have indicated that bullies are the product of homes that are not as well-grounded as they should be, and no matter how confident you are about your parenting ability, I urge you to read that chapter. What's more, remember that subparenting is also a problem. A self-effacing, successful young woman or man might be given a great deal of freedom and left to fend for himself on many occasions. Trust is a precarious thing, and many parents are coerced into believing that when everything looks good, their child should be allowed freedoms on many different levels. It's important to remember that children of all ages, no matter how confident or successful they might be, need regular boundaries, plenty of parental input, guidance, mentorship and communication.

Take a look, too, at the way your children interact together. Sibling rivalry can escalate into bullying without a parent noticing, and if your child has been the butt of his sibling's jokes, or been teased mercilessly, or even subjected to violence, he may well take that out on his peers or others. While it teaches good problem-solving techniques for children to be left to negotiate their own battles and learn to compromise, parents must also be alert to situations that have gone too far.

What is your communication like? Do you have regular times, every single day, when your child can share his problems, complain, get some recognition, support or appreciation, have an outlet for his emotions, or just chat? Do you feel that you know a lot about your child, who his friends are, what he gets up to in his spare time, what he worries about, what his goals are, and how he interacts with his peers? Do you look over his homework or coursework and show interest and enthusiasm? Do you praise things that may not be obvious?

And how about your responses to your child? Are you competitive for him, and want him to be the best, thereby ignoring his worries that he may not match your expectations? Do you dismiss his problems and say that they are 'part of growing up' or he will 'sort them out' himself? Do you take note when he shows weakness or vulnerability? Do you take him to task for being aggressive, racist, unfair, dogmatic or supercilious? In other words, how good is your feedback? If you hear things that are socially unacceptable and a precursor to bullying, do you tune out because you have other things on your mind, or do you actively parent? The most important element of parenting, apart from providing unconditional love, is to give guidance, in every and any situation. That doesn't mean storming in with moral lessons, or pointing out where your child has gone wrong, but, instead, looking at preconceived ideas and beliefs together, and working on making a child more tolerant, more loving, more empathetic and more in tune with himself.

Talking to your child

If you have reason to believe that your child has been bullying others, don't go in with the sledgehammer approach. This will only put his back up and encourage further and even more elaborate defences and lies. Many children feel guilty about bullying; others have a defence facility that allows them either to justify it or to subconsciously deny it; others know instinctively that you will not react well to hearing the truth about their actions, and they will use every ploy imaginable to ensure that you never find out; still others will be as subversive as they are at school, and play the innocent because they genuinely believe that they are. Whatever the case, tread lightly. If you show immediate anger or disapproval, you will never get anywhere, and you will lose the opportunity both to right the wrong and to prevent the behaviour from recurring. Moreover, you will lose the option of teaching a lesson, of presenting the empathetic and moral standpoint, of explaining and reassuring, and, most importantly, of working out the factors that have caused your child to behave the way he has.

Kids will not usually confess, so you need to be protector, detective, counsellor and ally all in one.

Go in with an open mind, and be prepared to listen. While bullies rarely deserve sympathy, they may have issues that are encouraging them to act the way they do, and unless they feel secure enough to divulge these, they can never be addressed. So you must present yourself as a non-judgemental, unconditionally loving, listening parent. No matter how angry you are – or how outraged or betrayed you feel – listen.

Like the parents of 'targets' or victims, you also must learn to read between the lines, and ask pertinent questions. Is there anyone bullying at your school? Are there any children you don't like? What happens when you don't like a particular child? Do any of your friends pick on kids they don't like? Is it OK to bully at your school or will you get into trouble? What did you do after school today? Was there any trouble at the bus-stop/on the school bus/in the playground? What do you do when someone makes you really angry?

Innocent questions, put forward on a daily or weekly basis, help you to keep in touch with what your child may be doing and/or hiding from you. Keep the channels of communication open, and don't express dismay or surprise if he divulges something you don't want to hear. Use it as a vehicle for further discussion in a calm, dispassionate way. Use his answers to teach emotional literacy, with responses such as: that must have made you feel very angry/jealous/hurt/crazy/frustrated, etc.

If your child does admit to having bullied others, you are entitled to ask some hard-hitting questions, but your responses must remain the same. Remember – and this is important – the more open and reflective you are, the more your child will confide.

(continued on page 134)

Girls and violence

Parents of girls may be particularly upset to hear that their daughter is a bully, as bullying falls so fully outside what we, as a society, expect of women. Many women, growing up, have experienced the typical 'girlie' nastiness – the ostracism, the changing of allegiances, the neat little put-downs, the bossiness, and the fight to be the 'leader' within a group. Appearance rates heavily, as does compliance towards the 'leader', and the ability to add to the group in some measurable way. So, too, do popularity and other perceived qualities.

Girls have always been able to rely more heavily on 'turned backs', on gossip, notes and telling glances than boys have ever done. For this reason, many parents of girls will dismiss verbal and social bullying as just 'one of those things' that girls do. But does this make it right? The simple answer is no.

Girls are rightly taught that they are as important as boys and have the right to the same code of behaiour. However, in recent years a growing number of girls, for various reasons, have begun to replicate and emulate the actions of boys by becoming as physical and violent as they are (see page 19). And we must ask ourselves whether we are in danger of creating a nation not of 'supergirls' but of girls trapped in a world that embraces violence, glorifies people 'standing up for themselves', rejects overt femininity, and celebrates women who behave like men. No wonder there is confusion, and no wonder girls feel obliged in many cases to behave like their more violent peers. It's a sign of parity, of being one of the gang, of being capable of doing anything a man can do, and a ticket to the overvalued world of men.

If you have a daughter, think carefully about what you teach her. Don't make her give up her feminine side in the pursuit of equality. Let her play with her dolls and her crafts; let her keep her makeup and 'dressing-up' clothes. She needs to learn that being a woman is a positive and pleasurable thing, and that female concerns and values could be adopted by the rest of the population to great effect. Parents of daughters should take great care to raise them as women – capable women, certainly, women who are able to reach their goals on every level, and match the achievements of men when required, but women who also maintain the important aspects of humanity.

What you can do:

- Apply the same rules for girls as for boys – violence is not acceptable under any circumstances. It doesn't make a girl more of a 'lad' or make her stronger in any way; in fact, it makes her someone who complies and reacts rather than uses innate intelligence to negotiate or communicate her way out of difficult situations.
- The general advice in this chapter relates to girls, but with girls you may need to delve deeper; girls bullying with violence is a relatively new phenomenon, and finding out why your daughter needs to behave this way is of paramount importance.
- Encourage your daughter to celebrate being a woman rather than changing key values to behave like violent male peers. If she is self-confident and self-respecting, she will learn to believe in herself and the obviously positive qualities of women.
- There is nothing wrong with being a 'tomboy', and embracing traditionally male activities; however, becoming violent is unacceptable no matter what the sex.
- If your daughter is hanging out with a male crowd, and feeling pressure to conform to its values, you may need to look carefully at finding alternative activities and friends. This may take some effort, but you can enrol her or suggest that she goes to different clubs, after school events or extracurricular activities.

Girls will bully as often as boys, and the more subversive means they use are highly dangerous and distressing. Don't go in easier because you are dealing with a girl. If your daughter has been bullying, whether by isolation tactics, gossip, notes, or emotional abuse, it is wrong, and it must be addressed. Remember, it is not part of life.

- Girls tend to bully in gangs rather than on their own, so it may be necessary to ensure that she is not hanging out with a big crowd and causing trouble. Encourage smaller groups of friends by inviting them round, by taking one or two of them to the cinema or the theatre, or suggesting small sleepovers or shopping trips. The smaller the group, the less likelihood of real trouble. That's not to say that girls won't turn on each other in smaller groups, because they most certainly will – and this must be dealt with. But they are much less likely to cause great harm to others if they are on their own.

Kids will not usually confess, so you need to be protector, detective, counsellor and ally all in one. Ask how your child feels about himself, how he thinks things are going at school and at home. Ask if he is being bullied, and how he gets on with other kids. Ask how he treats other children, and what he would feel about being called a bully. If you know and he has admitted that he has been bullying, ask how he feels about himself, ask why he thinks he might need to bully, and ask what he thinks might help him to stop. The more information you get, the more you can help.

Assessing the cause

When you get to the point where you are fully aware that your child has been bullying others, you can then take steps to work out why. In Chapter 1 we looked at all the different causative factors of bullying. Take a look back now, and see if any of them is pertinent. Look at your family life, the way the kids work together, and who his friends are. Ask questions about the school and how they deal with bullying. Work out what he does in his spare time and whether or not more sanctions need to be applied. Does he have too much or too little freedom? Can he relate well to others on a general level, or does he have trouble interacting? Has he always been a little highly strung? If he appears to lack empathy, sympathy and compassion, why might that be? Have you been empathetic to others, sympathetic to his needs, and compassionate in your job as a role model? Has your child learned racist tendencies at home? Is your family discipline consistent? Are your penalties or punishments too harsh or do they exist at all? What is your own approach to bullying? In other words, have you ever shown tolerance or acceptance of bullying in any manner (including statements, such as, 'Well, he had it coming', or 'He needs to learn to grow up', or 'He'll soon learn to fight his own battles', or 'It's a part of life')?

Look at the questions above and try to find motivation for anything to which you could confidently answer yes. It's a difficult job, and it may involve admitting things you'd rather not, but no bully can ever be helped without some honest assessment, followed by a plan based on his individual factors.

Self-esteem

The question of self-esteem hangs high over the whole issue of bullying and to this day many experts still strongly disagree about whether bullies have high or low self-esteem. The simple answer is that in most cases research indicates that bullies have high self-esteem to the point of not caring about others. But any child who feels the need to steal from his peers, to cause physical harm or damage, or merely to want to undermine another child, does not have good emotional health. So though self-esteem may be high, the chances are that self-respect is not. And, ultimately, self-respect is much more important.

Furthermore, not every type of bully will have self-esteem. Take the bully-victim, for example – the chances are that his self-esteem was low enough for him to appear initially to be a target for bullies. Similarly, passive bullies – those who sit on the sidelines until the action begins – will not necessarily be high in self-esteem or even be popular. They are playing by the rules, and siding with whomever they feel is the most popular or prominent member involved. Unlike bystanders, however, they will get involved and join the fracas – whether it be name-calling, physical violence, extortion or something else. It lifts their self-confidence and makes them feel important and part of a group.

So there are two questions to ask here – does your son or daughter have an inflated opinion of himself or herself? Are they 'high' on their own self-esteem; do they feel that they are invincible? It's not an easy question to answer, but if they show scant regard for other people, compete relentlessly and care nothing for the underdog, have no compassion for or empathy with others, and perceive others to be inferior or weaker, you may have a demon on your hands.

The second question is: Does your child lack self-esteem and make up for it by joining in bullying, or by bullying himself? Does he feel important and powerful because he's in charge? Does he have something to gain personally by abusing others? Look at the list in Chapter 3, which outlines the characteristics of genuinely low self-esteem. If your child suffers from these, he needs some help.

But remember, self-esteem is not necessarily the aim here. Self-respect is much more important and, with almost all types of bullies, it is lacking or entirely missing. For details about how to raise self-respect, see Chapter 7. Children with high self-esteem should, by all rights, be emotionally healthy, but that is not always the case.

One thing research shows is that high self-esteem can make people more resilient, make them keep on plugging on after initially failing at something. So that's good. According to self-esteem expert Roy Baumeister, 'The main thing self-esteem does for us, apparently, is to make us happier people. It makes us feel good, at least for a while.' Feeling good about oneself can be a fine thing, he said, particularly when troubles arise, as they inevitably do in all our lives. A genuine sense of self-esteem can give people a stock of positive attitudes that can help them cope with life's trials. People who don't have this handy psychological care-package are likely to be more vulnerable to stress and depression.

So, self-esteem has an important role in creating resilient children, and it's important for parents of victims to note this as well. However, when it goes too far, or when a child believes that he is superior, there is a problem. Furthermore, it fails to address the crucial issue of self-respect, which necessarily involves a respect for others, including their property, and a respect for self. A child with high self-esteem may bully because he needs to feel more powerful, which doesn't mean that he doesn't feel good about himself, but that he lacks the respect necessarily to interact with others on a healthy level. Let's look at a classic scenario below:

Case history

Robert *'I suppose I was the classic bully. I came from a wealthy home, went to a top private school, and every single thing I did was praised over and over again. I felt like I was the best thing since sliced bread. My parents constantly pushed me to be the best, and they backed that up by being so obviously sure that I was the best. They made sure I ate well, and got to sleep on time. I wasn't allowed out too much on the weekends, and because I was doing sports all weekend long, I had to go to bed early then too. My mum chose my clothes; my dad chose my activities. It was a tightly run ship, and I was pretty much a credit to them – I got good grades, I did my homework, I followed the rules, I was a nice guy to their friends. In fact, my social skills were immaculate. They thought they had it made, really.*

'To be honest, I did feel pretty good about myself. When you have so many people believing in you, it's hard not to yourself. But what really irked, as I got a bit older, became a teenager, was that I didn't have any power at all. I was not really my own man at all. Just a puppet, and if I gave the right responses and did the right things, I was happy and so were my parents. All my decisions were made for me, my life was planned down to the last minute, I was questioned at length if I did anything that fell outside 'the brief'. I suppose, in hindsight, that was the reason why I started bullying. It wasn't even a conscious thing, but there were a few things that bugged me. The first was seeing kids who were free to do

what they wanted – some of them were really successful, and others were just nothing but themselves. I felt jealous and angry, so they were the people that I targeted, I suppose. The second thing was just feeling this huge lack of power – lack of control over anything in my life. So if I stood up to other kids, and made myself into a bit of a ringleader, controlling their activities, being the guy who chose what we did, made the master plans, organised our time, and, embarrassingly now, choosing victims – maybe stealing a bit of their money or some of their stuff, maybe sending out nasty notes about them or passing on untrue gossip; maybe even giving someone a good beating if I was in the mood. It created a bit of a high. I was in control. And the amazing thing was that it seemed, for a while, to make me even more popular. Even though I was being nasty, I had this bunch of kids who hung on my every word, who did what I said, and who supported me whenever I chose someone to pick on. I can see now that they probably acted out of fear, but the great thing for me was feeling powerful.

'Now I feel badly of course. And do you know what? Because I was an A student, and on the varsity squad; because I was popular and had lots of friends, and because I had money and worthy, interested and intelligent parents behind me, no one ever squealed. They weren't so into bullying intervention in those days. But I feel like shit for what I did to so many kids. And now that I have kids of my own, I realise what a nasty piece of work I really was and how I probably ruined the schooldays of more than one kid in my class.

'But I've had some counselling – and the reason is that I took things a bit too far in my office on a few occasions. I suppose I was the bully there, too, because I learned at a pretty young age that being in charge and making other people do what you want is a huge buzz. I nearly got fired. I was the golden boy in a lot of ways, but got it all wrong in the way I dealt with people. I know now that it's power I've been looking for, because throughout my whole entire childhood, I never had any. I also know that I get quite jealous of people who have what I don't have – and I'm not talking about money here, because I had all that. I'm jealous of people who are self-sufficient, independent and completely in control of their lives even if they rub people the wrong way. I guess I never had the chance to rebel because I was so 'good', but my form of rebellion may well be the most dangerous of all.'

Insecurity

Even bullies with high self-esteem can feel insecure. They may feel powerless in their own environment, or they may feel threatened by their peers. Moreover, many bullies have had insecure attachment as children (see page 71), harsh or punitive disciplinary methods in their home, or, alternatively, overly lax parenting; they may have been victimised by others, or never had an emotional outlet, or a voice in their homes. All of these things can lead to insecurity, and make a bully irrational, jealous or easily riled, because they see things in a negative light, and perceive hostility where there is none, as well as having an overwhelming need to prove their own importance. Girls may use indirect bullying techniques in their social group in order to isolate others whom they perceive to be a threat, or of whom they are simply jealous. No matter how confident these girls may appear, insecurity is at the root of much of this type of bullying.

Most kids feel insecure to some extent as they grow older, and deal with these feelings by seeking validation of their actions and beliefs through persuading peers to adopt the same actions and beliefs. This is one reason, perhaps, why bullies tend to be so intolerant of people who don't 'fit in', or come from different classes, races or religions. They are, in fact, a perceived threat to an insecure child.

Even under stable family and societal conditions, an adolescent's passage into young adulthood is fraught with challenges. As adolescents move away from the prescribed moorings of family to stand on their own, they experience heightened vulnerability, loneliness and insecurity. Simultaneously, adolescents are bombarded by internal pressures and simulations. Under these pressures, they seek experiences and feelings of power, peer affiliation and certainty.

Numerous studies have identified the importance of attachment security in teenagers, linking poor attachment security to a range of significant mental health outcomes from criminal behaviour to substance abuse, even across decades. And, interestingly, a 2004 study found that adolescents became increasingly insecure in the face of stressors that overwhelmed their coping abilities while also cutting them off from opportunities to rely on close relationships for support.

Attachment security has long been recognised as one of the hallmarks of adaptive social development in infancy and childhood, and is increasingly being recognised for its similar role in adolescence and adulthood. In adolescence, attachment security reflects the ability to openly and straightforwardly seek out and value close relationships while maintaining perspective and balance within those relationships. And we all know that bullies often fail to have that perspective and balance.

Not all bullies are insecure, but many are. Try to work out whether your child feels good about herself.

? What can you do?

• Stress is an important cause of insecurity in children and adolescents. Take steps to deal with it, and to make your child more resilient to the demands made upon him (see pages 88–89).

• Adolescence in particular is a time of great emotional ups and downs, and insecurity, as identity and independence are established, often occurs in children who were fairly robust in earlier childhood. What children need, more than ever (though many will actively resist it), is the support and approval of a loving family. Communication becomes harder in these years, but continue as best you can and offer unconditional love, no matter how annoying your child becomes!

• Spend time together as a family. Children's sense of security is mostly founded on their relationships with their parents and family. It stems from being with people a child trusts in an intimate relationship. But a child needs to have enough time with you to feel that the everyday world you live in is a reliable and safe one in which he feels protected. This can only come from warm, nurturing relationships.

• Express feelings. Help your children express their feelings and concerns. This means giving them the time, empathy and support to do so. Quick, hurried reassurance does not allow children to get all their feelings out. Listen, empathise, and help children share what's on their minds in play as well as in verbal exchanges. It's reassuring to know you are being listened to.

• Allow your child plenty of opportunity to become a confident decision-maker. An 8-year-old is capable of deciding if she wants to invite lots of friends to her birthday party or just a close pal or two. A 12-year-old can choose whether she wants to join the choir or the school band. As your child becomes more skilled at making all kinds of good choices, with your support, she will feel more secure.

• Work on the jealousy aspect, which is often how insecurity manifests itself. Ask your child some pertinent questions, such as why does that bother you?

Are your fears or worries about this particular person/group realistic? Are you being tolerant, knowledgeable and respectful about the differences between you? Is fear leading you to do disrespectful or hurtful things to others? Are you using the same standard to judge your friend's/enemy's behaviour that you use to judge your own behaviour? If not, why not?

- We need to teach children that all people are equal, and that jealousy is really just fear, or placing undue emphasis on what other people are or have. A child needs to learn that everyone has the same basic abilities. Everyone has the same wish to be happy and to succeed, and not to be unhappy or to fail. And everyone has the same right to be happy and to succeed and the same right not to be unhappy or to fail.

- Point out the good things about your child, and often. Children are less likely to become jealous if they are aware of their own strong points, and accept themselves. A strong self-image is part of this (see page 94–96).

Temperament

You can do little to change your child's temperament. Hot-headed, easily frustrated, easily angered and impulsive children have been shown, in many studies, to have a propensity for bullying.

Temperament is a set of inborn traits that organise the child's approach to the world. They are instrumental in the development of the child's distinct personality. These traits also determine how the child goes about learning about the world around him.

These traits appear to be relatively stable from birth. They are enduring characteristics that are actually never 'good' or 'bad.' How they are received determines whether they are perceived by the child as being a bad or good thing. When parents understand the temperament of their children, they can avoid blaming themselves for issues that are normal for their child's temperament. Some children are noisier than other. Some are more cuddly than others. Some have more regular sleep patterns that others.

One reason why avoiding 'labels' (see page 95) is important is that many of your child's temperamental attributes (high energy, impulsiveness, etc.) may have been labelled in a negative light from an early age. Your child may grow up thinking he's 'bad' or 'different' or that he is unacceptable in some way. Children can't 'change' their temperament, so it can be a mortal blow to find that his defining characteristics are somehow wrong.

? What can you do?

- Remember that one of the most important jobs a parent can do is help his child develop self-esteem and self-respect (see page 200–207). That doesn't mean over-inflating his ego but rather helping him develop a positive sense of himself with a fair sense of his strengths and weaknesses. Understanding a child's temperament is the first step towards enhancing his self-esteem because you will be able to deliver praise sensitively in accordance with his innate tendencies and help him build upon those traits in a positive way.

- Learn to distinguish between behaviour that is temperamentally induced and that which is learned. If a child knocks over your best vase by mistake because he is a high-energy child and was running gleefully through the living room, your response should be different than if he broke your vase deliberately.

- Develop specific plans ahead of time to cope with troublesome behaviour and then enforce them in sympathetic but consistently firm ways. If your child tends to get wild on family occasions or when he's with friends, be sensitive to this tendency and take steps to quiet it before it escalates.

- Self-awareness is a first step towards modifying behaviour, so use your experience to talk with your child about his temperament. Help him understand how his own temperament affects his feelings and behaviour, as well as the impact this has on others.

- Talk with your intense, active and distractible child about the situations in school that in the past have led to problems. Did your high-activity child often get into shoving matches with other boys when standing in a queue? Did he have problems settling down to work first thing in the morning or after coming in from the playground? Discuss other ways he could handle stressful or challenging situations. Identifying together when and where problems occur can help your child anticipate and avoid confrontations.

- Set firm limits when you discipline, and remind your child of your expectations constantly. Hot-headed, high-spirited, strong-willed children may be more difficult to discipline because they often learn differently and need to experience the consequences of their own choices and behaviour. Also, because regular discipline methods don't usually work with these children, they can bring out very strong reactions in parents. But the crux of the matter is that they do require more discipline, with firm boundaries, than more compliant children – that's not to say being stricter or unfair, just standing your ground and being consistent, no matter how difficult it may be.

Perception

Involved in the idea of temperament is the subject of 'perception'. Many bullies simply do not perceive situations or interactions in what we might consider a 'normal' light. They see threats and danger where there are none; they are quick to judge without learning the facts; they often brim with hostility which can explode without warning. Much of this is temperament based; however, there's more.

'Aggressive children also seem to have a perceptual blind spot for their own level of aggression,' says psychologist John E. Lochman of Duke University Medical Center. In one study, he had boys previously rated as aggressive or non-aggressive listen to a story about two kids who bump into each other in the hall and begin to yell and fight. The boys identified which child had caused the fight, speculated about what the characters were thinking and feeling, and prescribed a way to resolve the incident. Lochman then paired one aggressive and one non-aggressive boy, telling them that when they talked over their reactions to the story, they should defend their opinion. Afterwards, they rated their own and their partner's level of aggressiveness.

Lochman found that aggressive boys underestimated their own aggressiveness. They also described their partners as the aggressor more frequently than did non-aggressive boys. 'Aggressive boys had distorted perceptions,' Lochman says. 'These kids overperceive hostility in their peers.'

Bullies tend to misread social cues and put the worst construction on them, so a brush in the hallway will be interpreted as a deliberate challenge rather than an accident. Because these kids 'jump to conclusions that others are out to get them', Lochman says it's important to teach them to read social cues, and then to teach them social problem-solving skills. 'We help them think about different solutions that are available to manage problems without aggression,' Lochman says. Even kids who normally can solve problems verbally 'many times have not acquired very socially skilled ways for talking with others about disagreements' in the heat of the moment. 'They become so aroused, they're not able to do that.'

? What can you do?

• Look at Lochman's programme for dealing with anger management (see page 150–51), which helps children to change their perceptions and deal with others in a more constructive and acceptable way.

- Consider the issue of social skills (see page 98–101). Many bullies appear to be socially adept when, in reality, their behaviour and their perceptions prove otherwise. Teaching problem-solving may also help. If a bully is riled by very little, he may need to learn to negotiate, to interact normally, and to manage problems himself rather than lashing out at others.

- Similarly, stress can make a child more 'touchy' and quicker to react; if your child is in a calmer frame of mind, he may not see things in quite the same way.

- Teach empathy (see page 144). Bullies react rather than think things through, and do not consider feelings and motivation, or the impact on the victim. If children become used to looking at things from others' point of view, walking in their 'shoes' for a while, and thinking about what it is that irks them about another child, it makes a difference. No one hurts someone they understand.

- Use television, books, DVDs and even games to impress on children the fact that other children have rights, codes of behaviour and even irritating habits. But always to assume they are aggressive is misguided and misperceived. Say: 'Do you think he "deserved" that?', and, if they say 'Yes', ask why. Then use the opportunity to explain another person's point of view. The more often your child is able to see another person's point of view, the less likely he will be to react in a negative fashion.

- Talk about whose 'fault' things are when problems occur in daily life, and try to impress on your child that some things are not anyone's fault. Sometimes we come across people who simply rub us up the wrong way, but that is a state of affairs that must be accepted rather than used as an excuse for causing pain.

- Look at your own tolerances and intolerances. Do you go mad if someone cuts you off when you are driving? Do you blame others instead of taking responsibility yourself? Do you use racist, homophobic, elitist talk? Ever? Kids pick up their cues from parents, and if you are intolerant, or quick to blame, they will be the same. Similarly, if you show tolerance and an understanding of others, your children will get the message that everyone is worthy of respect. More importantly, perhaps, they will learn to understand that other people's actions are not designed to irk them, nor are they usually hostile. Other people rarely think about the impact they have on other people in the course of daily life, and most certainly do not set out to cause trouble. If your child learns to see it that way, rather than assuming that there is a personal vendetta against him, he'll be much more relaxed in his social encounters.

The importance of empathy

Almost all studies show, without fail, that bullies lack empathy and com-passion, and, simply put, do not have the conscience that most of us do. They cannot see things from anyone's point of view but their own. Some of this may be due to the fact that they have never been taught empathy as children, and see little of it in the world around them. We live in a competitive society where the message is often 'look out for number one' at whatever cost, and this mes-sage undoubtedly filters down. The overemphasis on self-esteem may also be partly to blame, creating a generation of kids who think they are superior to their peers, have a divine belief in their own ability to do and get what they want, and the full support of parents who think they are 'wonderful' and 'the best' no matter how they behave. I also question the motivation of some parents to encourage self-esteem. For many years, it was believed that creating high self-esteem in children made them 'superkids' and able to do or be anything they wanted. Many parents are highly competitive for their children, often living their own unrealised dreams through them. Some have actually considered the development of self-esteem to be a tool for success, rather than something that will make their child a well-rounded, happy and positive member of society.

In his book, *Empathy and Moral Development*, Dr Martin Hoffman says the most advanced stage of empathy involves the ability to catch nonverbal and verbal messages from others, their cues in social interactions, and to use these to understand lives outside your own. Bullies can't do this. They see things only from their own point of view and they care only about their own feelings. They are not good at sharing, caring about others, or making friends. They are not good at empathy. All these are behaviours that can be taught and learned.

？ What can you do?

• Many experts suggest that teaching very young children to empathise is the key to discouraging aggressive behaviour, and there are several studies back-ing this up. Instead of showing anger or aggression when a child hurts some-one, the idea is that you say things like: 'Ouch. Oh, that hurts. Oh, that's so painful,' rather than losing your temper and punishing the errant or aggres-sive child. Even young children are able to make the connection that their actions can cause discomfort or pain in others, and it's an important lesson in cause and effect that helps to teach empathy.

- Again, for younger children (though I suspect that this would have some effect on older ones as well), ensure that all attention is given to the hurt party when dealing with aggression, in order to make the aggressor's bid for attention fail. You can encourage the offender to offer a soft toy for the victim to hold, or to hold ice on a bump – all in all, to be attentive and affectionate. This takes the focus away from negative behaviour, helps a child to feel better about himself by being kind, but also pushes home the message that bullying others hurts.

- In a classroom or home scenario, much the same thing can work with older kids and teens. Don't hesitate to show your emotions when your child is rude to you, or if he is violent in any way. Although this is in direct opposition to what we suggest for younger victims in a school bullying scenario, in the context of a supervised environment with adults, it is very important that bullies learn the effect and consequences of their words or actions. A cold, angry parent responding to a cold, angry child will end up in a power struggle rather than anything positive. A warm parent who shows the occasional chink of weakness, and the ability to be 'human' can help to teach children compassion for others.

- Similarly, if your child hits another child, or bullies a sibling in your presence, ensure that he is involved in the 'mopping up'. Ask him to run a warm bath, or get a cold cloth. Ask him to explain to you how you think the victim feels – and wait patiently for an answer. Focus your attention on the needs of the victim, and, once again, use emotive words: 'Ouch, that must have hurt,' 'Poor you, that looks dreadful,' 'You must be very upset.' Only through teaching can children learn empathy.

- The American professor Dr Adam Blatner, an expert in empathy, teaches it through role-playing. This can be undertaken in a less formal way at home (using the questions he suggests below while watching TV or in response to violence or violation of any nature), or in the classroom to good effect. He says, 'Role-playing is a natural vehicle of learning because it's an extension of the imaginative, pretend play of childhood. It should be noted that this approach is often neglected in the course of traditional education, because it addresses a different type of learning than that which can be easily tested in exams. Role-playing builds a deeper type of understanding and a more flexible type of thinking, qualities which will become increasingly important in the coming years. However, what most kids learn involves memorisation and calculation, logical composition, and other more didactically taught skills.'

For more information on this technique, visit *www.blatner.com*. Interestingly, one of the other things he does is to teach children to think a little outside the box, asking not only how a victim feels, but also how his parents, siblings, the people watching and his teachers feel. Getting a handle on the repercussions of bullying can be very important in teaching a child some compassion.

- The younger you can teach your children empathy, the better. Begin by putting a name to your child's behaviour so he can recognise emotions. Say, 'Oh, you're being so kind,' when he kisses your hurt finger. He'll learn from your reaction that his responsiveness is recognised and valued. He needs to understand negative emotions, too, so don't be afraid to calmly point out when your child is being less than caring. Try saying, 'It made your baby brother really sad when you grabbed his toy. What could you do to help him feel better?' Use this technique, too, for older children, but in a slightly different way. For example, when your child does something nice, whether it's apologising for actions (even grudgingly), or trying to make up for bad behaviour, offer plenty of praise and ensure that he realises that his actions are spot on. Similarly, when he does do something objectionable, ask him how he could rectify it. If he's caught bullying, ask him what he can do to make things better for the child he has picked on, and make sure you praise any efforts, no matter how meagre.

- Point out other people's behaviour. Teach your children to notice when someone else behaves kindly. For example, if someone returns your stolen purse or phone, or runs after you on the street with something you've dropped, point it out. Say: 'That was so helpful. She really made me feel better.' Even older children will get the message that other people's actions can affect us emotionally. Books, TV programmes and films are also vehicles for this – talk about how someone might be feeling, and ask them what they'd feel like in that position. Ask what he might do to make things better for that person. Any opportunity you have to point out that what we do and say can have an impact on others – positive and negative – will get the message across.

- In the classroom, or in your home, create opportunities for children to work together – on assignments, household chores, etc., – anything that requires sharing and collaboration.

- Praise your child for acts of kindness and respect. Although this alone is unlikely to make a massive difference, it can teach your child that he is a valued and respected member of the family.

- Show empathy yourself. If your child wallops a sibling, or is caught out bullying, show him first and foremost that you identify with the fact that he must have been feeling angry, upset, frustrated, jealous or whatever emotion motivated him to behave the way he did. It teaches children that others can see their point of view. It's not condoning the behaviour, because you can then move on to say that you 'understand' the motivation, but that the behaviour was unacceptable, and you would like to know how he thinks he can make up for his actions. Don't hesitate to take the opportunity to point out how the other person felt as well. So, 'I know you were angry, but you hurt and frightened Susan, and you will need to apologise to her.'
- As often as you can, give your child the message that there's almost always something good about other people. Choose anyone and everyone, even a crotchety neighbour, to make this point. For example, 'I know she's a grump, but she's probably sad and lonely because her husband died a while ago and her children never visit her. But she's so kind to the cats in the area – did you see how she always leaves out milk for them?' Point out kind things that others do, and try to explain to your child – or give a word for – why they are doing what they do and how it makes you or others feel.
- If someone winds your child up or upsets them – perhaps a catalyst for bullying behaviour of your own child – be sympathetic and understanding, but when your child is feeling better, examine the other child's behaviour. Is he being bossy because he's insecure? Is he a new boy and trying to find his place? Is he having trouble at home? Is someone else bullying him?
- Finally, let your children know that they don't have to like everyone. Not everyone can be a friend. But it's not acceptable to be mean to those you don't like, and it's never right to join others who taunt unpopular kids.

Violence and aggression

Bullies are, by nature, more violent and aggressive than their non-bullying peers, whether or not they choose less physical types of bullying and rely on verbal or even social abuse. The simple reason is that violence and aggression manifest themselves in negative behaviour – largely because the bully cannot control his feelings or actions, or perceives hostility where there is none.

Bullies may have been exposed to abnormal amounts and types of TV violence, in which case the parents have not taken responsibility to censor certain types of viewing. Some fathers may even encourage their children to engage in bullying behaviour by play fighting, which, though it may seem harmless, can in the extreme teach children that this is an acceptable way to behave. Even more importantly, perhaps, children who are physically disciplined learn the overwhelmingly confusing lesson that if you are angry or frustrated it's OK to lash out, and that violence has a place within a relationship.

Psychologist Marjorie Roberts highlights the work of Gerald Patterson of the Oregon Social Learning Center, who, with his colleagues, have studied families in which children resort to aggression because it seems the only way to get along at home. 'People teach one another when they interact,' Patterson explains. A family may learn that coercion works, for example, when a sibling squabble erupts: a young girl teases her brother, he retaliates by punching her and she quits taunting him. Thus he learns that aggression works. Then the mother steps in and in turn hits her son as punishment. Temporary peace and quiet may result, but each family member has had a lesson in the value of physical force. Patterson says: 'Even a couple of minutes later, these patterns are more likely to occur again.' Thus as both initiator and victim of aggression, children may unintentionally train their parents to punish them severely or even to abuse them.

Aside from their often troublesome home lives, some aggressive children may have difficulty interpreting the intentions of their classmates, another body of research reveals. In a 1980 study, Vanderbilt University psychologist Kenneth Dodge gave aggressive and non-aggressive boys a brief hypothetical story to read. Each boy was asked to imagine that a classmate had spilt a lunch tray all over his back. Dodge asked them whether the classmate had hostile or benign intentions and how they would respond if this really happened to them. The aggressive boys read hostile intent into the story 50 per cent more frequently than did the others, and they had aggressive retaliation in mind more often.

This isn't just fantasy – countless studies, including the seminal studies undertaken by Kris Bosworth and K. Kumpulainen in 1999 and 1998 conclusively show that bullies have higher levels of anger, they lack confidence in the use of non-violent strategies, and accept aggression as being justifiable and satisfactory. No big surprise, then, that they fail to feel remorse for behaving in more or less the only way they know.

A recent US study set out to discover whether bullying is related to other forms of violence-related behaviour. The results were not unexpected, but made fairly frightening reading nonetheless. For example, researchers found that both children who bullied and their victims were more likely than youth who had never been involved in bullying to engage in violent behaviours themselves. However, the association between bullying and other forms of violence was greatest for those who bullied others. For example, among boys who said they had bullied others at least once a week in school, 52.2 per cent had carried a weapon in the past month, 43.1 per cent carried a weapon in school, 38.7 per cent were involved in frequent fighting, and 45.7 per cent reported having been injured in a fight. By comparison, of the boys who said they had been bullied in school every week, 36.4 per cent had carried a weapon, 28.7 per cent carried a weapon in school, 22.6 per cent said they were involved in frequent fighting, and about 31.8 per cent said they had been injured in a fight.

The issue of media violence cannot be underestimated. Most children watch TV (and most of them watch some violence), and not all of them turn into bullies or axe-murderers; however, some children are more susceptible to the effects of violence in the media – because they have issues of their own in the home, because they are temperamentally inclined to find this type of thing exciting, or because they are under pressure and in the right frame of mind to take it on board. Children view an average of 10,000 acts of violence yearly on television alone, including *South Park, Beavis & Butthead* and *The Simpsons*! Children spend 16–20 hours a week playing video games, and 4–8 hours watching movies. In general, 57 per cent of all TV programmes have violence in them, 73 per cent of which goes unpunished, and for 58 per cent no pain is registered at the violence. Research at the Menninger Clinic in Houston, Texas, shows that children who have conduct problems show responses to violent movie clips that indicate a type of numbing-out of violence. Sometimes a smile indicates that responses to the violence have been suppressed. Whereas this could be a survival tactic of some value when conscious, if it becomes too much of a habit, it creates an apparent remorselessness and lack of empathy in the child. Overall, the evidence is that repeated, merciless violence in the media – newspapers, movies, television, or the internet – may predispose a child to violent thoughts and acts both in their current life and perhaps even in later life.

❓ What can you do?

• Parents of bullies need to look long and hard, no matter how painful it is to do so, at their home environment. Aggression is not created out of thin air, and you may find that there are a few things you can do to change the balance.

For example, look at your discipline programme. If it's harsh, inconsistent or physical on any level, make some changes (see pages 216–19). Your child may be angry because he lacks respect – either from you or his siblings. He may feel that he has no voice or that he is powerless, all of which can stir up rage.

• Consider whether or not you tease your child mercilessly, or use sarcasm to discipline or make your point. These can create negative feelings in a child, which manifest themselves as anger or aggression.

• Consider your TV viewing habits, and even the PC or games console games that he has. Kids can become sensitised to violence when they see it often enough – some games put a child in the position of being the bad guy, and efforts to kill or wound others, or damage their property, win points. This is wholly unacceptable. If the viewing certificate says 15, your 9-year-old should not be playing or watching. Kids live what they learn, and if violence is a normal part of their lives, they'll be more likely to act it out.

• Look at some of the anger management programmes around. They may genuinely help. For example, John Lochman has worked on three techniques to defuse anger once it develops. Obviously a child has to be aware of what he is feeling first, so it is important that you teach your child some self-awareness, how to identify his emotions, and give him the words and understanding to do so. It's important to explain that it is not wrong to be angry, and that anger is a normal feeling; but it's equally important to explain that anger is a negative emotion, that it will not have any happy outcome either for the sufferer or for anyone at the receiving end, and that when it results in aggression, there is a real problem. Anger is OK; dealing with it is OK; but aggression is not.

• Lochman's first suggestion is distraction: 'If you feel yourself start getting angry and recognise that it's a problem, you focus on something else, such as what you're doing later that day,' Lochman says. The classic distraction, counting to 10, actually seems to work. Then, 'self-talk' or 'self-instruction' can be repeated silently, carrying a message such as, 'I'm going to keep cool, I won't let this person get me into trouble.' Self-talk can act like a little recording, he adds. 'We do role plays, they practise being taunted and teased.' He then suggests a little short-term relaxation therapy – working on relaxing the muscles and mind, perhaps going to a happier place in your imagination for a short while. The programmes seem to work. In a three-year follow-up of the Anger Coping Programme, held in 18 group sessions for kids aged 8 to 14, 'The most notable finding was that the boys had lower rates of substance abuse at age 15,' Lochman says. There were some improvements in problem-solving and self-esteem, and a modest reduction in delinquent behaviour. Obviously these are just 'plastering over the cracks' solutions, in that they don't actually address the cause of the anger; however, if a child learns self-control and self-awareness, he is learning a valuable lesson for life. There will always be times when we feel uncontrollably angry, and we all need to learn to deal with those feelings in a positive way.

- So, getting to the cause is important – why does your child have a lot of aggression? Why does he need to project that aggression on to other children? Why has he not learned to interact with other children in a non-violent way?

- As with any problem behaviour, the first step is prevention. Infants and toddlers tend to become aggressive in predictable patterns. Rough play, crowded conditions, being tired, hungry or uncomfortable can all provoke aggressive outbursts in a young child. When rough-housing with a youngster, keep a special eye out for the point where the 'play aggression' moves beyond play. When young children get over-excited, they are likely to forget the rules. Remind young children constantly when they cross the line, and tell them what is acceptable and what is not. Similarly, older children who have been stressed by exams, or problems at school, need an outlet. If they aren't given one, they may channel their feelings of stress into aggressive behaviour.

- As always, reward positive behaviour whenever you see it. Hugs, gentle touches, sharing and cooperation should be noted and rewarded with lots of attention.

- Help children find acceptable outlets for their anger – for example, give them a particular object, such as a pillow, that they can hit instead of another child. Talk to them about what they are feeling so that they learn to express their anger and frustration through words, not through aggression. Repeat and affirm what they say to you. Help them express how they would like the problem to be resolved, then help them develop a realistic solution.

- Also, make sure children experience consequences for aggressive behaviour, as they should for any misbehaviour (see page 217).

- Children often express anger towards other children when they are feeling angry or upset over something they cannot control. A new sibling, a move, a divorce (or fear of it), or starting a new school may all contribute to aggressive behaviour (often called 'acting out'). Help children discuss and resolve these deeper problems and usually aggression will diminish. For very serious problems, counselling may be necessary to help children deal with the difficult emotions they are facing. The earlier problems are handled, the more easily they will be resolved.

• Social cognition (see page 98–99) as well as problem-solving (see page 84–88) can be learned by children of any age, and all bullies, no matter how clever, astute or confident, will benefit from being taught these skills in order to interact on a more positive level with their peers.

Peers and peer pressure

Many bullies seek attention from their peers, or feel the need to exert power or authority over them. Other bullies begin to victimise others in an attempt to join in with the crowd, to avoid being bullied themselves, and as a response to peer pressure to conform. Either way, it is clear that the peer group has a great deal to do with bullying, and it can't be overlooked as a causative factor when considering why your child has become a bully.

The need for acceptance, approval and belonging is vital during the teen years. Teens who feel isolated or rejected by their peers – or in their family – are more likely to engage in risky behaviours in order to fit in with a group. In such situations, peer pressure can impair good judgement and fuel risk-taking behaviour, drawing a teen away from the family and positive influences and luring them into dangerous activities.

Several studies have shown that 85 per cent of bullying episodes occur in the context of the peer group, and though a 1997 study found that 83 per cent of students indicate that watching bullying makes them feel uncomfortable, observations indicate that peers assume many roles in the bullying episode: joining in, cheering, watching and occasionally intervening. In fact, peers who form the audience for bullying may be critical in starting and supporting it.

Peers tend to give positive attention to the bully, rather than the victim. Their reinforcement of the bully may serve to maintain the bully's power over the victim and within the peer group. Two studies have found that boys are more likely than girls to be drawn into bullying episodes, and become actively involved in the bullying. But studies have also shown that by intervening, peers have the capacity to stop and reduce the bullying. In playground observations, one study found that peers intervened in significantly more episodes than adults did (11 per cent of episodes versus 4 per cent).

Don't underestimate the effect that peer intervention can have on a bullying episode. According to researcher Dr Debra Pepler, 'Children want to be on the side of status. They don't want to be the next victim. I also think it's engaging, it's very arousing. Children become very excited. The more children who are in the audience, the longer it continues.' However, she goes on to say that when a child intervenes to stop the bullying, the bullying stops within 10 seconds, 57 per cent of the time. She feels there is tremendous potential to engage children in addressing the problem.

? What can you do?

- Interventions must aim to change attitudes, behaviours and norms around bullying for all children in a school. Under teachers' guidance, students can recognise the problem of bullying and their potential contributions. With teachers' support, they can develop strategies for intervening themselves or seeking adult assistance to stop bullying. Promoting attitudes in the peer group which support empathy for the victim and condemn aggression will reduce bullying. In a nutshell, unless peers are involved in an anti-bullying programme, it simply won't work.

- Fellow peers also need to take responsibility and turn in bullies. There are many bystanders who do not want to get involved due to fear of being next. Peers need to stand up to the bullies and show them that they do not have control over these victims.

- The classroom is the appropriate place for discussion of the moral implications of bullying. It is in classroom discussions that students can talk about human rights and the expectation that in a free, democratic society, no one should feel unsafe or be unable to enjoy that freedom. Discussions about 'might versus right', and the equality of all people, are ideal vehicles for shaping attitudes and values that will harness positive peer pressure to reject bullying as a method for solving problems or satisfying one's needs.

- You can get to know your child's peer group, and work out his role within it – is he a 'henchman' or a 'leader'? Do kids follow his example, or is he quick to act in response to a more popular or powerful child's leadership? Use this as a talking point and explain that although peer relationships in childhood (and often into adulthood) are always very political, and there is often a defined pecking order, it is wrong to lead others into trouble, it is wrong to follow the lead of someone who is causing trouble, and it is always wrong to hurt others.

- Raising your child's self-respect and self-image can make him more resistant to peer pressure and less willing to follow a gang mentality (see page 200–207).
- Teach your child that a big part of being an individual involves making decisions based on what is best for him or her. It can mean we take ownership and responsibility for what we do and how we think. Being an individual can still mean that your child is a valued part of a group, but he must have the confidence to believe in himself, and the self-respect to stand up for himself. Children with self-respect ultimately gain the respect of their peers, even if they are taunted a little along the way.
- Encourage your child to spend time with peers who like doing the same types of things and share common interests. It isn't essential to hang out with the football team thugs just because you are on the team, nor is it essential to choose the most popular clique and do whatever you feel you have to do to stay on their right side, and belong. This may help to avoid a situation where children feel pressured into doing things they don't want to do. Remind your child that the 'in' crowd may not be as much fun as it looks.
- Teach your child to say no, and to have the strength to say no. Teach him to explain in a calm way why he doesn't want to be part of something, and impress on him the fact that sticking to beliefs does actually earn respect. Show this in the way you deal with your child. When you believe firmly in something, say no. Explain your views, listen to counter-arguments calmly, but show fortitude. Having the strength to say 'no' may be hard. However, it may also feel good to stick with what you believe in.
- Encourage your child not to place judgements on other people's choices. If he is tolerant of others, peers will be more likely to respect his choices.
- You can support positive peer relationships by giving teenagers the love, time, boundaries and encouragement to think for themselves.
- Encourage a positive relationship with your child – and keep it up into the teenage years. When parent–teen interactions are characterised by warmth, kindness, consistency, respect and love, the relationship will flourish, as will the teen's self-esteem, mental health, spirituality and social skills.
- Being genuinely interested in your child's activities is crucial. This allows

parents to know their children's friends and to monitor behaviour, which is essential to keep kids out of trouble. When misbehaviour does occur, parents who have involved their children in setting family rules and consequences can expect less flack from their children as they calmly enforce the rules (see page 222). Parents who, together with their children, set firm boundaries and high expectations may find that their children's abilities to live up to those expectations grow.

- Encourage independent thought and expression. In this way, children can develop a healthy sense of self and an enhanced ability to resist peer pressure.
- Do not attack your child's friends. Remember that criticising his choice of friends is like a personal attack.
- Help your child to understand the difference between image (which is an expression of youth culture) and identity (who he or she is).
- If you are concerned about your child's immediate peer group, check whether your concerns are justified. If you believe they are, talk to your teenager about behaviour and choices – not about the friends in question.
- Encourage your child's independence by supporting decision-making based on principles, not on other people.
- Encourage reflective thinking by helping your child think about his or her actions in advance and discussing immediate and long-term consequences of unacceptable behaviour.
- No matter what kind of peer influence your child faces, he or she must learn how to balance the value of going along with the crowd (connection) against the importance of making principle-based decisions (independence).

The power equation

Much bullying is about 'power'. Bullies feel powerful by being in charge, and by using whatever means to get others to submit to their demands or their abuse. The bulk of research indicates that bullies have an extraordinary need for power, and this is one of the things that drives their actions. We have seen already that there are many reasons for this (see page 35).

As children grow older, the intensity of the power dynamics within the peer group becomes much greater as groups of children adopt the bully-victim-bystander roles. Competition for leadership of groups and, later on, as the child grows up and becomes sexually mature, gender and ethnic battles and games, all add fuel to this fire. Thus, being humiliated in front of a girlfriend or being rejected by a boyfriend has very intense emotional implications and can often lead to despair and humiliation. Even worse, it can sometimes lead to suicide, or to revenge and retaliation that may take the form of homicide, as the recent spate of school shootings so dramatically illustrates.

Children try out their social power – the power to command attention, obedience, respect. Bullying occurs on a continuum from mild to severe; mild cases are most common.

? What can you do?

- The good news is that kids who are bullies can learn to change their behaviour. Teachers, counsellors and parents can help. So can watching kids who treat others fairly and with respect. Bullies can change if they learn to use their power in positive ways. And this is important. Many bullies are persuasive, dynamic individuals with strong views and easy expression. Get them on the debating team, get to them to sell advertising for the school newspaper, give them a top job in the student union – not as a reward for bullying, but as a channel for their positive abilities. Gaining success at something they do well is a huge boost for a child who needs some form of power in his life.
- Bullying is a complex social dynamic that requires a combination of large group interventions that target improving the school, social and home climates by having a zero tolerance for bully-victim-bystander behaviours. Interventions need to target the school climate because the problem is created among normal, healthy children who need to learn positive alternatives to negative power struggles. Bullying needs to be exposed as destructive behaviour rather than glorified, modelled and ignored by adults.
- In Chapter 8 we look at how to parent and discipline in a way that gives your child some power. If you offer plenty of opportunity at home, and ensure that the family power dynamic is a healthy one, your child will feel increasingly less need to seek power elsewhere.
- Offer your child plenty of choices and responsibilities, to give him some control over his environment, and a sense of power over his life. That doesn't mean removing boundaries or rules, but enforcing them in a way that your child has some say in his own fate (see page 217–19).
- Talk to your child about what it feels like to be powerful, and why it may feel good. But turn the question around and ask your child how it might feel to be at the end of bullying. If your child has ever felt powerless in any situation

Changing the school climate

In Chapter 8 we look at the type of initiatives that work in the classroom, and the need for a whole-school approach to bullying. You can work hard on your own child, and remove a great deal of the causative factors, but if the school climate is still dictated by fear, and there is a problem with the power dynamic, the bullying will not stop, and your child is likely to be drawn in again. Unless bystanders and witnesses can report with confidence, and feel certain that they will be backed up by peers, authority figures and a strong anti-bullying policy, they will continue to keep their heads down and go about their own business – probably in fear. Parents and teachers can do a great many practical things to change a bully into a respectable citizen – and many of them will work on a fundamental level. But the process must be supported by the school environment.

One key thing that can be undertaken is the concept of mentoring. Many schools have set up a staff/student mentoring system, where staff members act as mentors to students during the school day. Students have an opportunity to form a healthy relationship with a professional adult who can assist them on a regular basis and support them in dealing with issues that arise, including stress, peer pressure and bullying. Staff help to teach bullies to treat other students with respect by helping them to focus on their own self-image and confidence. This type of programme seems to work because there is a great deal of one-to-one attention for the children, which is empowering and reassuring, because there is a hands-on approach to a bullying problem and an opportunity to set it right in a personal way, and because there is necessarily more supervision, as staff members interact directly with pupils.

(and all of us have) ask him to remember and relate those feelings to you. Does he remember being dropped from the basketball squad without being given a second chance to change the coach's mind? Does she remember being shunned by a bunch of girls and not invited to the biggest party of the year? How did that make her feel? She couldn't do a thing but accept her fate.

- Educating and empowering a child to have a strong sense of self is very important. It is imperative that children know that their opinions matter and that, even at their young age, they have something positive to offer to others. This is not achieved overnight: it is a long and arduous process.
- Give your child a reason to feel good about himself, and in charge – taking over responsibility for a pet, working at the local kennel or old people's home, reading to local schoolchildren, doing some babysitting, helping an elderly or sick neighbour with shopping or housework. Anything that makes him feel important and valued is empowering.
- Don't hesitate to notice and use realistic praise for achievements and effort. Children who feel good about themselves simply do not have the overwhelming need to be in control all of the time, or to exert their authority. In a nutshell, they are often happy just being them.

Other practical steps you can take

We've looked so far at the many factors that can lead your child to bully others, and some of the ways that you can overcome them. There are still, however, a number of practical things you can do yourself, and with the help of your child's school, to deal with a bullying issue. Let's look at some of these now.

- Experts recommend that parents and teachers take a hard-line approach to childhood aggression. Adults must make it clear that aggressive behaviour in school, the neighbourhood, or at home is not acceptable and will not be tolerated. Children should be encouraged to report aggression and threats. Parents and school staff must deal with these incidents seriously. When aggression is tolerated, everyone loses – the bullies, the victims and the bystanders. They are all learning that violence is acceptable, and that is not the lesson we want to teach our children.
- Be sure to express strong disapproval of bullying when it occurs or comes up in conversation. Be sure students know that you don't condone any kind of harassment or mistreatment of others, whether it be teasing, social exclusion or physical violence. Teachers should, as much as possible, reassure students that the classroom is a safe and supportive place.
- Avoid physical forms of discipline. Hitting children when they misbehave reinforces the belief that violence and intimidation are appropriate ways to get what you want. Model non-violent means of resolving conflicts (see page 213).

- Parents and teachers would benefit by keeping a log of bullying incidents, including who was involved, when it occurred, how often, and what strategies were used to address it. Over time, this log will help to identify any patterns in bullying behaviour, as well as what kind of interventions worked best to stop it. Teachers may discover that more bullying takes place around exam time, when the students are stressed, or when they haven't had any physical outlet for a week; they may discover the same culprit over and over again, stirring things up. Parents will have to rely on the honesty of a child as well as the support of the school in order to complete a log with any success, but it can help you to keep tabs on your child's behaviour, work out when he's most difficult, what the catalysts might be, and which methods of dealing with the problem at home are actually having some effect.

- Make sure your discipline system in the home is consistent, with praise and reinforcement for good behaviour, and fair penalties (never violent) for violation.

- Ensure that you model the type of behaviour you want to see.

- Build on your child's talents and help him or her develop less aggressive and more appropriate reaction behaviours.

- Maintain contact with your child's school. Support the school's efforts to modify your child's behaviour. Enlist help from the school to try and modify your child's behaviour.

- Although certainly not all bullying stems from family problems, it's a good idea to examine the behaviour and personal interactions your child witnesses at home. If your child lives with taunting a from a sibling or from you or another parent, it could be prompting aggressive or hurtful behaviour outside the home. What may seem like innocent teasing at home may actually model bullying behaviours. Children who are on the receiving end of it learn that bullying can translate into control over children they perceive as weak.

- Constant teasing – whether it's at home or at school – can also affect a child's self-esteem. Children with low self-esteem can grow to feel emotionally insecure. They can also end up blaming others for their own shortcomings. Making others feel bad (bullying) can give them a sense of power.

- Emphasise that bullying is a serious problem. Make sure your child understands you will not tolerate bullying and that bullying others will have consequences at home. For example, if your child is cyberbullying, take away the technologies he or she is using to torment others (i.e., computer and mobile to text-message or send pictures). Or instruct your child to use the internet to research bullying and note strategies to reduce the behaviour. Other examples of disciplinary action include restricting your child's curfew if the bullying and/or teasing occur outside of the home; taking away privileges, but allowing the opportunity to earn them back; and requiring your child to do volunteer work to help those less fortunate.

• Teach your child to treat people who are different with respect and kindness. Teach your child to celebrate and understand differences such as race, religion, appearance, special needs, class and sexuality. Every child needs to learn that all people have rights and feelings. Teach a little history – show how oppression has affected countries around the world (parts of Africa, for example) and how intolerance has led to wars and horrific crimes against humanity (the Holocaust, for example). Sometimes children need to learn that intolerance and disrespect have very serious consequences.

• Find out if your child's friends are also bullying. If so, seek a group intervention through your child's school.

• Observe your child interacting with others and praise appropriate behaviour. Positive reinforcement is more powerful than negative discipline.

• Be prepared to talk to your child's school about how they can help your child to modify his behaviour. They may have some excellent ideas, that are in line with the school's anti-bullying policy, and which will be backed up by other pupils and staff members. It can be very upsetting to have to admit that your child is a bully, but if you show humility and a willingness to set things right – perhaps even explaining problems your child may have experienced outside the school gates, and which may have contributed to his attitude and behaviour – you are likely to receive the support you need. Keep in touch with the school so that you can monitor and report, and they can do the same.

• Tim Field, bullying expert, feels that, 'School environments tend to be one of "exclusion" rather than "inclusion". Children are left to form their own groups, or gangs, and you are either "in" or "out". I believe children should be taught at the outset to show dignity and respect to other children regardless of whether they are "in" or "out", and to be proactive in their relationships to other children, especially those who "do not fit in", for whatever reason.'

• Remember to keep your cool. If you become angry, you will get nowhere – either with your child or with the school. Your child will not confide in you, and you'll never come to terms with the causative factors without appropriate communication. Show patience and unconditional love at all times; make it clear that you still love your child, even though his behaviour is not lovable.

- Bear in mind that your child will be very likely to deny any wrongdoing, and/or minimise his involvement. It's a natural reaction, and you will need to be patient and persistent to get past this.
- If your child has been involved in extortion, ask yourself some questions about his material status – if he doesn't have anything that his peers have, he may be stealing to keep up with the crowd; if he doesn't have a lunch made for him, or any lunch money offered, he may be hungry and angry about his position, and take it out on others. If he doesn't have an appropriate amount of pocket money for his age and is therefore unable to keep up with normal social requirements, he may resort to stealing. Be realistic, and ask some questions of your child – and the parents of your child's peers.
- Increase your supervision of your child's activities, whereabouts and associates. Spend time with your child, and set reasonable rules for curfews.
- If your child is viewing violent television shows, including cartoons, and is playing violent video games, this will increase violent and aggressive behaviour. Change family and child's viewing and play patterns to non-violent ones.
- Make sure that your child is not seeing violence between members of his or her family. Modelling of aggressive behaviour at home can lead to violence by the child against others at school and in later life.
- About 1 per cent of all bullies have a serious sadistic nature, in that they enjoy the pain of others. Such children tend to be rather unfeeling when they bully and are not anxious, nor is their self-esteem low. They often have serious problems with criminal behaviour later, and can become quite abusive. If you think your child may have sociopathic tendencies, ask your GP to refer you for counselling. Your child may genuinely need help.
- Parents may inadvertently support bullying by accepting it as just a normal part of growing up and leaving children to solve their own problems. Don't make that mistake. Bullying is wrong; this message needs to be repeated and reinforced in your home, and guidance needs to be offered at all ages.
- Find out exactly what it is that your child has been doing. What has your child been accused of doing? What does he admit to doing?
- Ensure appropriate adult supervision at all times. Be aware of your child's involvement in activities inside and outside of school. Make certain that adequate adult supervision is present in every situation.

- Report any incidents of bullying behaviours to school officials, even if your child is the one engaging in those behaviours. This will teach your child that he or she is accountable. Engage school officials' help in monitoring and addressing these behaviours. This will show your child that you will not tolerate it, and that you want to help your child avoid it.
- You need to give them some feedback, make them accountable for their behaviour and help them accept responsibility for it. You will need to raise their understanding of how they made it happen and enable them to look at the impact of their behaviour. Help them plan not to do it again, identify the situations to avoid and suggest alternatives to bullying.
- Try to avoid threats and warnings, which will shut your child up. You need to get cooperation without building resentment. Concentrate on passing on responsibility not blame, focus on the behaviour not the child, solutions rather than problems. Don't bully your child.
- Make it very clear that it is OK to stick up for yourself, but that bullying is not acceptable.
- Assess what your child does and what he gets from it – what need is the bullying performing in his life?
- Try very hard to see your child's point of view. It may be a complete anathema to side with a bully, but you need to understand in order to get anywhere. There may be genuine reasons for his behaviour.
- Encourage your child to see the victim's point of view, and to try to make up for his behaviour in some way. Ask them to think of a way they can make amends with the victim, perhaps by apologising. Perhaps if the victim is timid and shy they can befriend them and be protective towards them.
- Look at yourself, too. Make sure that you never, ever, blame a bullied child, or show any type of bullying behaviour yourself (such as using sarcasm, or joining in with teasing or name-calling as a joke). Avoid having favourites within your family unit. Do not embarrass or humiliate your child in front of others. Most importantly, perhaps, have a reasonable and rational approach to the problem – don't ever tell your kids not to tell tales or not to get involved. All kids today face bullying, whether as bully, victim or bystander, and they need to know that they have rights and the ability to get some help.
- Offer to talk to the victim's parents and school staff, if the bullying has been happening at school. But do not defend him. Even if he was not the ringleader, the fault is still his. If you do determine that your child is using controlling,

aggressive behaviour, experts agree that the responsibility lies first with you to teach your child non-coercive ways to negotiate.

- Many experts recommend setting a regular family time in which issues can be addressed and lines of communication opened. Asking an aggressive child – or the entire family group – to comment on unacceptable behaviour, and then ensuring that his or her response is listened to, without judgement or interruption, can help get messages across in a more positive way than slamming down hard on individual children. Ultimately, every child in the family will have views, and hopefully morals and values will have been installed by parents. When these are shared amongst the family group, the message about what is acceptable and what is not becomes clear.
- If your child is very young, read aloud books about bullies. Let him or her take care of a pet. Invite other children over to your house and monitor them. Let them play in a non-competitive way.
- Enrol an older child into groups that encourage cooperation and friendship, such as social groups or Scouts. Have him or her volunteer to learn the joy of helping others.
- Remember: you are not alone. Other parents have had this problem and fixed it. One parent said the best thing that ever happened in her son's life was when he changed from being a bully into a compassionate human being.

The more positive you are about the changes you can make, the more likely you are to inspire change in your child's behaviour. Bullying is serious, and can have extremely grave consequences, so don't be tempted to play it down. Be honest with yourself, fair with your child, consistent in your approach to discipline, and take all the steps you can to teach your child the important lessons of life. It's not easy, and many parents make mistakes. Busy parents can also easily overlook signals that all is not well with their child – and it sometimes takes a shock in order to set things right. There are many other factors apart from parenting that can have an impact on your child's life – including the various stresses and demands that are now placed on children at increasingly young ages. Perhaps we are simply asking too much of our children. Let's look at this next.

6

The Stress Equation

In all our efforts to provide 'advantages' we have actually produced the busiest, most competitive, highly pressured and over-organised generation of youngsters in our history – and possibly the unhappiest.

Eda J. Le Shan, *The Conspiracy against Childhood*

NOT SO VERY LONG AGO, we would have laughed at the notion that children feel stress. Childhood used to be a time of freedom and development, when children explored their environments and learned life's lessons at an easy, relaxed pace. As adults, most of us look back on our childhood years with fondness; our memories are of fun and play, testing our parental boundaries, schooldays and sports, laughter and an overwhelming sense of timelessness.

That's not to say that bullying did not exist; in fact, most adults have a strong memory of one or more bullying experiences that took place at some point in their childhood, and for some that memory has had long-lasting repercussions. But bullying was not as rampant as it is today, nor, more importantly perhaps, were there so many other factors causing us to experience stress.

These factors are manifold. They include children being forced to grow up too fast in a rarefied environment, and being forced to witness and/or be party to acts of violence in society and in the media. They also involve overtesting and overcompetition in schools, and living with stressed parents who are statistically more likely to be experiencing marriage problems, raising a child on their own, facing their own stress in our 24/7 society, or finding it difficult to cope without the benefit of extended family networks. We'll look at these in detail later in this chapter, but it's important, from the outset, not to underestimate the effect of stress on children, and its intrinsic relationship with bullying.

The relationship between stress and bullying

There can be no doubt that a bullied child will experience stress, and in an already stressful lifestyle, this can tip the balance between, on the one hand, coping or adjusting, and, on the other, suffering often severe symptoms. Put another way, as children we may have suffered episodes of bullying, and though they may have left a stark emotional memory or affected our self-esteem, the chances are that we were more able to cope because we had fewer other elements of stress in our lives. Too much stress causes illness, both physical and emotional.

However, the stress–bullying equation is not as simple as that. Children who are stressed suffer low self-esteem, begin to doubt themselves, or are fearful, shy, or prone to cry easily. These are common symptoms in children who internalise stress, who 'hold it in', and they are, as we saw in Chapter 3, some of the characteristics that define a victim – which make a child victim 'material'.

Some children, on the other hand, do not internalise the stress, but 'act it out', losing their tempers easily, becoming demanding or destructive or, not surprisingly, teasing or bullying other children. Research shows that under high-stress situations, boys tend to become more aggressive and disruptive, while girls become anxious or depressed, though the latter situation has undoubtedly changed over the past few years as an increasing number of girls show violent tendencies. So children who are under stress – particularly those with the potential or predilection to become bullies – are more likely to show aggression and to persecute others.

So stress is, in many cases, both the cause and the effect of bullying. Stress in children is one very good reason why bullying is on the increase.

Nor should we underestimate the impact of bullying on bystanders and witnesses. A 1992 study found that children who are in contact with other children who are being bullied feel compelled to be drawn in, suffer guilt because they are not being bullied, and experience a range of negative emotions. So even kids who aren't bullied themselves, or bullying others, will be affected negatively simply by being in a bullying environment. Stress is the result.

? How stressed are children?

Many parents will be genuinely surprised to learn that stress is greatly on the increase. The majority of children are unaware that what they are experiencing is stress, and symptoms are often put down to illness, poor behaviour or even emotional problems. Robert Dato is an American stress expert and pioneer who

Starting young

An extremely worrying study was published in 2006. Research by Adrian Angold, a leading British psychiatrist based in the USA, found that children between the ages of two and five (we are talking, effectively, about toddlers here) have the same rate of mental health disorders as teenagers, which is only slightly less than that suffered by adults. Mental health disorders include anxiety, depression and conduct disorders, and appear to affect one in ten preschool children – and older children, too. Children as young as three are being treated for stress-related illness and emotional problems.

A child suffering from stress is more susceptible to the effects of bullying, and much less likely to be resilient to it. This has the effect of increasing both the potential for bullying and bullying itself.

developed the 'Law of Stress' and the highly regarded and scientifically validated 'Dato Stress Inventory'. He says, 'Children and adults all have the same hardware. The symptoms of children, however, are often more extreme or frequent under the same pressure because adults have better software in place to manage that pressure. In other words, they are more adaptable.'

So children can be even more affected by stress than adults are. And another source of stress is the fear of failure, of letting down parents and teachers. To combat problems within their lives a child's subconscious will develop defences to keep the trauma of failure to a minimum – 'laziness', withdrawal, selective deafness, defiance, school avoidance, to name but a few. The fear of failure is in itself a major obstacle to learning. It may sound silly to assume that children are worried about failure, but so many parents today are hyperconscious of their children's development – that they are intellectually adequate, keeping up with their peers, good at everything from ballet and French to identifying colours and becoming a prefect – that many children soon pick up on the fact that they are not living up to expectations.

The behaviours that children adopt in an attempt to cope with stress are really just struggles to manage and react to stressful events. Children generally distance themselves emotionally from stressful situations by behaving in ways that diminish the stress (crying or being upset when a parent leaves them at school or nursery, for example), or acting out in ways that conceal feelings of vulnerability (being aggressive or disruptive). As they become older, children learn to use problem-solving strategies to cope with stress by asking questions about events, circumstances and expectations for what will happen and clarification of what has happened.

So what is the scale of the problem?

According to research published in October 2000, children as young as eight describe themselves as 'stressed'. More than 200 interviews conducted by a team from City University in London found unprecedented levels of stress in British people of all ages and 'worryingly high' levels in children. More than a quarter of those questioned by the researchers said they were often or always stressed. Half were 'occasionally stressed'. 'We were surprised by the extent of the prob-lem, particularly by the amount of stress reported by very young people,' said Professor Stephen Palmer, who led the study. 'If you had asked eight-year-olds about stress twenty years ago, they would have looked blank. Now they under-stand the concept and a significant number report experiencing it.' They also found that nearly a quarter of the under-18s studied said that they often got stressed, and only one in six never suffered from it.

In addition, according to a survey carried out by the Office for National Statistics in partnership with a team at the Institute of Psychiatry and the Maudsley Hospital, a quarter of young people in the UK had felt so unhappy or worried that they asked people for help.

In 1996, on behalf of the NSPCC, MORI Social Research interviewed a representative quota sample of 998 children aged 8–15 in England and Wales. The aim of the survey was to obtain a contemporary picture of children's experiences of, and attitudes towards, family and social life. Among the many surprising things that researchers found (many of which will be detailed later in this book), stress and anxiety were considered to be normal by almost half of those polled.

When asked about sources and frequencies of worries, academic pressures were the most commonplace (44 per cent) for all except the youngest children. Younger children were generally more likely to say they frequently worried about things and a fifth (22 per cent) were classified as 'anxious' on a composite scale, compared to one in ten of those aged 12 or over (10 per cent).

A recent report by the Mental Health Foundation revealed one in five people under 20 experiences psychological problems, from anxiety to psychosis. Research by Young Minds, the mental health charity, shows a huge increase in recent years in the number of children, some as young as four, seeking treatment for severe mental health problems.

? What is stressful about our children's lives?

Traditionally, stress has been defined in terms of its cause – in other words, whether it is 'internal' or 'external'. Internal sources of stress include hunger, pain, sensitivity to noise, temperature change and crowding, fatigue and over- or under-stimulation in a child's immediate physical environment. And according to a 2002 study, external stressors can include separation from family, change in family composition, exposure to arguing and interpersonal conflict, exposure to violence, experiencing the aggression of others (bullying), loss of important personal property or a pet, exposure to excessive expectations for accomplishment, 'hurrying', and disorganisation in a child's daily life events. Although many studies appear to focus on single stressors, such as grief, violence and change, for example, in real life children experience stress from all sorts of directions. A 2000 study found that 'multiple stressors' interact with one another, and can have a cumulative effect.

These are not isolated problems affecting small sectors of our society. Children from all social classes, in cities and in the countryside, in many, many countries, are experiencing stress from a variety of different sources, and the impact of that stress will undoubtedly have ramifications for the future.

The main causes of stress in kids
Parental expectations

One of the major features of modern-day parenting is a passion for excellence in our children. This is undeniably affected by our society, which focuses so heavily on being the best, coming first, winning. The problem is that this extends to children, who have little concept of balancing life's ups and downs. Childhood is a period of learning about the outside world, about experiencing defeat and coming to terms with our own strengths and weaknesses. The trouble is that weaknesses are no longer acceptable, and given that there can only ever be one winner, there are an awful lot of children out there who will be experiencing massive disappointment, dejection, feelings of failure and inadequacy at a time when their self-esteem and personal identity are being established. Far, then, from creating super-children who will be able to handle anything that life throws at them, we are creating children who will have fundamental flaws in their emotional foundation. If they never succeed as children, they will never have the confidence they need to try new things, to take risks, to believe in themselves, to make choices based on their own individual talents, skills and, yes, weaknesses.

While a certain amount of competition is essential in childhood, because, after all, we live in a competitive society, constant competition in all fields is undermining and exhausting. A child can no longer feel proud of a single achievement – in sports, perhaps. She's expected to be brilliant at everything, and if she can't do it naturally, she will be cajoled, encouraged, tutored, coached and pushed until she improves. Still, chances are she will never be the best, because there are always other children out there with a natural talent or ability. What does that say to our children? What about the child who

Over-scheduling is a serious problem in today's children, and it is partly driven by this focus on being the best.

struggles with maths, improves her marks with lots of hard work, and still comes last in a class of 30? If the only measure of success is being first, being the best, then she has effectively failed. What should be celebrated here is her achievement, rather than her place in the class, but in most cases it is not. If something isn't excellent, it's worthless. If your son doesn't make the A-team at football, then he's no good, even if he beat 40 other boys to a B-team spot. It's a pressure that is too much for most children to bear, and only part of what the modern child faces today.

Parents, often unwittingly, exacerbate the problem. Too often they focus on a 'failure' (a lack of excellence) as an indicator of long-term problems. If a child struggles academically, they are concerned that they are producing a potential misfit who will never get a job. This fixation on winning can lead parents to go to great lengths to give their children a competitive advantage, such as extra 'workbooks' at home, extra tuition, extra coaching, early reading programmes, baby swimming classes, infant music lessons.

All this does, however, is to fill a child's hours with activities at which he may never really be any good, or for which he may never have any interest or feel any passion. Over-scheduling is a serious problem for today's children, and it is partly driven by this focus on being the best.

The main problem, of course, is that children are enormously sensitive to parental approval, and will often pull out all the stops to ensure that they are performing according to expectations. The 1996 NSPCC poll showed that parental approval was extremely important to 78 per cent of children. This means that the vast majority of our children are performing with a view to achieving recognition from their parents. And since excellence in every aspect of life is now the norm, this puts intolerable pressure on young children.

Failure is part of growing up, and learning from failure is often just as valuable as learning from success. More importantly, learning how to cope with failure is a key step in maturation, and a crucial aspect of stress management in children and adults. There will always be failure in life; if our children are taught to avoid it, fight it and disparage it, they will never be able to accept the things that will ultimately go wrong.

Living through our children

If, as research shows, the majority of parents are dissatisfied with their lives and their jobs, they need to acquire feelings of happiness, success and achievement elsewhere. All too often, this falls on the shoulders of young children, who become the focus of their parents' unrealised dreams.

When adults first become parents, their identities often shift: they become a 'mummy' or a 'daddy', rather than a high-flying career woman or a top city lawyer. As part of that confusion of identities, parents often feel that their children's success – or lack of it – and achievement are reflections of their own status in society. The other dads on the football pitch may not know that you are a 'success' at work, and one of the good and great, but he'll sure know if your child is a lousy passer and let in three own-goals in the last match. This sort of public 'failure' doesn't sit well with most of us, which is another reason why we strive for excellence in our children. They become extensions of us. If we have a stumbling academician on our hands, we feel that we have failed. If we have a 'naughty' or 'disruptive' child, we are concerned that we will be considered inadequate parents. This type of neurosis is a common feature of most adults, largely because of the kind of society in which we live. But it extends to and affects our children greatly. They are shepherded into believing that success and excellence are the hallmarks of a happy future, and, not surprisingly, they experience enormous pressure en route.

Stressed parents

Most adults admit to suffering from stress, and parenting undoubtedly increases that burden. According to a UK survey of 5,000 women, 93 per cent of working mothers find it difficult to juggle a career with family life. Many of those questioned said they were overworked, underpaid and at 'breaking point' from stress, causing them to shout at their children. Mothers who work feel that by doing so they are emotionally damaging their children and putting their own health at risk. Three out of four believe that career stress is causing their health to suffer.

Many studies have shown how a mother's job can influence her child's development, but one conducted in 1999 showed that fathers' jobs can also affect children. Researchers at Pennsylvania State University in the USA studied about 200 working parents and their fourth- or fifth-grade children for three years. The goal of the study was to assess the effects parents' jobs can have on children's development. The study found that job pressure and marital stress can interfere with communication between parent and child, and that this applied to the father as well as to the mother.

What are the implications of parental stress? Once again, there are many. First of all, stressed parents are much more likely to 'snap' and take out their problems on their children. There might be a few saintly mothers who can face a long working day and cope calmly and energetically with demanding children at bedtime, but these are in the minority. Human resources are not endless, and if we are emotionally exhausted throughout the day, it's often difficult – if nigh impossible – to find the patience and even time required to parent the way we would all like to.

Feeling that we are inadequate parents in any way encourages us to 'make up for it' in other ways. One of these is through material goods. We can assuage guilt by giving our children the best things in life, whether we can afford it or not. According to a 2001 UK study by the research group Mintel, overworked parents are tempted to lavish expensive designer clothes on their children to compensate for their own busy and stressful lives. Working mothers in particular feel so guilty about not spending enough time with their families that they are spending less on clothes for themselves in order to be able to dress their children in the latest brandnames. Others are using their children as the 'ultimate fashion accessory' to display their own personal wealth and allow their offspring to 'stand out in the playground'. Based on interviews with 2,000 people, the study found that in the previous five years spending on children's clothes had increased by 34 per cent in real terms to £6 billion. This was expected to rise in the following five years to £6.8 billion.

Whether it's clothes, computers, games consoles, CDs or new sports equipment, the increased materialism affects our children now and will affect them in the future. First of all, they will develop a need for and interest in material goods, which they will begin to associate with affection and love. This focus can become obsessive, and children will require more and more to satisfy them, and to reassure themselves that they are important and loved. Secondly, it creates an instant gratification scenario, whereby children demand and receive. They do not learn the art of patience, of financial management, of working hard for something (which imbues a sense of achievement), and of looking after things. If things are quickly and easily replaced, they lose interest, and are on to the next 'big' thing. It throws them in the 'competition' ring with their friends, whereby they feel inadequate and upset when they do not have everything that their friends have.

This is undoubtedly stressful, and my own questionnaire, undertaken for my book *Kids under Pressure*, showed that all the children surveyed felt that their lives would be improved in some way, that they would feel 'cooler', if they had more of the things their friends had. This is a perfect example of consumerism run wild, when children begin to associate wellbeing with possessions.

Material possessions also create an 'image', which allows a child to feel that she is 'fitting in'. If she doesn't feel that she has what her friends have, she may suffer a loss of confidence that affects her ability to interact – setting up, in some ways, a classic 'victim' scenario. So, too young, kids are placing enormous emphasis on possessions rather than friendships and affection – a lesson sadly learned at home. This affects a classroom dynamic, and sets the scene for rivalry, jealousy and competition.

Busy parents

Following on from the effects of stressed parents on children, there is undoubtedly an issue of time. Hardworking parents have little time to spend with their children, and this in itself is stressful. Without the regular, patient guidance of a loving parent, children will often feel out of control and emotionally unstable. New experiences, concerns, fears and every other aspect of growing up can no longer be sorted out over the dinner table, on a family outing, or during a long bedtime chat. Children are not machines that can spill out the day's woes at the touch of a button. They often need to unwind, to be drawn out in order to express their emotions. If there is no time available, they will learn to shut it all away.

Not only is this stressful, it also has enormous ramifications for the bullying problem. Stressed children cannot 'let their hair down' or 'let out' their emotions at home, so they either internalise those emotions, or 'act out' (see above). What's more, we've seen from the earlier chapters in this book that parenting is an important part of what makes up a bully or a victim – lax or overauthoritarian parenting rather than consistent, loving parenting with a fair discipline policy has a dramatic effect on children. And don't forget – parents who don't have their finger on the pulse will never be aware of the signs that their child is being bullied, or that they have a bully on their hands.

Children need to learn to cope with conflicting emotions and problems by expressing them and then coming up with solutions. By burying them, they will ultimately begin to take a step back from reality, and 'pretend' everything is all right. If our children never have time to express their concerns, either because they are being ferried from activity to activity with no time to stop and contemplate, or because they simply don't spend time with their parents, they will feel stressed by even the most basic aspects of growing up, such as peer pressure, identity, marks, performance and relationships.

Many very good parents are shocked to see how little time they do actually spend with their children in an average week. Work it out. How much time do you really spend with your child: chatting, laughing, sharing and planning? How often do you get a chance to listen, really listen, with nothing else on your mind? Parents can't be blamed for this situation but they need to be aware that it exists. Children need parents, and never before have they had so little of the nurturing care they require. This isn't yet another poke at working mothers; at-home mothers are often just as busy, and with a hectic run of school deliveries, activities, homework, instrument practice and running a household, there is often very little useful interaction.

In fact, research shows that working parents often devote more time to their children than their non-working counterparts, partly perhaps because of an inherent sense of guilt, but also because the day-to-day running of their children's lives is turned over to someone else, such as a nanny, leaving them free to concentrate on the children themselves rather than struggling to keep them

How much time do we spend with our children?

- In the UK, research funded by Powergen found that 6 out of 10 parents do not have time to read to their children before bed. Dr Aric Sigman, the psychologist who ran the study, questioned 84 parents with 150 children to compare reading patterns between generations. While almost three-quarters of parents recalled being read to regularly when they were young, only 40 per cent of their children heard a story most nights of the week. One common complaint from children is that their parents – especially dads – fall asleep themselves before they have finished reading a story.

- In the USA, the situation is even worse. According to research supported by the National Institute of Child Health and Human Development, less than 53 per cent of parents read to preschool (aged 3–5) children every day, and the average American child spends 4.4 hours every day watching television, usually without a parent.

- A survey of 1,000 households by the Food Foundation, the UK's healthy eating group, found that only 15 per cent of households sat down together to eat every day. A later study, published in April 2001, showed that parents considered this trend to be worrying: more than 80 per cent of parents felt that family dinners were a vital part of home life. Over 33 per cent thought that the dinner table provided the only opportunity to discover what their children were thinking. Despite this belief, only 75 per cent of the sampled group, in a survey carried out by the Consumer Analysis Group on behalf of Paxo, managed a family meal once a week. Does it really matter if we eat with our kids? Studies show that it does. In particular, a large federal study of American teenagers found a strong association between regular family meals and academic success, psychological adjustment, and lower rates of alcohol use, drug use, early sexual behaviour and suicide risk.

- While most children in the UK claim to take part in regular family-based activities, a fifth of all children reported that they had not done anything with their father in the last week.

- In a 2000 UK poll, 21 per cent of teenagers rated 'not having enough time together with parents' as their top concern.

busy. *Allaboutparents.com* commissioned a report in 2000, which showed that working parents spend nearly as much quality time with their children as mothers and fathers who stay at home. They spend between two and five hours a day 'one-to-one' with their children, against three to five hours for non-working parents. Less than a quarter of working parents questioned said that they devoted less than 30 minutes a day to their children.

A modern lifestyle

We've already looked at some of the reasons why children's lives tend to be over-scheduled, but there are other factors that add to the pressure placed on them. Some of these are societal: in particular, the breakdown of the family. Others are caused by well-meaning authorities, such as educational institutions, which create situations where children are intensely pressured.

Before we look at some of these factors, it is important to remember that childhood and adolescence are themselves inherently stressful. It is a time of change and learning, of seeking to find one's place in the world, learning to forge relationships, deal with peers and peer pressures, cope with issues such as bullying, and establish moral beliefs. At the same time, hormones rush madly around their bodies in preparation for growth and eventual adulthood. Every parent will remember the insecurities, the feelings of embarrassment, the faux pas, the lack of confidence in certain situations that characterise childhood and adolescence. We recall first crushes, the overwhelming need for approval from parents and peers, the trauma of falling out with best friends. We remember coveting the newest boots or jeans, experiencing sibling rivalry, and battling with parents to be allowed to express our own ideas and individuality.

None of this has changed. Children still experience the same emotions and undergo the same stages of development as they have always done. The difference is that today there are an increasing number of other factors that affect their wellbeing and their ability to adapt to stress.

Education

There are several elements here, and most of them exhibit the current trend for excellence. League tables put teachers and the education system under increasing pressure to perform. Not surprisingly, this pressure is passed down to the children themselves, who face a battery of exams and tests at increasingly younger ages.

Caroline Wigmore, national president of the Professional Association of Teachers in the UK, says that youngsters are treated 'like products on a conveyor belt' by the stringent testing requirements. School staff report increased stress among pupils. Half the teachers in a recent survey had seen entire classes suffer mass anxiety or panic attacks caused by testing and exams.

This is a complex situation, driven partly by a parental and societal demand for success and achievement, and partly by a genuine need to improve national standards for the benefit of every child. However, the means by which this task is being undertaken are open to criticism. No child should be pressured to perform for anyone other than himself. In other words, school standings in league tables, and working for parental approval, leave a child not only susceptible to failure, but likely to fail. Children do not live in a cocoon. This intense focus on academia undoubtedly affects the way they approach their work, and the emphasis that is placed upon it. The 1996 NSPCC poll showed that academic success was most likely to engender self-pride in 88 per cent of those children surveyed, while marks and performance were the greatest cause of 'worries'.

SATs
Standard Attainment Testing was first established in the UK to monitor the overall standards of children at different ages, ostensibly to find areas of weakness within educational systems and individual schools. Once again, this has become yet another way of evaluating individual and collective performance, and many children are under pressure to perform to ensure a school's league standing. Parents also use SATs as a benchmark of their child's overall ability, and long-term potential.

Researchers at the Institute of Education in the UK are to undertake what is thought to be the first nationwide study of stress in schoolchildren, following a preliminary survey commissioned by the BBC which revealed alarming levels of stress in seven-year-olds who took national tests in 2000. Teachers reported pupils in tears, feeling sick and tired, and refusing to work. Other symptoms included stuttering, tantrums, sulks and psychosomatic illness. Six out of 10 said that there was no doubt that stress was generated by the Key Stage One SATs. One in five of those believed that stress levels were 'very high'. The children most likely to suffer the highest stress were those who were not tested by their usual classroom teacher.

All the teachers who reported highly stressed pupils said the children were also under pressure from their parents. A senior educational psychologist at the Institute of Education, Alan Jensen, one of whose specialities is stress and stress management, described the findings as 'alarming'. 'I thought there would be a few tears and a tiny proportion of other symptoms,' he said, 'but here we had children not wanting to come to school. My gut reaction is: What are we doing for these youngsters at six and seven years old? What is it all about and how can we prepare children better?'

The institute now plans to conduct a study of stress levels in older children too. Among other things it will be interviewing parents at length about the extent to which they put pressure on their children.

It's not surprising, of course, that parents are concerned about results. Far too much emphasis is placed on individual grades at increasingly younger ages. No longer 'on the spot' tests, SATs have become a focus for parents already concerned about their children's performance. Parent meetings are organised to warn of upcoming tests; SATs predictions are allegedly raised artificially year on year to satisfy national education watchdogs (regardless of the fact that results vary according to pupil intake and staff changes); there is rivalry between some teachers for best SATs scores, following UK government announcements about performance-related pay; extra coaching is used to improve statistics; classwork, sometimes a year early, consists mainly of SATs papers, with priority given to English, maths and science; and scores are benchmarked against test levels. Robert Dato claims that standard testing has produced a generation of 'cheats', in which grades are artificially raised to satisfy parents and educational authorities. He says, 'Grade inflation is rampant in both public schools and at the university level. Now this feeds into the wish of parents to have superior children, and the narcissistic wish of children to be perceived as more powerful than they really are.'

Growing up too soon

One of the side-effects of the modern get-it-now, faster-is-better society is the fact that children have been drawn in on the act. No longer content to wait until appropriate ages for activities, clothing, possessions and freedom, today's children expect to be (and are) treated as miniature adults, complete with miniature versions of everything adult. With this comes inevitable responsibility and a need for acquisition. The majority of children are too young and immature to deal with either of these.

Learning the art of patience is an important part of childhood. Childhood and adolescence are marked by various rites of passage, experienced at appropriate points across the years. Children have always wanted things to come sooner. They can't wait to be allowed to go to 'big school' like a sibling, or to make a football team. They can't wait to be permitted to stay up until 9.30, they can't wait to get driving licences, to be allowed to go out alone with friends, to move away from home, have some freedom, earn their own money. This type of

When children are exposed to an increasing number of experiences at an early age, they become bored with routine, average activities.

yearning for the future is normal, even healthy, but children have to learn to wait for each of these stages, and to feel a sense of pride and empowerment when they arrive.

Today everything is pushed on more quickly. Children go to school younger, and learn to read earlier. Weekend sporting events are organised, with full 'adult' equipment and replica kit, and sometimes even overseas tours. Children have CD players and all the latest top 10 hits; they wear mini-Calvin Klein and Paul Smith; they have mobile telephones and their own computers. Advertising encourages them to look and be seductive and cool; young girls dress in the same style as their heroines, many of whom are scantily clad and earning a buck by being overtly sexy. The inevitable question is 'What next?' How can a child who has already toured Europe with his football team be content with playing for his school? How can a child who is bombarded with sexual messages through the media be content to hold hands at a school dance?

The pressure on children to become more grown up, more quickly, tends also to suit our modern style of parenting. If we treat our children as if they were older, dress them as if they were older, and push them on to achieve things at increasingly earlier ages, we can justifiably expect 'adult' behaviour.

According to David Elkind, author of *The Hurried Child: Growing Up Too Fast Too Soon* (1981), the normal stress of growing up is increased when children are hurried into taking on adult behaviours and responsibilities. Elkind believes that today's middle- and upper-class parents push their children to grow up too quickly. These children now live under the kind of pressure that has long been experienced by lower-class children – they are required to become self-sufficient as soon as possible. Children are urged to read to excel in school, regardless of their readiness for academic tasks. He claims that the most stressful responsibility that hurried children are asked to undertake is to listen to and to share adult's problems, as if they were their parents' contemporaries.

There are several other problems with the adultification of childhood. The first is the boredom factor. Many children now complain of being bored, largely because there is very little to look forward to in terms of personal goals. They have 'been there, done it all'. They travel, they eat out, they wear designer clothes, they have all the trappings that matter. They take part in ambitious school productions, play in international sports tournaments, surf the internet and set up their own email accounts. They have bank accounts into which their pocket money is paid, and they use their considerable purchasing power to get whatever they need.

When children are exposed to an increasing number of experiences at an early age, they become bored with routine, average activities. What fun can be had in the park with your parents, if you could be watching satellite TV in your room with your mates? How boring a trip to the seaside will seem after a two-week holiday in the Caribbean. Who wants to watch a 'PG'-rated film, when you've seen an adult-rated movie with your friends?

Once children become accustomed to a steady diet of stimulation, it's very difficult to turn back the clock. This is stressful in itself; the need for constant stimulation indicates a need to keep adrenaline flowing. It can only be detrimental to the emotional and physical health of our generation. Many adults now find it hard to relax on holiday and seek out 'thrilling', 'risky' activities to satisfy a growing need for stimulation. If children have done it all by the age of 12, what effect will it have on their ability to switch off?

More importantly, however, stress becomes a factor because of the emotional and physical demands that this type of lifestyle necessarily comprises. It is literally an assault on young and impressionable bodies and minds. What's more, many children are being left to make the transition from child to adult on their own. So-called latch-key kids are a modern-day phenomenon, and many children are essentially raising themselves: they come home to an empty house, organise their own time structure, often make their own meals, and choose their own entertainment.

Even children who are at home with parents during the day and after school have unhealthy pressures placed upon them by media such as television. If most children in the USA are spending an average of 38 hours a week exposed to media outside of school, by the time they reach the age of about 11, the average child will have witnessed more than 100,000 acts of violence on TV. Children may be exposed to as many as 5 violent acts per hour during prime time and an average of 26 violent acts per hour during Saturday morning children's programmes. And that's just violence. What about advertising, where even 12-year-old starlets have nothing between them and their Calvin Kleins?

There are sequential steps in a child's development, and ignoring or disregarding these stages can have serious consequences. Children need to be parented and allowed, and encouraged, to be children. Parents have an obligation to take charge and become involved so that children can learn something along the fast lane to adulthood, and avoid the stress that comes with it.

Leisure activities

Tied into the concept of adultification is the issue of leisure activities. When children are constantly stimulated, they require constant stimulation. When their hours are filled by activities, they need a busy schedule to keep them occupied. When they do have a little time to spare – and we'll discuss this later – it tends to revolve around artificial stimulation: games consoles, computers and television.

There is nothing wrong with any of these activities – in moderation – but when they become the sole way that a child 'relaxes' and 'recharges', we have a problem on our hands. None of these activities will do anything to reduce stress in the short or long term. They also take the place of healthy occupations, such as unsupervised play, exercise and quiet reading, thinking or simply daydreaming. They also disrupt sleep, which adds to the stress load.

In the UK, children spend more than five times as long watching television as they do playing outdoors, and over half of all 10- to 15-year-olds have a TV in their bedroom. Given the long hours spent at school, doing homework and being involved in extracurricular activities, there is little time left for the type of activities that every child requires to be emotionally and physically healthy. Think about your child's life. Is there really time for positive interactions, for personal growth? Have you allowed the stresses and technological advances of modern life to overwhelm the significance of your family?

The fact is that children have much less leisure time than they once had, and, having lost confidence in our ability to rely on the family and the household for entertainment, we fill their days with a multitude of 'improving' activities. William J. Doherty, author of a landmark paper entitled 'Overscheduled Kids, Underconnected Families', has summed up the statistics. He found that children have an average of 12 hours less free time per week, with a 25 per cent decline in playing, and a 50 per cent decline in unstructured outdoor activities. Over the same period, structured sports time has doubled, while passive, spectator leisure (not including television, but including watching sports) increased from 30 minutes per week to over three hours.

What does this have to do with stress? If children are not relaxing in the true sense of the word at any stage of the day, their stress levels, far from being reduced, are actually being increased by the constant stimulation. Overstimulated kids are stressed – and, once again, that stress can be internalised (setting up a victim scenario) or acted out (as in the case of a classic bully).

Broken families

Dr Robert Dato blames the rise in stress on the changing family unit. He says, 'The main reason why stress is on the increase in children is the disintegration of the nuclear family. One-parent and blended families are on the increase. This is confusing and destabilising to children. Yet children cannot attack the family directly because it is so valuable to them. So they turn their anger inward, which generates depression, anxiety and anger. These, of course, are all forms of emotional stress.'

Broken families are not necessarily dysfunctional, but the family members involved often do not have the same network of close, loving carers on which to rely. Extended families are often hundreds of miles away. Children frequently grow up without regular contact with grandparents, cousins, aunts and uncles, all of whom can, at times, play an important role in development and, of course, stress relief. When children often feel under-confident about relating negative information to their parents, close family members can be a godsend, providing an outlet and offering advice without recrimination and with unconditional acceptance and love.

We should not underestimate the effect of divorce on children. Dr Richard Harrington argues in the *Journal of the Royal Society of Medicine* that there is little evidence that children who are bereaved suffer mental health or behavioural problems. He believes evidence shows that children who have to witness their parents separating or divorcing are much more likely to develop depression than those who have experienced the death of a parent.

So while many children may appear to take divorce in their stride, there may be deep-seated concerns that are never really expressed. The situation becomes particularly damaging when parents continue their battle post-divorce. Studies have shown that staying in the same community and school post-divorce is less disruptive for children. Unfortunately, many families have to move, and have less money to live on, so children have to adjust to a different lifestyle.

The post-divorce stress load relates to more than the simple, immediate loss of a parent. Children may also feel that they have to be more self-reliant, to take the pressure off an unhappy home life or a tense, upset parent. Their basic security system becomes flawed, and one of the bricks of their emotional foundation is effectively loosened. It's also common for children to feel guilty, particularly if they have heard parents arguing about them at any time. They may also feel angry, frightened and worried that they will be abandoned by or 'divorced from' their parents.

Given that the family is the bedrock of humanity – a stable environment that allows growth, self-understanding, comfort and love – it's not surprising that today's children feel more unsettled and under pressure when the very basis of their lives could conceivably change at any given moment. They will find it difficult to learn the trust that is necessary for self-acceptance, friendship, successful relationships and security – all of which are necessary for maturing into young men or women who can react to, interact with, and adapt to the surrounding world.

Violence

We've already looked at the idea that violence on television, and in other leisure pursuits, can increase the stress load. But what about the violence that many children from good families are now accustomed to seeing, hearing about and witnessing on a daily basis? Quite apart from the increasingly violent music lyrics, and the violent nature of TV programmes and video/computer games, children live in a society where acts of violence are the norm. While few children actually experience murders and shootings in their schools, their awareness of them is likely to increase both fear and stress. If the once-safe sanctuary of school holds the possibility of danger, feelings of fear become more common in youngsters who are unable to evaluate the actual risks or potential dangers.

The NSPCC calculates that 40 per cent of abuse on children is committed by other children, and the true problem is much larger than that because not all such abuse is reported.

This type of violence can be one of the causes of post-traumatic stress disorder in children (see page 192) and it can add to the stress load of an ordinary child, living an ordinary life,

In addition, of course, children are now becoming victims of crime and violence on their own doorstep – bullying.

Lack of exercise

The importance of exercise cannot be understated. Children who do not exercise enough are missing an important way of letting off steam and releasing the adrenaline that builds up in the course of a busy day. Children are forced to sit for long periods at desks, concentrating and 'behaving well'. Even preschool children are often carted from one activity to another without being given any time to expend physical energy. Not only does this increase stress levels by disrupting normal, healthy sleep, it also causes dips in concentration, focus and even brain function which make normal schoolwork much more difficult and demanding.

Peers and peer pressure

Children always rate their peers highly, and their status among their peer groups will always be an issue. A recent study showed that most children (61 per cent) spent time with their friends either every day or most days, and over two-thirds (68 per cent) felt they had extensive friendship networks. This type of peer relationship is healthy and normal.

Peer pressure becomes a problem only when a child is forced into situations in which he feels uncomfortable. There will always be 'pressure', but it can be stimulating rather than stifling or frightening. The key is self-esteem. A child has to respect and believe in himself. He needs the courage to stand up for himself, and to challenge his peers when he feels threatened or uncomfortable.

It's important also to remember that peer pressure can be positive. The peer group is a source of affection, sympathy and understanding from people who

Peers and stress

Several studies indicate that during early adolescence, the function and importance of the peer group change dramatically. Adolescents, seeking autonomy from their parents, turn to their peers to discuss problems, feelings, fears and doubts, thereby increasing the salience of time spent with friends. However, this reliance on peers for social support is coupled with increasing pressures to attain social status. During adolescence peer groups become stratified and issues of acceptance and popularity become increasingly important. Research shows, for example, that toughness and aggressiveness are important status considerations for boys, while appearance is a central determinant of social status among girls. Many researchers believe that the pressure to gain peer acceptance and status may be related to an increase in teasing and bullying. This behaviour may be intended to demonstrate superiority over other students.

Research with primary school children supports the view that peer group members reinforce and maintain bullying. For example, a 1997 study showed that participation of peers in the bullying process was clearly evident when aggressive and socially competent children in grades 1 through 6 were videotaped in the playground; they found that peers were involved in bullying in an astounding 85 per cent of bully episodes.

The stress element becomes increasingly clear in the transition between primary and secondary education. Some researchers speculate that this transition can cause stress that might promote bullying behaviour, as students attempt to define their place in the new social structure. For example, a 2001 study found that changing from one school to another often leads to an increase in emotional and academic difficulties, and found that bullying may be another way that young people deal with the stress of a new environment, and with the difficulties they may have with 'fitting in'. We touched on this in Chapter 3 – when we showed that not 'fitting in' was considered to be one of the key reasons why kids were bullied.

So kids under pressure or stressed by the change to a new school often react by copying peers. They do whatever it takes to appear to 'fit in'.

are experiencing the very same emotions, situations and outlook. Peers act as guinea pigs, as adolescents and children experiment with different personalities and behaviours in the normal course of development. The peer group helps them define themselves, and it's a step away from being dependent upon parents. In fact, it's a normal feature of development.

Nevertheless, peer relationships can be stressful, largely because adolescents and children invest so much in them. They experience, for the first time, affection and acceptance that are conditional. Until then, their main relationships will have been with family and close friends. They are also often, for the first time, meeting and developing friendships with people who have different morals, values and goals. There may be a sense of competition firing it all (see page 178), as well as new types of relationships, romantic or otherwise, with the opposite sex.

These elements of the peer group can often make children feel uncertain about themselves, and force them to confront and perhaps even challenge their own ideals. Not surprisingly, this puts pressure on familial relationships, for as adolescents begin to explore, experiment, question and define themselves, they often contradict parental expectations and even values. The whole issue of peers is, then, a difficult one for children to manage, and can be a source of great stress.

The impact of bullying

The negative effects of bullying have been investigated in a number of studies. New research even dispels the popular myth that a bully's words will never hurt you. Research into bullying and post-traumatic stress in adolescents at secondary schools by Dr Stephen Joseph, a psychologist at the University of Warwick in the UK, reveals that verbal-victimisation has a particular impact on the victim's feeling of self-worth, and that name-calling can significantly reduce self-esteem. In fact, verbal abuse can have more impact on a victim's self-worth than physical attacks or attacks on a victim's property.

This study assessed 331 school pupils in England and revealed that as many as 40 per cent were bullied at some time during their schooling. It suggests that one-third of bullied children may suffer from clinically significant levels of post-traumatic stress (see page 192) – so rather than helping to toughen up school pupils, bullying could seriously affect their mental health. The research paper examined the levels of post-traumatic stress experienced and the impact of bullying on the self-worth of victims.

The results indicate that different forms of abuse have distinct effects on victims. To analyse the effects of different types of aggression, a 'Victim Scale' was used to assess the experience of physical victimisation, verbal victimisation, social manipulation and attacks on property. All types of bullying result in lower self-esteem, but social manipulation, such as excluding the victim from taking part in games, is more likely to lead to post-traumatic stress, and verbal taunts typically lead to lower self-worth.

The study also suggests that verbal bullying or social manipulation can lead to victims feeling helpless and that they lack control over their own feelings and actions. Those who feel that power and control lie with the bully, rather than internally, are much more likely to suffer from post-traumatic stress or lower self-worth.

Dr Joseph says: 'This study reveals that bullying and particularly name calling can be degrading for adolescents. Post-traumatic stress is an anxiety disorder that can develop after exposure to a frightening event or ordeal in which physical harm occurred or was threatened, and research clearly suggests that it can be caused by bullying. It is important that peer victimisation is taken seriously as symptoms such as insomnia, anxiety and depression are common amongst victims and have a negative impact on psychological health.'

Symptoms of stress in children

In the short-term, stress produces the hormone adrenaline, which causes the body literally to shut down as it prepares to fight or flee. This is the reason why we lose concentration, feel irritable, and suffer from digestive problems and high blood pressure. With adrenaline surging through our bodies, we also experience tension, headaches, shakiness, tearfulness, anger and even fear. The symtoms of stress in children are varied and can include the following:

- over-eating and obesity
- loss of appetite and anorexia
- substance abuse
- irritability
- difficulty making decisions
- suppressed anger
- difficulty concentrating
- loss of sense of humour
- paranoia
- feeling out of control
- feeling unable to cope
- inability to finish one job before starting another
- tearfulness

- lack of interest in hobbies
- constant tiredness, even after sleep
- headaches
- chest pains
- palpitations
- indigestion
- nausea
- loss of appetite
- diarrhoea
- constipation
- flatulence
- stomach cramps
- tremors and shaking
- fainting
- nervous twitches and ticks
- foot tapping
- nail biting
- jumpiness
- insomnia and other sleep disorders
- muscle cramps and spasms
- neck pain
- increased sweating
- menstrual irregularity
- frequent urination
- increased susceptibility to viruses
- frequent colds and flu
- itching
- worsening of chronic conditions, such as asthma and eczema

Can stress really cause all of these symptoms? It certainly can. Even emotional stress has a profound effect on the workings of the body. The mind–body relationship is now firmly established, above and beyond our knowledge of the hormones that are secreted during periods of stress. An argument with a loved one, or a falling-out with a best friend at school, can be as physically detrimental as long hours working at a computer, or facing exams. When children are under pressure, they respond in exactly the same way that adults do.

In the short-term, stress can cause enormous problems with emotional health. Children learn to recognise symptoms and know that they are associated with feeling unhappy, unwell, nervous or frightened. Several potential scenarios can result from this. In the first instance, children can literally become phobic or intensely preoccupied by events that they know are stressful. For example, if a child faces a difficult test when he's seven, and experiences a host of debilitating symptoms, he'll learn to dread tests, and these feelings and symptoms of stress will be exacerbated with each ensuing test.

Secondly, if children find it difficult to cope with relationships and experience distress, they can literally 'opt out'. This means choosing not to commit or to put themselves in a position where it matters so much. Normal emotions are heightened under stress, and, rather than experience paranoia, distress, anger or loss of control, many children will resolve not to put themselves in that situation again. This is a short-term problem with long-term ramifications.

Thirdly, stressed children may give up more easily, learning never to push themselves to a point where they experience unpleasant symptoms. This is unfortunate for a number of reasons. They will, for one thing, never experience the joy and sense of achievement that comes with mastering something, and adapting successfully to the normal stresses of day-to-day life. They may also become fearful and reluctant to try new experiences. Taking risks is a part of life, and every child needs to learn to make rational decisions based on his or her abilities. If children learn at a young age to avoid anything that leads to unpleasant feelings, they'll never understand that it's possible to overcome those feelings, and to succeed.

At the opposite end of the scale are children who become 'addicted' to stress. Like many adults, they love the feeling of adrenaline surging through their bodies, which can, for some people, provide a 'buzz' and a sensation of power. While this quality can often be controlled and even harnessed in adulthood, in children it can be manifested as manic behaviour, a 'what next?' mentality and easy boredom. It also leads to a superficial 'high' and then 'crash' cycle, in which children swing from feeling fantastic to feeling dangerously low.

Preschool children

This is a difficult age to assess because toddlers and very young children are naturally and inherently curious, erratic, developmentally unique and, most importantly, unable to verbalise emotions.

There are, however, some things to watch out for. Remember that every child is different, and a change in behaviour could indicate illness, or just a simple phase of development, involving some anxiety or rebellion.

Some behaviours may include:

- irritability
- anxiety
- uncontrollable crying
- trembling with fear
- eating problems
- sleeping problems
- regression to infantile behaviour, such as bedwetting, thumb-sucking
- loss of control that frightens them
- uncontrollable anger
- fear of being alone or without a parent
- withdrawal
- biting
- sensitivity to sudden or loud noises
- inexplicable sadness

- aggression
- nightmares

- suddenly becoming prone to accidents

Primary-school children

Once again, it's normal for children to exhibit a wide range of behaviours, including tantrums, when things don't go their way; aggression when they are angry and do not have the maturity to cope with conflicting emotions; persistent questioning; whining; a healthy fear of new experiences; loss of concentration; nightmares; and the normal complaints about friends, siblings, discipline and, of course, school.

These responses are all normal, and part of development. Children are coming into contact with a wider and more frightening world, and they are bound to have worries and fears. They are also leaving behind the comfort of having a parent or carer by their side almost constantly, and probably a favourite blanket or stuffed toy as well. At school, they begin to master simple and then more complex tasks, which involve reasoning and logic. A huge range of skills are developed, and for the first time they may experience peer competition, a need for intense concentration, while becoming more self-aware and conscious of differences, performance and achievement.

So expect doubts, normal fears, questions, self-doubt and feelings of inferiority during this period. Watch out, however, for the following:

- withdrawal
- feeling unloved
- distrust
- showing a constant fear or dislike of school
- failing to establish friendships, or withdrawing from regular friends
- difficulty in expressing their feelings
- a need to know exactly what the future holds

- chronic worrying
- headaches or stomachaches
- trouble sleeping
- trouble unwinding
- loss of appetite
- frequent urination
- regressive behaviours
- constant aggression and/or outbursts
- becoming prone to accidents
- worsening reports from school

Adolescents

Adolescence is a period of great physical and emotional change; we enter as children and emerge as adults. The course of adolescence is necessarily bumpy, with many rebellions, cries for independence, experiments and periods of self-definition. Self-image becomes increasingly (and almost obsessively) important, as do appearance, peer relationships and status. This period is also characterised by great physical development, complete with skin problems, growing pains, weight issues and the onset of puberty, in which hormones often win the battle for self-control. Sexuality becomes an issue, and this can be at once confusing and elating for adolescents.

The message is: expect some irresponsibility, disturbances in sleep and behaviours, rebellion, arguments, sulking, agitation and selfishness. Although some of these may be linked to the stress of growing up, they are normal and not usually cause for concern.

Some children sail through the transition from childhood to adulthood. This may have something to do with genes, conditioning and stress tolerance. Furthermore, children with a strong family background, good relationships, high self-esteem and a strong self-respect will normally find it easier than others to cope with the rigours of growing up. A wide variation of behaviour can be expected from adolescents, but every parent needs to look out for sudden changes in behaviour, personality, temperament, levels of activity and approach to life.

If the following symptoms are a common feature of your adolescent's everyday life, he or she is more than likely to be under too much pressure:

- long-term and seemingly inexplicable anger
- lack of self-esteem
- lack of self-respect
- extreme behaviours, such as committing crimes, overt rebellion, lack of respect for authority and figures of authority
- feelings of disillusionment
- drug abuse
- depression
- suicidal tendencies
- truancy or refusing to go to school
- distrust
- a marked change in grades at school

Post-traumatic stress disorder and bullying

Post traumatic stress disorder (PTSD) is a natural emotional reaction to a deeply shocking and disturbing experience. It is a normal response to an abnormal situation, and bullying is one such 'situation' that can leave a child deeply shocked and stressed. Moreover, prolonged bullying does not need to be the cause; it is now known that a single, life-threatening (or what a child perceives to be life-threatening) event can be as dangerous and can act as a catalyst for PTSD. It can involve lack of control, repeated violation of boundaries, betrayal, rejection, confusion and disempowerment, all of which can be experienced in many common bullying situations. It is the overwhelming nature of the events and the inability (helplessness, lack of knowledge, lack of support, etc.) of the person trying to deal with them that leads to the development of post-traumatic stress disorder. There are several types of PTSD, including 'complex PTSD', which seems to result from situations such as bullying, harassment, abuse, domestic violence, stalking, unresolved grief and exam stress over a period of years.

According to Tim Field and his team at bullyonline, little (or no) attention has been paid to the psychological harm caused by bullying and harassment. According to Field, common symptoms of PTSD and Complex PTSD reported by sufferers include:
- hypervigilance (feels like but is not paranoia)
- exaggerated startle response
- irritability
- sudden angry or violent outbursts
- flashbacks, nightmares, intrusive recollections, replays, violent visualisations
- sleep disturbance
- exhaustion and chronic fatigue
- reactive depression
- guilt
- feelings of detachment
- avoidance behaviours
- nervousness, anxiety
- phobias about specific daily routines, events or objects
- irrational or impulsive behaviour

- loss of interest
- loss of ambition
- anhedonia (inability to feel joy and pleasure)
- poor concentration
- impaired memory
- joint pains, muscle pains
- emotional numbness
- physical numbness
- low self-esteem
- an overwhelming sense of injustice and a strong desire to do something about it

Untreated, PTSD can lead to a 'breakdown'. Field is quick to distinguish between the two main types:
- nervous breakdown or mental breakdown is a consequence of mental illness
- stress breakdown is a psychiatric injury, which is a normal reaction to an abnormal situation

He says, 'The two types of breakdown are distinct and should not be confused. A stress breakdown is a natural and normal conclusion to a period of prolonged negative stress; the body is saying "I'm not designed to operate under these conditions of prolonged negative stress so I am going to do something dramatic to ensure that you reduce or eliminate the stress otherwise your body may suffer irreparable damage; you must take action now". A stress breakdown is often predictable days – sometimes weeks – in advance as the person's fear, fragility, obsessiveness, hypervigilance and hypersensitivity combine to evolve into paranoia.'

So someone with PTSD is not necessarily suffering from any diagnosable mental illness; he is suffering from being subject to humiliation, loss of power, virtual captivity, confusion, rejection, and a deep sense of poor self-worth that may have occurred over a long period of time, or may be the result of a bullying experience that has left a traumatic mark on his psyche. While many children do not go on to suffer from PTSD, it is crucial that you look out for the symptoms. PTSD has been blamed for many children taking their own lives, and each of these deaths was preventable.

Assessing your child

It's extremely important to remember that children behave differently at different stages of their development. Their behaviour, approach to life and even happiness will dip and soar. Remember also that children do not go through life with a map. They need constant guidance, reassurance, interaction and experiences with adults along the way, to keep them on track and to ensure that they are developing into happy, healthy people.

While it's crucial to keep an eye out for inexplicable or worrying changes across each of the developmental stages, it's also important to look for niggling or insidious changes that may indicate a problem. Not all health and emotional problems caused by stress are clearcut, and you may have been overlooking a series of small issues and health problems that form a clear picture of a child under stress.

We live in a society where ill-health is rapidly (even instantly) relieved with a variety of drugs and other quick-fix solutions. Your child has a headache? You pop him a teaspoon of paracetamol, or put him to bed. If he has a tummy ache, you offer an effective anti-acid, anti-nausea or anti-diarrhoea agent. If he's having trouble getting up in the morning, you put him to bed earlier, or warn him that TV is off the leisure menu if he doesn't start getting up on time. We also tend to blame emotional symptoms on poor behaviour (she's so ratty at the moment; she's a complete nuisance these days), rather than looking for the cause.

And this approach is crucial if we are successfully to recognise and deal with stress in children. We need to look for causes rather than cures, and we need to look at the whole child, rather than the individual symptoms. Many parents will be aghast to find that their children are suffering regularly from a multitude of symptoms associated with stress. And it's only when these symptoms are highlighted that we can see what's really going on.

I'm not suggesting that parents knowingly ignore symptoms; indeed, most parents are quick to offer comfort and treatment when their children are distressed, feeling out of sorts or physically unwell in even the slightest way. Once again, however, this does not get to the crux of the problem. Until a link is made between the various physical and emotional symptoms, until a clear picture of your child's overall health and wellbeing is available for scrutiny, you cannot really know whether or not your child is under too much pressure.

Take a look at the following checklist. In my book, *Commonsense Healthcare for Children*, I asked parents to complete this to work out whether or not their children were emotionally healthy. It's equally relevant here because a stressed child will not be emotionally healthy, no matter how well he seems to be coping with day-to-day life.

It's impossible to define emotional happiness in a way that applies to all children. Some children are naturally exuberant, whereas others find contentment in quieter pursuits. Some children whistle and sing in the morning, others prefer to curl up with a good book, or to daydream. No one of these scenarios is 'correct', and it's important that you don't try to create a lively, bubbly child from an introspective dreamer. What you can do, however, is look for signs that all is not well.

❓ How is my child's emotional health?

Answer the following questions honestly:

1. Can my child tell me how he is feeling? (This doesn't mean coming out with a pat 'I am sad' or 'I am happy' in response to your questions, and it doesn't mean that your child volunteers information upon request. It means that your child can express his feelings – at bedtime, in a quiet moment, or in the throes of an argument – without being prodded.)

2. Does my child exhibit signs of stress (see page 187)?

3. Does my child seem listless or withdrawn on a regular basis?

4. Does my child laugh less than he used to?

5. Does my child smile or show delight easily?

6. Does my child become frustrated easily, and want to give up?

7. Does my child push himself too hard, to be the best, the top of the class, the best player on the pitch, or the winner of the prize?

8. Is my child reluctant to take on new challenges or activities that he would normally enjoy?

9. Does my child become extremely upset if criticised or corrected?

10. Does my child put himself down regularly?

11. Is my child overly critical of others?

12. Does my child try too hard to please people (teachers, friends, family members)?

13. Is my child clingy?

14. Does my child suffer from inexplicable fears, or is he afraid to face new situations?

15. Does my child need continual approval?

16. Does my child boast?

17. Is my child aggressive or attention seeking?

18. Is my child impatient and unappreciative?

19. Does my child suffer from a series of low-grade infections, abdominal pains or headaches that cannot be explained, but appear regularly?

Judging the results. If you answered yes to the first question, and no to all the others, you have a supremely balanced child who is clearly not under stress to any adverse degree, and is obviously coping well with his lifestyle, commitments, relationships and sense of self. Chances are, however, that you will have a blend of yes and no answers. This isn't a test, but it provides a basis for understanding the signs of emotional ill-health, which can have an impact on your child's life in many ways. Remember that almost all cases of bullying – for both victim and perpetrator – have their roots in emotional ill-health to some degree, whether it is the result of stress in various areas of their lives, the product of inconsistent, over- or under-parenting, or simply a predisposition. There are many things you can do to help, including providing a structured, loving home with interaction, consistent discipline techniques, and, of course, dealing with stress in order to ensure that your child is both resilient enough to cope with the demands on his life, and happy enough to be a positive member of your household, his classroom and society in general.

Much has been written in recent months about the importance of respect. Raising respectful, tolerant children is just one way that we can address the bullying epidemic, and we'll look at that in the next chapter.

Case history

Robin was the product of an apparently happy home, with aspirational parents and a well-rounded social life, including many activities. He was fairly popular at school, with a good group of friends. When he was 11, he moved house – the same year that he was due to take his exams in order to get into the 'best' local school. He knew no one in the new area, and found himself increasingly alone. Worse, however, his parents began to panic that he might not meet the necessary mark in order to get into the school, and arranged extra tutoring, extra music lessons, and they took a new and rather overwhelming interest in his homework, his results and his potential. Robin was shocked by this new input, and felt that he would never be able to live up to his parents' demands. He'd suffered a number of events that caused stress in his life, and felt inundated with too many new things, without having the support of his old friendship network. His marks started to suffer as he lost confidence, he withdrew into himself, resisted going to school, and began wetting his bed and crying for no obvious reason. His parents became more frustrated with what they perceived to be 'giving up' and applied more pressure for him to 'sort himself out'. Feeling powerless, Robin started acting up in school – which irritated his classmates, all of whom were working towards the same goal of passing the exams. He became the target of their stress, and a way of making themselves feel better. His lunch money was taken, and he was given short shrift when he tried to make new friends. He developed the classic 'victim' mentality, and had a wary look about him – as though he knew that he would be targeted sooner or later. He was soon subject to physical abuse by older boys who noticed his apparent weakness. Robin was too embarrassed to tell his parents, and spent an increasing amount of time alone, without any support. It was not until Robin failed his exams, and became uncontrollably hysterical, that the story came out. His status, and the mentality he developed, were the product of stress that he could not control, in a situation where he had no one to turn to. His parents failed to see the damage that had been done until it was almost too late.

7

Getting It Right at Home

The strength of a nation derives from the integrity of the home.

Confucius

I F YOU ARE READING THIS BOOK, there is a strong likelihood that your child has been either a victim of bullying, or involved in bullying as a perpetrator. You may have a child who has been affected by bullying problems at school or in the neighbourhood, either as a bystander or witness, or simply because escalating tension, violence or fear has left a mark. All of these are indications of problems with emotional health and wellbeing, and must be addressed.

There is no doubt that your child's home life will affect his emotional health on many different levels, as well as his likelihood of becoming involved in bullying. Overwhelming evidence points to the fact that both parenting techniques and disciplinary methods have an impact on whether a child becomes a bully or develops characteristics that label him as a potential victim. Family characteristics such as low involvement with children, low parental warmth, low family cohesion and single-parent family structure have been found to be related to increased bullying among young people. Childhood experiences more relevant to aggression – such as smacking and other physical discipline, inconsistent punishment, family violence, bullying and/or victimisation by siblings, and a father's history of bullying – have all been related to bullying behaviour. What's more, neighbourhood safety concerns have been positively linked to increased bullying behaviour, while having positive adult role models has been associated with less.

This is not to say that your home life or discipline techniques are necessarily to blame. Some children are naturally more resilient than others, and can bounce back from stressful situations and slights more easily than shyer, less robust children. But when there are problems with bullying – or if your child appears to be struggling to cope – it is extremely important that you keep the home fires blazing, and take steps to create an atmosphere where your child feels confident and good about himself, where he can retreat from stressful situations or problems, where unconditional love and acceptance are the governing features, and where there is balance, consistency and an outlet and opportunity for him to accept himself.

So the environment you create within your home – the interaction you offer to your children, your availability for regular communication, the level of warmth and friendship, as well as the methods with which you choose to discipline – will all have an impact on your child's resilience, his ability to cope with stress, the way he interacts with his peers, his levels of aggression, his ability to deal successfully with his emotions, and his overall emotional health.

We'll start with everyone's favourite word: self-esteem.

The importance of self-esteem

Parents can have a direct impact on their children's self-esteem, and it is worth looking at how you interact with your children on a daily basis. A child with low self-esteem is not necessarily the product of poor parenting. There are many factors in this big, bad world that can affect the way your child views himself, but from the very first words you utter to your child, you can encourage or discourage a positive self-image.

When a child is born, he trusts his parents completely. He asks questions about his world, and they are answered. Parents are the all-powerful source of knowledge, and children learn by watching and listening. You tell your child that the sky is blue. You tell him that 1, 2, 3 is counting. You tell him that shoes go on feet. You tell him that night-time is for sleeping. You tell him that cats have kittens, that books are for reading, that a cow says 'moo'. He believes you, and this belief is validated by the fact that the outside world seems to be in agreement. His grandmother gives the same response to his questions; his babysitter confirms that cows do say 'moo'. His trust is complete. Everything you say will be taken seriously. He will believe you.

Take this one step further. In the throes of a chaotic day, your child feeds his toast into the video player. You lose your temper and shout, 'How could you be so

Is all well?

As many as 10 per cent of children and adolescents have some sort of mental disorder, according to a UK government survey of 1999. The research, published by the Office of National Statistics, included emotional, behavioural and overactivity disorders, but it showed that one in 20 children in the UK has a 'clinically significant' disorder, with more boys than girls being identified. The survey involved face-to-face interviews with 10,500 parents of children aged 5–15, and 4,500 children aged 11–15. Emotional disorders include a wide range of problems such as over-anxiety, phobias, social phobias, panic attacks, obsessive compulsive behaviour and depression. Behavioural disorders include awkward, troublesome, aggressive and antisocial behaviours.

stupid!'. Or your child runs into the street to collect a favourite ball: 'How could you be so naughty?', you cry. Your daughter gets a C for a crucial GCSE exam, and you go mad and rail at her for ruining her future by being lazy. Think of some of the things we say to our children: you are a very bad girl, you are a spoiled brat, you are silly, badly behaved, jealous, stupid, impossible to control, selfish, always late, irresponsible ... you get the picture. When parents are angry, upset, frustrated, busy or just exhausted, things come out that we don't intend. This is obviously the source of much parental guilt, and we make up for it with kisses and cuddles and even apologies later. But stop and consider this: your child believes everything you say. If you tell him he is stupid, even in a burst of anger, he will believe you. If you tell him he is selfish, he will think it's true. Every time we use negative words to define our children, they take them on board and file them away for future reference. No child will remember a particular incident, or be traumatised for life by being called stupid, but these occasions form faulty bricks in the foundation of his self-image. No matter how much you try to compensate for it afterwards, if you have said something, your child believes it, even if it is on an unconscious level.

No parent can ever be completely calm, or show a level of self-control approaching sainthood, particularly with small children about. What we need to do, however, is learn to think about how we say things in order to prevent labels from becoming self-fulfilling prophecies.

Here's what to do:

- Change personal attacks to more general messages about behaviour. You love your child, he's bright and clever, but his behaviour is unacceptable. So, instead of your child being naughty, his behaviour is naughty. Instead of your child being selfish, he is acting in a selfish way. This has the effect of distancing the criticism and making it more constructive. Children can accept that they are behaving badly (which can be changed) more easily than they can accept a damning critique of their personality or character (which cannot).
- Consider whether the behaviour or action is really that bad. For example, if your child fed his toast into the VCR, he probably had a very good reason for doing so. Ask him why he did it. Children do all sorts of things as part of the developmental process (and remember that this extends right through the adolescent years as well), and they learn by trial and error, and by example. He's probably never seen you push your breakfast into that slot, nor has anyone ever told him that he shouldn't do it. So, why not? Let's see what happens. Many of the things that send parents around the bend are the very things that enliven memories of our children's childhoods. Try not to be too judgmental. There are very few children who are wilfully naughty without good reason. If he isn't harming himself or others, try to understand rather than lash out. You'll be a lot more likely to teach your child what is acceptable if you are calm.
- Change the emphasis from attack to explanation, from you to me. For example, if your child runs into the street, say, 'I was very frightened. I was worried that a car could come along and run you over.' Or if your child throws a tantrum in the middle of the supermarket, say, 'I feel very sad and upset when you do this, and I am worried that people will think you are a naughty child when I know how nice you really are.' If your son stays out all night with his mates and 'neglects' to ring, you can begin by explaining that you were worried and upset, and go on to explain the effects of his actions. By explaining, rather than attacking, and drawing attention to your concerns rather than his shortcomings, your child will have a better understanding of what is and is not appropriate behaviour.
- Remember too that 'cause and effect' is a difficult lesson for anyone to learn, and kids will make mistakes, errors of judgement and even behave in a foolhardy way on occasion, well into adulthood. Chances are that you did too.

Self-esteem vs self-respect

The emphasis on self-esteem that has littered self-help books for the past few years has created some unholy monsters. Parents bend over backwards to ensure that their children are praised, rewarded, adored, and even worshipped, in order to find the holy grail of self-esteem.

Now self-esteem is undoubtedly important. It involves having a positive self-image, and feeling good about ourselves. We want that for our children, but many parents go in completely the opposite direction and give children a false sense of their own worth. They pump them up to the extent that they believe they are omnipotent and all-powerful, and from that point on they have their parents over a barrel. They've learned how to express themselves emotionally; they've accepted that they are the best; and they have very little time for anything other than praise and anything that increases the good feelings about themselves.

Remember that many, many studies have shown bullies to have a higher-than-average sense of self-esteem. So going too far in the 'you are great' direction can have the opposite effect of what is intended. Humility, pride in 'real' achievements, a sense of responsibility, empathy, compassion, generosity of spirit, a realistic belief in their own abilities (which takes into consideration weaknesses, too), and a willingness to try new things in all situations shows self-respect. Children with overly high self-esteem have an inflated opinion of themselves that shows no regard for others, or any real understanding of their own strengths and weaknesses. This 'omnipowerful' attitude is the root of much bullying.

So, the most important quality with which you can imbue your child is self-respect. It differs from self-esteem in several key ways. While esteem is awarded, respect must be earned through responsibility, cooperation and achievement. If we avoid the use of self-respect and substitute self-esteem, we have a convenient way of avoiding the effort required to succeed. For example, giving everyone a trophy simply because he or she participated in a race would increase everyone's self-esteem, but not their self-respect.

Another problem with disproportionately inflating your child's sense of self-esteem is that the 'real' world may not recognise your child's genius, and he will be set up for a nasty fall when he reaches adulthood, and even his late teens. The other problem is that discipline becomes more a question of softly, softly, rather than a realistic set of tools on which your child will rely as he makes decisions throughout his life. We'll talk about the importance of discipline later in this chapter.

And self-respect *is* the linchpin of successful discipline. When a child learns to respect himself, he also learns the ability to respect others – and other things, such as property, motivation, emotions, responsibility and authority. The reason is that he has earned his self-image and he can respect that. The process that led him there will be etched in his mind, and he will be able to draw upon that in different situations throughout his life, when dealing with others and when acting in society as a whole. A bully does not respect himself because he has no respect for others. Similarly, a child with no respect sets himself up to be a victim by failing to interact normally with others, by lacking the social skills that are a definite part of self-respect (children who respect themselves have been shown respect, and that requires regular and consistent communication and guidance; children who learn communication skills at an early age have the social skills necessary to carry them through difficult periods in their lives and come out the other side with their integrity intact).

You can't 'give' your child self-respect, but you can ensure that he earns it by offering him opportunities to take responsibility, by giving him unqualified attention and unconditional love (hence enhancing his belief in himself as a unique individual, worthy of such attention); by providing realistic goals and praising their attainment; by rewarding genuine effort and achievement rather than blindly praising things that show no enterprise, initiative or effort; by encouraging him to feel good about himself and his body; by praising the things that make him special; and by teaching him respect for others, so that he can find the same qualities within himself.

How do you go about it? Set realistic expectations, and respect the efforts your child makes to attain them, whether they involve matters of discipline, school work, sports, interaction with family and peers, work, responsibility or just about anything else. It's a time-consuming process, but good parenting takes time. Explain why things matter – why jumping on someone's sofa might be offensive, why rustling sweet wrappers in the cinema is disruptive, why hitting someone makes them feel bad about themselves, why bullying or unkind words wound others, why the destruction of someone else's property is insulting and hurtful … Put it in their terms, and help them to feel empathy and understanding for those around them, in all kinds of different situations.

Realistic praise

Every adult knows how good it feels to be praised, and in our society there is far too little of it. Everyone is too busy to stop and appreciate, to comment on the little things that make us feel good about ourselves. Think of a typical child's day: he's rushed through breakfast and into clothes, out the door and off to school. He comes home with a new painting or an 'A' grade on his GCSE paper, and you glance at it and say 'how lovely' and urge him to do his homework, or to watch his little brother while you finish the ironing. He might have a music lesson, or gymnastics to fit in before dinner, and then there is the battle over what he will and won't eat – a battle over computer games, or the ubiquitous mobile phone. Everything is running late, so bathtime is

Praise produces that warm feeling inside that makes your child think: I am all right. He learns to feel good about himself, to appreciate, and to see good in the world around him.

nothing more than a quick splash, and if there's time for a story before bed, things are looking up. Lights out and most parents breathe a sigh of relief. Older children tend to compound parental stress by being up later, and being an all-consuming responsibility – the reminders to set out kit or books or uniform for the following day, the battle to achieve a regular and acceptable bedtime, the long hours on the telephone or the computer, the arguments over weekend arrangements and homework, the urging to bathe – it's all rather hard work, and, once again, parents are relieved when children disappear and they can relax.

So look back at your child's day. How often did you praise him? How did you make him feel good about himself? Probably not much, and maybe not at all. If he was overexcited, grumpy or 'difficult', you probably blasted him. He may well have been disciplined, but he probably wasn't praised.

I can't overstate the importance of praise. Praise produces that warm feeling inside that makes your child think: I am all right. He learns to feel good about himself, to appreciate, and to see good in the world around him. He feels loved, and valued, and worthy of your attention. He sees that he can do good, and that you will recognise it, and him, for his efforts. He learns to like himself and he develops confidence.

Fit praise into your day as often as you can. If you only praise good grades, he may become obsessed with schoolwork as a way to please you. If you only praise his efforts on the football pitch, he may drive himself too hard to get your attention. If you never praise him, he will continue to do whatever gets your attention, which probably means 'naughty', sulky or insolent behaviour. If, during a day, the only time you give your child your full attention is when he won't eat his dinner, he slaps his sister, plays his music too loudly, slams his bedroom door, or spends hours on the telephone, you can guarantee that these behaviours will be repeated. Negative attention is better than no attention at all, and all children thrive on attention. Make no mistake about it – we are talking about adolescents as well as young children here.

Be liberal with your praise. From morning to night, notice and dwell on the good things about your child's behaviour, his actions, his personality and his views. Praise him for remembering to put down the seat of the toilet after he's finished, even if does forget to wash his hands. Praise him for eating his cereal, even if the fruit remains untouched. Praise him for putting on his shoes without being reminded, even if they are on the wrong feet. Praise him for getting his gym bag by the front door, even if he forgets it on the way out the door.

Praise his artwork, his homework, his spelling test results, his appearance, his memory, his organisational skills, his sense of humour, his silly jokes, and really mean it. Don't just glance at a proudly displayed piece of artwork or coursework, even if it is exactly the same as every picture or project he's showed you all week. Point out aspects that you like, and ask questions. Show interest in him and his world. Be thrilled for his achievements, even if they don't live up to your expectations. If your child gets a report card full of Cs, but his teacher says he's really trying, make a fuss. If your child fails everything, but gets a glowing personal report, focus on the fact that he is a nice, popular child. Praise everything good about your child and what he does. If he feels good about himself, if he believes you like him, flaws and all, he will develop healthy self-esteem and the type of self-respect that will spill over into every part of his life.

This is not to say that praise should be unrealistic. A teenager who gets a series of terrible marks in French or maths and is clearly making no effort, should not be praised. But if he spends an hour or so revising, then praise the effort. Show interest and enthusiasm in his interests and enthusiasms in order to create a bond, and a point of contact. But avoid offering praise for things that are clearly unworthy of it. You'll raise his self-esteem, again, but you will not give him self-respect, which is so very important.

It is very important not to praise one single aspect of your child – his grades, for example – which can put pressure on your child to perform at a consistent level. Psychologists at Columbia University, New York, conducted six studies of 412 11-year-olds in which they compared children praised for intelligence with those praised for effort and hard work. They looked at children under conditions of failure as well as success. They found that commending children for their intelligence after good performance might backfire by making them highly performance-oriented and thus extremely vulnerable to the effects of subsequent setbacks. On the other hand, children who were commended for their effort concentrated on learning goals and strategies for achievement. The researchers found that children who were commended for their ability when they were successful learned to believe that intelligence is a fixed trait that cannot be developed or improved. They blamed poor performance on their own lack of intelligence. When children praised for their hard work performed poorly, they blamed their lack of success on poor effort and demonstrated a clear determination to learn strategies that would enhance subsequent performances. The answer? Use both general and specific praise, so that your child has plenty to feel good about, even when one aspect of his life slips.

Most importantly, however, praise your child for just being himself. Praise his appearance (you are such a good-looking boy, your hair looks nice today, you've got such a great smile, you look good in those jeans, what gorgeous eyes you have ...) constantly. Children will define their bodies by how others perceive them. If you make them feel that they are attractive, you will improve their confidence and their self-image. Fat children, skinny children, adolescents with acne – everyone needs to feel that they are lovable and nice to look at. You won't create a big-headed child by praising appearance, you'll simply ensure that your child feels comfortable in his own skin.

Physical affection

Nurturing touch plays a strong role in infant and child development and research suggests that it continues to be important as a way of communicating love and caring between parents and their older children. Most parents continue to share some level of physical closeness with their daughters during the growing-up years, but this can change dramatically for sons. Parents of boys (particularly mothers) find that their physical contact with a son grows more awkward and less frequent around the age of eight or nine, but the shift is most dramatic when the son moves into adolescence. Many children naturally withdraw at this stage, particularly in front of their friends, and this reaction must be expected and respected. However, it doesn't mean that we should give it up altogether. Like many other aspects of parenting, physical closeness remains important throughout a child's life. A parent is one of the few people who can give a child the emotional comfort of physical warmth in a non-sexual context.

A hand on a shoulder, a pat on the back, a tousle of the hair, or a quick squeeze are all ways of showing affection. A child who is not touched will feel ignored, ashamed, unworthy of attention, inferior and misunderstood. Touch is important throughout childhood and into adolescence and beyond, and it has a language of its own. It can offer reassurance and love that go beyond words. Watch for signs that your children need a little reassurance, and make it natural. Sit down together with a book and put your arm around your child. If he's watching television, stroke his feet. If he's struggling with homework, give him a hug. If he cries, don't expect him to be more mature. Get down there and be physical. There is safety in physical affection, and all children will benefit. Children need to experience physical tenderness if they are to be able to be physical themselves as adults.

This brings us to the question of bodies. Children need to feel good about their bodies and themselves, and physical affection can provide reassurance that they are attractive and lovable. No one touches things that they find distasteful, and if you fail to touch your child, he will get the message – even if only on a subconscious level – that he is something with which you would rather not be in contact. Touch raises self-esteem and self-respect and it costs nothing to give.

Communicating with your child

The cornerstone of any relationship is communication, and it is important that you take time to establish communication that you both understand. Look back on your day. Have you had any real interaction? Many days are spent chivvying children along, asking questions but not really listening to the answers, expressing your viewpoint without really taking theirs on board. When is the last time you sat down and had a satisfying conversation? And when you do speak to your child, do you get the message across satisfactorily, and is he able to put forward his own message?

In even the most hectic lifestyles, it is important to make time for conversation and interaction. Make it part of an evening routine, when your child is relaxed and calm. Give every child a chance to speak at the dinner table, and have a rule about hearing everyone out before interrupting. Encourage communication, whether it is positive or negative. It is crucial that you give children space in which to express emotion, and that you offer a non-judgemental, reassuring ear.

Children need to learn to communicate without being afraid of the repercussions. If your child confesses that he's broken a window, eaten his brother's chocolate, ruined your best shirt or even, in the extreme, tried a recreational drug, don't blast him. Honesty is extremely important to successful long-term communication and if your child believes that he can tell you the truth without a lecture, an argument or a punishment, he will continue to do so throughout his life. If your child has done something serious, let him know how you feel, but stay calm. If he has broken a rule, ask him how he thinks you should deal with it. Most children will willingly offer a suitable punishment, given the authority to do so. They will feel less chastised if they have had a part in the proceedings, if they have been the instigator of justice.

Physical punishment

Physical punishment has no place in the upbringing of any child. However, no parent can ever maintain full control and there may be times when you lash out. This type of physical aggression is much less serious than a planned physical punishment. If you give your child a clip around the ear in a moment of complete and utter frustration, admit that you've lost control. Apologise and explain that you felt so angry you just couldn't help yourself. He'll understand that you don't consider it to be acceptable behaviour, and he'll be less likely to use violence himself. But if you use violence in a premeditated way – smacking a child as a form of discipline, for example – you are sending conflicting and negative messages. I have watched mothers slap a child for slapping someone else. What an extraordinary contradiction this presents. You cannot teach a child that violence is unacceptable and then use it yourself.

In the case of bullying, this is crucial. More than 100 studies show a link between authoritarian parenting and bullying. Hostility and violence in the home is the catalyst for many bullies, and can also result in children becoming victims. Do not underestimate this. Violence begets violence; governing by fear

(continued on page 212)

An emotional vocabulary

Children need to be taught to express themselves, and they need to learn the vocabulary with which to do so. Boys have been much neglected in this area. In fact, if you ask the majority of boys 'How do you feel about that?', you are likely to get nowhere. They might talk about how they approached a problem, or divulge a plan for setting something right, but most boys do not express emotion easily, largely because our culture discourages emotional development in boys.

As they get older, most children are dissuaded from showing outward displays of emotion, and learn that it is better to hide feelings than to incur the teasing or wrath of a tired parent, a sibling or a peer. Without emotional literacy, children are left to manage conflict, adversity and change with a limited emotional repertoire.

Here's what to do:
- From an early age, help your child to express himself. Start by expressing your own emotions: I am feeling sad, tired, excited, happy, frightened ... and explain why. Children learn by example, and if they see that it is acceptable for parents to express themselves in emotional terms, they will be much more likely to do it themselves. Show them that emotion is a part of life, not a sign of weakness or imperfection.
- Help your child by giving him the words ('You must be feeling very disappointed'; 'That must have made you very sad'; 'I can see that you are excited'; 'You must feel proud of yourself'; 'You should be thrilled'; 'It's no wonder you are feeling angry'.) Give them the words and teach them how they are used.
- If your child is reluctant to express himself, encourage him. Open conversations and let him continue them ('You must be feeling very cross about being overlooked for the football squad'; 'You must be feeling very sad that you weren't invited to X's party'; 'If I were you, I would be very proud of myself'). Use the words that he needs to learn: proud, happy, excited, angry, frustrated, confused, distressed, sad, lonely, jealous. Let him know that it's OK to feel even negative emotions, as long as they are expressed rather than used in aggression, or withheld – which can be as damaging.

- Share your own experiences. If your child is having difficulty in any situation, try to find a similar situation that you experienced as a child (or even as an adult). Describe the way you felt, and ask how your child would feel in the same situation (even if you know full well he's feeling that way now). If a child learns that it is acceptable to feel that way, he won't be ashamed to admit it.
- Most importantly, however, listen! There is no point in encouraging honest emotional vocabulary in a child if you brush it off. If you teach a child to express feelings, you must acknowledge them, offer reassurance and spend time finding ways to make your child feel better about himself and a situation. For example, if your child says that he is upset because his sibling is going to a party and he is not, don't say 'How ridiculous. you've been to three parties this month and he's been to none'. Accept and validate his feelings. Show understanding: 'I would be upset, too. It's hard to see other people having fun when you've got nothing planned. Why don't you and I do something nice together instead.' If your child tells you when he feels jealous, don't become angry or judgmental. Accept his feelings and let him know that they are normal.
- Much aggression is caused by an inability to express feelings. When we suppress emotions, they have a tendency to boil over from time to time, and, in children in particular, they can come out as violence and physical loss of control. Most aggression can be curtailed by regular expression of feelings.
- Remember: most bullies are 'acting out' and most victims are 'withholding'. Communication is essential to redress the balance. When a child has a voice he learns to stand up for himself – ensure that you offer that voice, and that he gets used to finding the words to express himself.

And in the context of bullying, research leaves us in no doubt that children who can communicate, negotiate, stand up for themselves and deal with anger or other negative emotions in positive ways, are much less likely to be involved in bullying. Communication is essential.

may work in the short-term, but in the long term it breeds resentment, hostility and anger – all of which feed a bullying situation.

Try to remember a time when you were physically punished as a child. How did you feel? Angry, embarrassed, invaded, distressed, frightened? Did you lash out or did you withdraw? Did you feel intense rage or hatred for the perpetrator, or did you feel guilty and unworthy? This is an important exercise. Most of us have been hit at some point in our lives, and the feelings we experienced are the very ones that we will create in our children if we use violence. No positive feelings ever come from physical discipline, and you can undo a great deal of good work by degrading your child in this way.

The effects of smacking

Studies show that many children who are smacked at home are more likely to be physically aggressive at school. They feel a greater need to gain 'power' and are therefore more likely to be bullies, or use bullying tactics. Studies also show, however, that some children do not necessarily turn that shame and anger into violence. They turn those feelings inward, which makes them incapable of sustaining healthy, loving relationships.

Research has also consistently shown that severe or frequent parental use of physical punishment is associated with an increase in a child's aggression. The more children are smacked, the more likely they are to be physically aggressive with siblings, in school and, as adults, with spouses and children, according to psychologist Terry Luce, a professor at the University of Tulsa in the USA, whose area of research is aggressive behaviour. He says children as young as pre-school age will hit other children as a result of being smacked themselves. In teenage years, there is a high correlation between smacking and delinquency.

All smacking does is teach a child to 'Do what I tell you'. As a result, children learn how to avoid getting smacked (including by lying and cheating), but not how to regulate their behaviour. They are less likely to internalise the difference between right and wrong or to develop a conscience. Longitudinal studies also show that children who are smacked are more likely to do poorly at school, and less likely to finish higher education.

What is particularly troublesome is that smacking is often done by otherwise loving parents. So the message becomes, 'When you are angry with people you love, hitting is OK'. Therefore when you smack you are modelling violence as an acceptable way to solve problems. This behaviour has an enormous impact on society as a whole, and may, in part, explain the huge problems we have with violence and lack of respect. Respect is mutual: if you are disrespectful of your child, you will never gain his or her respect. In addition, he or she is unlikely to respect authority figures in general.

A punished child becomes preoccupied with feelings of anger and fantasies of revenge, and is thus deprived of the opportunity to learn more effective methods of solving the problem at hand. He learns little about how to handle or prevent similar situations in the future. As children grow older, consider, too, the invasiveness and the loss of integrity involved with physical violence. A teenager who is hit will feel an enormous resentment. And when a situation arises where he might feel threatened, or perceive an injustice, he will respond in the way he has been conditioned to respond – with violence.

Disciplining with confidence

Never before has discipline been such an apparent problem in our society. Teachers complain of the impossibility of maintaining classroom control with increasingly delinquent pupils. Many parents feel overwhelmed by children who appear to show little regard for rules and acceptable behaviour. More worryingly still, lawlessness is rife among children. A 2002 poll by the Youth Justice Board in the UK found that one in four children admitted to committing a crime in the last year. The most common crimes were fare-dodging, shoplifting, graffiti, criminal damage and carrying a weapon. One in five also admitted stealing from school, handling stolen goods, or stealing from home.

The blame for the slide appears to shift between parents and teachers, with no one taking real responsibility. I believe that discipline is firmly rooted in the home. Teachers and schools have a responsibility, too, but their role is more one of maintenance and reinforcement. The reason for this is that discipline is not about controlling children, or laying down the law. It's about guiding children to adulthood, and investing them with respect for themselves and others. Indeed, as already stated, giving our children self-respect is the linchpin to any healthy discipline policy and the key to empowering them to make the right choices in life. One of the most important jobs a parent has is to teach life lessons to their child, and behaviour is part of that. For people to live together in harmony, there has to be a basic level of respect for others.

All children need discipline. It defines their world, and makes it a safe place in which to live. It shows them their boundaries and allows them to express themselves and show some independence within those boundaries. Children without discipline are effectively thrust into the world without a guide and are forced to make decisions and choices that they are not equipped to make. There is a curious divide in the way modern parents approach discipline. Some underparent, giving their children too much freedom, leaving them to their own devices for long periods of time, and expecting them to behave in an adult fashion – literally looking after themselves. Some overparent, giving them no personal freedom, over-disciplining them, and expecting them to behave beautifully at all times, and to achieve and succeed. Both extremes can produce equally disastrous results. You've seen what the studies say: under-parenting and overparenting can both cause bullying behaviour.

The best parents are those who allow their children some free rein, some scope to be children, some freedom to be themselves, while still respecting the rights and needs of others. What children need is guidance, and an understanding of the world around them. This requires time and patience. Constant explanations are required to give children a realistic reason why certain behaviours are unacceptable or disrespectful.

Parents represent the first relationships our children have in their lives, and these must be healthy and built on the sound principles of love, respect, care, nurturing, guidance, acceptance, understanding, communication, mutual expression and, above all, security. Most of what our children do in their lives revolves around relationships and interactions with other people – with friends, classmates, teachers, coaches, other family members, peers, babysitters, carers and even shopkeepers. If they learn the lessons of healthy relationships and the ability to interact early on, they will have the tools they need to find their place in the world.

What all parents need to do is to provide their child with an understanding of how other people feel and think, and what will be expected of them in certain situations. No child knows instinctively how to behave, and, with even the best guidance, there will always be times when emotion overtakes logic, or exuberance overtakes wisdom, or temper overtakes self-control. This is where patience comes in.

Patience is sometimes intolerably short in today's hectic, stressful lifestyles. No one can exhibit patience when they feel exhausted, tired, fed up and powerless, and this has a dramatic effect on the way our children learn to see themselves. Because we take our parenting responsibilities seriously, our expectations tend to be high, and we often see any rebellion or bad behaviour as a reflection of our poor parenting skills. We often lose a lot of the joy of parenting because we become overly caught up in the role of disciplinarian. We also often misplace our sense of humour, which is one of the best tools we have to negotiate the parenting minefield.

We do not let our children be children; we control rather than teach; we expect adult behaviour and decision-making in children who have little understanding of what is expected; we punish and penalise rather than focus on the good things. The result is that many children feel powerless, valueless, disrespected and unloved. They develop poor self-identities and never acquire the self-respect required for them to be confident and caring members of society. A cause of the bullying epidemic? I suspect it's certainly one of them.

I've praised him, what happened?

It would be idealistic to think that praise will make your child a perfect person, and even children with a healthy sense of self-esteem and confidence need guidelines for behaviour. One of the most important jobs parents have is to teach life lessons to their child, and behaviour is part of that. For people to live together in harmony, there has to be a basic level of respect for others. You need to respect your child, and he needs to learn to respect you, and everyone else around him. Teaching respect is the art of discipline.

First and foremost, consider your expectations. You cannot make a lively child into a quiet conformist, and you cannot turn a dreamer into an outgoing conversationalist. One of the most important things to remember is that you are working with a unique personality, and your expectations have to be geared to those characteristics. A lively child should not be 'controlled', but taught appropriate behaviour in various situations. A shy child should not be expected to hold a long eye-to-eye conversation with an adult, but he can be taught to be polite.

Parental expectations are crucial to discipline, and you need to assess whether they are appropriate. Do you expect your child to sit quietly through a play at the theatre, or during an adult dinner party? Do you expect your child to walk by your side in the supermarket? Do you expect your child to behave beautifully in all situations? If so, your expectations are probably too high. Children have abundant natural energy, and while it can be channelled, it should never be suppressed. Many parents feel the need to control their children because of the way they will be perceived by others. 'Bad' behaviour is too often considered to be a sign of poor parenting, or lack of parental control. Be realistic in your expectations. Make allowances for age and temperament, and ensure that you have made clear your expectations before every situation. If they let you down (which they inevitably will, from time to time), you need to consider methods of discipline that will get the message across in the most positive way possible.

? Which discipline?

- Gear your discipline to the individual child. A highly strung, rambunctious child will probably not respond to a quiet word in the corner. Maybe 'time out' is appropriate. He may long to be part of the action, and even the threat of a few moments alone on the stairs will be enough to calm him down.
- A less confident, quiet child might be devastated by the thought of time out, or away from you and the rest of the family. In this situation, a quiet word in the corner, explaining why behaviour is unacceptable, might just work.
- Whatever you do, don't assume that a method is appropriate for your child without trying it out first.
- Prepare your child in advance of every situation by letting him know what you expect. If he knows the game plan, he can make choices accordingly.
- Set up some household rules. Sit the whole family down at the table and work out what is expected from every member (see page 222).
- Give warnings! If your child is behaving badly, don't slam down a punishment. Give him a warning of what is to come. In our household we use the football disciplinary system of red and yellow cards. Yellow cards are a warning. A red card means big trouble, and a pre-arranged penalty. For example, if one of my sons is picking on the other, and causing trouble, I'll call out: yellow card. They know what comes next. Two yellow cards, and they see red! We have only ever got to red card stage two or three times over the past two years, so it is a system that definitely works.
- Try not to shout. It can be hard to control your own emotions in the heat of a frustrating or distressing situation, but it can turn up the temperature and make things much worse. Some children are terrified when their parents shout, whereas others just develop a thick skin, which means the decibel levels continue to rise over time until everyone is shouting to get a point across. Shouting also creates negative energy that can compound a situation. Try to

be calm and positive whenever possible, and, if necessary, remove yourself completely from the situation. If you are going to lose it, count to 10, and try again.
- Don't use physical violence, whatever the problem.

Power and discipline

Respect your child and give him choices. Allow him to have some control over his environment and his own behaviour.

- In terms of discipline, this means allowing him to choose how he behaves. In the middle of a temper tantrum, for example, offer a choice: 'You can stop shouting now, and I will be able to finish the shopping and we'll have time for a trip to the library. Or you can continue to shout and scream; I will be cross; and we will be too late to do anything other than go home. Which do you choose?' Give your child time to think, and then respond accordingly. Whatever you do, be consistent. If you say that you won't have time for the library, don't go. If you say that you will, you must make the trip.
- This technique also works well for older children: 'If you can sit down and explain your plans, we can discuss them. If you shout and slam your door, then the simple answer is "no".'
- Again, for an older child, the same method works in a variety of situations: 'If you do your homework now, you can watch an hour of television after dinner. If you don't do it now, you will miss out.' 'If you come home at 10pm after your party, I will trust you and allow you to go to a film on your own on Saturday. If you don't come home on time, I will not be able to trust you on your own.' Whatever the situation, give a choice and let your child know the consequences of either one.
- Don't be 'afraid' of your children. Most children will react when they are faced with discipline – when they are instructed to do something that goes against their own wishes or plans. Children love their parents – and that love is almost always unconditional. So when they lash out, they are testing boundaries, and will feel more secure when those boundaries remain consistent. With teenagers, you will always have battles about what friends are doing, and what should be allowed, but your remaining calm and consistent will benefit them in the long run, and will not threaten the integrity of your relationship. Parents who give in in order to maintain harmony, or to try to curry favour with a child, do them no favours. Inconsistent or lax parenting are associated with bullying.

- All children need to know that you (or another adult: teacher, babysitter, policeman, whatever) are in authority. That doesn't mean you have to be authoritarian, it simply means that your child must learn to respect people in charge. Establish early on that they have rights and choices, but within certain guidelines. No child will benefit from being allowed to run wild. Emotional health and freedom need the confines of a structured environment. Children of any age feel more secure when they know where they stand, and too much freedom can be alarming. Children and teenagers do not have the emotional maturity to make correct decisions every time. They will often feel confused and out of their depth. It's important to remember that your confident 16-year-old may not actually be anything like what he purports to be. Guidance is as essential at this age as it is for toddlers.

- Children need to be given licence to debate and to ask questions, and you must be willing to negotiate on the basis of a sound argument. However, rudeness or argumentative behaviour suggest disrespect, and every child needs to learn that they are always inappropriate. It is important to be consistent, to stick to the family rules, and to ensure that your child respects your authority to make overall decisions.

- If you do have a problem with lack of respect for authority, empowering your child can help. If he feels that he has some control, and some scope for making choices and decisions, he will be less likely to challenge you on everything. For example, if your overall rule is that your child must dress himself in the morning, and you face a battle every single time, use choices. 'Would you like to wear the red trousers or the blue trousers?' 'Do you want to put on your vest or your underpants first?' 'Do you want to get dressed before your breakfast or after?' Allowing choice makes him feel that he's in charge to some degree. You haven't changed the rule – he still has to get dressed – but you have given him some personal power.

- It works for older children, too. If your child regularly refuses to do his homework, offer choices. 'If we do it now, I can help you, or you can do it on your own after dinner.' 'Do you want to use the computer or write it out?' 'Do you want to do maths first or reading?' 'Do you want to do it in your bedroom or at the kitchen table?' Present it as an accepted fact that the homework will be done, but offer him some choices as to how, when and where.

- The concept of learned behaviour is central to discipline. Children who regularly receive praise and are given liberties when they behave in an appropriate manner continue that behaviour. If they never get a shot at being 'good' or are harshly punished without any choices, without any recourse, and without any positive attention, you can be sure that they will learn that being out of order is the 'order' of the day – gets them attention, gives them kudos with their peers (who become increasingly important when parental attention is lax), and helps to dissipate the resentment and frustration they carry. No power means powerlessness, and all children who are powerless will feel cornered and respond in kind. One of the ways children respond when they are powerless is by lashing out and becoming aggressive. Alternatively they react in the opposite way – they turn inwards and refuse to communicate. What do you have? Bully or victim.

- Model appropriate behaviour. If you shout and lash out in anger, you can expect your child to do the same. If you constantly lose your temper, interrupt your child when he is speaking, show little respect for his view or needs, you cannot expect him to act any differently. If you adopt a calm, reasonable approach to dealing with your children, they will learn that this is the way to behave. Children who live with fairness learn that there is justice.
- Above all, give your child an outlet, and don't expect him to behave angelically all the time. Everyone needs to let off steam. Children need to be allowed to be children. Children do not have the self-control or the sense of propriety of an adult, or an understanding of societal expectations. As they grow up, they learn, through you, and through the reactions of everyone else around them, what is appropriate. Until then, give their natural enthusiasm room to blossom, within guidelines that your child understands and accepts.

Giving children an outlet

I've heard countless parents complaining that their children are so good at school, but a complete nightmare at home. If this sounds familiar, take heart. Your child has learned appropriate behaviour for the school environment and has probably worked hard for the whole day at keeping his emotions and enthusiasm in check. In the comfort of his own home, he can let down his defences and let out all that energy. This is the way it should be! A child's home is his castle – where he can be himself.

Don't expect the rigid routine of school to be followed by an equally rigid routine at home. Time has to be allowed and, indeed, encouraged, for fun, high spirits, laughter, shouting, cheering, crying or just lying about. If your child is exhibiting signs of stress, he does not have an appropriate outlet, and you will need to create one. Organise some enjoyable exercise. Throw him out into the garden to run and explore. Laugh, tell jokes, wrestle, play, relax – anything that lets the energy flow. Let him turn up his music and sing or dance.

Creating a healthy family life

- Spend time together. If you can't manage it every day, block off time to be together as a unit. As children get older, they will want to have a say in activities and you should encourage this.
- Try to eat at least one meal together every day. An alarming survey recently revealed that a large proportion of children never sit down with their families to eat. Not only does this have repercussions for their diet, it also means that many children do not have any time to interact with their families – a crucial part of family life.
- Keep the atmosphere calm and loving. Every family needs to ensure, when a child is dealing with negative elements in his life (stress, upset, trauma, emotional problems), that these do not have an impact on the family environment. As a unit, you can work together to make sure that every family member is happy and supported in times of trouble.
- Encourage time alone. Don't insist that your child is by your side every minute of the day. Encourage responsibility and freedom, and allow time for growth and learning by experience and experimentation. Let him dig in the garden, water the lawn, splash in the kitchen sink, read on his bed, make a magnificent snack, mess up the playroom, listen to his very loud music, ring up his friends, have some time on his bike or skateboard – have fun!
- Computers, microwaves and voicemail are all examples of tools and technologies designed to help us be more efficient and effective. Despite their usefulness, however, people seem to be struggling even more with lack of time. The tyranny of the urgent too often leads to stress and leaves insufficient time and energy for the truly important things in life. This often results in feelings of fatigue and frustration. Busy people feel unfulfilled when life is overrun with activity but has little meaning or purpose. Others struggle with a sense of guilt and frustration over conflicting demands. Balancing work demands, time for taking care of ourselves, and time for relationships and family can be a huge juggling act. In a happy family, every member needs a voice. As a unit you need regularly to determine your priorities and values. Ask yourselves what is

important in your life and why this is so. Then compare those priorities and values with how you are actually living your lives. Set realistic goals and know your limits. Make time for the important things in life.

- Watch your child carefully for signs of overscheduling. If he isn't getting pleasure from his activities, change them or leave them out altogether. If he's under pressure at school, talk to his teacher and make sure that your expectations are not compounding the problem.

- Balance a technologically busy life with an appreciation of the natural world. Take walks together, watch a sunset, get a birdfeeder, or watch a bird preparing a nest. Go to a nature reserve or a campsite for a holiday.

- Don't instil a desire for material possessions; they're not essential to happiness. Many parents struggle to give their children everything – the newest technology, trading cards, bikes, toys and games – at the expense of family life. As the old saying goes, the best things in life are free. Your child will benefit far more from your presence, affection and interaction than he will from a lot of material goods that keep you working all hours of the day and night. Children are less materialistic than we might think. According to new research, receiving more pocket money does not make children any happier, and family wealth makes no difference to children's worry levels. Professor Jonathan Bradshaw of York University has been studying the relationship between family wealth and a sense of mental well-being in children aged between 11 and 15. The study measured poverty in a number of ways – including income, lack of possessions and whether a family was on income support – and found that children's levels of sadness, worry or happiness weren't affected by these variables. Although there was no doubt that poverty had a terrible effect on children, it was not necessarily the most important factor when talking about children's mental health. 'The key determinants of children's mental well-being are relationships with parents and peers, rather than the level of income they are living on,' Professor Bradshaw said, 'Young people are not just victims of their circumstances but are able to be resilient actors in their own right with the support of their parents and peers.'

- Encourage your children's friendships and welcome their friends to your home. Children need experience in dealing with their peers, and they learn how to be themselves in the company of others. Peers and friends are an important part of the process of learning to be self-aware and confident, as children will be faced with new and different situations in which they must use their own

Family rules

Establishing expectations can have a dramatic effect on your children's behaviour, and you will need to sit down as a family to decide what is and is not appropriate. Focus on problem areas. For every rule, decide upon the behaviour you would like to see. Here are some examples:

- I won't play my stereo loudly past 10pm at night. I will respect the fact that other people in the family need to relax and sleep.
- I won't make a fuss about getting dressed in the morning. I will get dressed before I watch cartoons or eat my breakfast.
- I won't fight with my brother. I will treat my brother the way I would like him to treat me.
- I won't come home after 10/11pm (adolescents). I will call if I am running late and I will always tell my parents where I am going to be.
- I won't argue about doing my homework. I will do my homework after school (after dinner, after 10 minutes on the computer, etc.).

For every rule that is satisfactorily maintained, offer a 'reward'. Obviously it would be impractical to give a treat for everything done properly, but there are many ways of rewarding children. One of the best ways (for younger children) is a star chart, where a star can be given for everything done well. Ten stars can mean some pocket money or a magazine. A hundred stars can mean a family day out to a theme park or the beach. Encourage your

resources. Remember that human beings cannot live happily in isolation. Although your child may eventually choose a relatively solitary path, the quality of his life will largely be defined by his relationship with others.

Within the family unit, children learn the lessons of life: forgiveness, the capacity to trust, familiarity, relationships, honesty, empathy and appreciation.

child to choose what would be the best reward for consistently sticking to the rules. For older children, use much the same technique, but make the rewards a bit 'cooler' – an extra night out on the weekends, maybe a new CD, or going halves on a pair of sought-after trainers.

Remember that these rules will soon become a way of life, and, when they do, you can drop them. To be effective, family rules will need to be updated constantly. There's no point in giving stars for getting dressed in the morning if your child has been doing it successfully, of his own volition, for a month. There's no point in continuing to offer extras to an adolescent who is playing by the rules. Change the rules, dropping and adding, as your child grows and develops.

For rules that are broken, a penalty will be required. Encourage your child to choose his own. You'll find that children are much harder on themselves than you will ever be. For example, losing playtime on the computer, missing out on a trip to the library, giving up an after-dinner treat, being 'grounded' on Saturday night, or missing a trip to the cinema with friends. Whatever your child chooses (within reason), let it stand. Try to keep the penalty in line with the rule. There's no point in banning television for a night if your child doesn't eat his dinner, but that might be appropriate if he has beaten up his brother!

Make it fun! Don't go wild, but choose, say, five or six rules for each member of the family, and talk about them at length. Make sure everyone is happy with the rewards and the penalties, and hold family meetings from time to time to reassess.

That is the family's crucial role. It is a place of mutual self-discovery, communal growth and learning, where children discover the good and the bad within themselves and within other people. It is the spiritual sanctuary, where children begin to understand what it means to develop spirit, heal heart, clarify mind and purify intellect. With its love and acceptance, they are free to grow.

8

Bullying Initiatives

First they ignore you.
Then they laugh at you.
Then they fight you.
Then you win.

Gandhi

THERE CAN BE NO DOUBT THAT SUCCESS in tackling bullying involves the full-scale support of the school community. If teachers and other educators turn a blind eye to the problem, students will rightly perceive that they have no back-up or set code of conduct and will develop their own social hierarchy and methods of retribution and justice. No victim will ever feel comfortable coming forward and requesting assistance if his fears and experiences are belittled or disregarded. No bystander or witness will stick his neck out to stand up for a victim if he fails to receive the support of the adult community. No bully will stop his actions if he can get away with it. In fact, in a climate of fear and violence, bullying increases because students begin to believe that they have to be tough, to stand their ground, and have control over others both to achieve status in the pecking order, and to protect themselves from being bullied. More importantly, perhaps, if children are never taught appropriate means of social behaviour in the context of school; if they are never given rules or codes of behaviour to which they should conform; if they walk the corridors in fear of being the next target, and with the knowledge that they are powerless to do anything about it, the entire purpose of school life – the development of social skills, successful social interaction, education and learning – is destroyed. No child can learn in a war zone. And to redress the balance, not only do 'orders' have to come from 'the top', they must also be maintained by every single member of the school community.

Psychologist Dan Olweus looked at a number of successful anti-bullying programmes, and found that the most effective involve the entire school community, rather than focusing on the bullies and victims alone. His research shows that where programmes involve school staff, parents and every student, bullying has been reduced by up to 50 per cent. In addition, schools that implement programmes also report a decrease in other anti-social behaviour, including vandalism, fighting, theft and truancy.

Many different bullying initiatives have been developed worldwide, some more successful than others. Some studies show that initiatives and interventions have been hugely helpful in combating the problem; others are more circumspect, indicating that the problem is so pervasive that little can be done to stamp it out without addressing the moral values, code of conduct and violent tendencies of today's children. We'll look at some of the research below. For now, however, what is certain is that unless schools take bullying in hand, there can be no hope of eradicating it forever. Perhaps such a hope is idealistic – perhaps the fact that bullies come from all classes and ethnic groups, and infiltrate every element of society, from school through to high-level employment, means that they are here to stay and what we need to do is create resilient children who can cope with them, now and throughout their lives. Bullies will always exist, but the real issue here is ensuring that children get a childhood, that they achieve what they set out to do when they go to school, that they have a right to a life without fear, and a right to be safe, no matter where they are.

The bottom line is this: without the active involvement of parents, teachers and students, it will never be possible to create a safe and fear-free school environment.

The best anti-bullying programmes

Olweus found that the best programmes involve the following:

- Surveys. The schools conduct surveys of students and adults. The surveys create awareness of the problem and are used to measure improvements after new programmes are put in place. They also allow students and teachers to be honest, thus shedding more light on the problem.
- Parental involvement. Parents are kept abreast of all developments, and made aware of both the problem itself and the school's policy for eradicating it. Campaigns are held throughout the year, through newsletters, at parent-teacher meetings, and at PTA events and activities.

- A school committee. A committee is established to develop a school bullying policy and coordinate bullying prevention activities. The committee might be an already existing group, such as the school safety committee, or one established just for this purpose.
- Class activities. Teachers work with students to write class rules against bullying. Role-playing exercises are used to teach those students directly involved in bullying other ways to solve conflict. Students who are bystanders learn how they can help.
- Individual work and learning activities. Individual work is undertaken with both the bullies and the victims; learning activities are aimed at reducing social isolation; and there is more adult supervision during breaks and lunch.

We also know that the following measures help to establish a successful anti-bullying initiative within the school environment:

Putting clear policies in place. These should be designed to prohibit bullying, and should give a full definition of bullying, one which leaves students and teachers in no doubt as to what is acceptable and what is not. It should be written into the school's code of conduct, and communicated (and re-communicated) to parents, students, staff and every other person working within the school environment. The possible consequences of bullying should be outlined, as well as details of what actions both victims and bystanders/witnesses should take.

Ensuring any programmes or initiatives are pupil-friendly. This means they must be easily understood and it must make sense. Highbrow, jargon-laden initiatives will not work. Kids need to know, in the simplest terms, what bullying is, what is and is not acceptable, what the expectations are, how they can get help, and what happens to bullies as a consequence of their actions. Teaching moral values, compassion and tolerance are equally important to create a strong, unified and happy school environment, but these, too, must be put forward in terms that the students can understand and relate to.

Reiterating the code of conduct regularly and making it a regular part of the curriculum. Through school-wide drives, campaigns, fundraisers and other activities, student and staff awareness should be raised so that the issue becomes a central part of the school community. When students are involved in making the policy clear – for example by making posters setting out a comprehensive list of consequences for bullying, or by debating the issues frequently – it keeps the subject fresh, and provides an essential driving energy.

The most effective initiatives are those that allow students anonymity. Children are much less afraid of 'reporting' incidents if they feel they can do so without having to face the bully, or risk being discounted, or endangering themselves further. There is an important codicil to this, however: although anonymity should be provided, there must also be a general climate of accountability. That is to say, students must learn that they have a responsibility to defend their peers and to report incidents when they see them. If this is a regular, accepted and encouraged part of the school policy, students will feel less nervous about coming forward. But in the lead-up to getting the programme off the ground, students should be allowed to report as often as required in order for teachers and administrators to establish a clear picture of the problem: where it is taking place and who the main instigators are, as well as which children tend to be witnesses or involved in some other capacity, and which children are being victimised.

Supervision is essential. It is well known that bullying usually takes place in the playground, or in more isolated areas – often where teachers are not normally 'patrolling'. So hallways, locker areas, student common rooms, lavatories, bus-stops, lunch areas and quiet corners should all be adequately supervised. CCTV, used to cover areas where regular supervision is inadequate, has in many cases proved to be a useful deterrent.

Don't assume that teaching staff, no matter how experienced or well-educated, will be able to pinpoint bullying, or pick out a bully. Bullies can be sly and subversive, and ostensibly popular members of the peer group, so it takes a canny teacher to see what is going on. Training is essential: to recognise the signs of bullying; to be familiar with the characteristics of the classic bully and victim; and to know what steps to take both to prevent the problem and to deal with it when it arises.

At any age, bullying should become a part of the curriculum – with regular lessons, projects, discussion and debates within the class group. Ask kids to examine some of the long-term effects of bullying (on both victims and bullies); some of the more dramatic and tragic cases of bullycide, or homicide caused by bullying; and even the factors that lead children to bully. The more knowledge children have, the better. A bully might feel less inclined to target others in an environment where it has been made clear that most bullies have home problems, have been abused themselves, and have anger issues and difficulty with social skills and problem-solving. What kid wants to be labelled with that?

Using school time to examine feelings and emotions is also helpful. Again, role-playing will help – as well as working out motivating factors, what a victim may be feeling, what the victim or bully should have done differently, and how the problem could be solved. If problem-solving and poor social skills are at the root of many cases, it can only help to broaden the horizons of students and teach them these important skills in the context of the school day. Similarly, teaching basic morality and a value system will help to get the message across that bullying has no part in a successful school or in society at large.

Remember the importance of bystanders. School staff may be unaware that bullying is taking place, but 'on the ground' it will be witnessed by many

Take every single report of bullying seriously, whether or not you have your doubts about its accuracy.

students. Empower kids to support victims. Make it a responsibility rather than just an option. Point out that when they intervene, bullying usually stops, whereas when adults become involved, it goes to ground and the wrong children are often earmarked for punishment. Through various means – supplying a box into which reports can be posted anonymously; holding a regular open-hour at which kids can discuss problems or report incidents to staff members; or even teaching kids how to stand up to bullies, and praising and reinforcing this behaviour (it takes a brave kid to stand up to his peers) – you can help to keep bullying at bay.

Parents are important – not just for reinforcing the school message, but also in coming forward with any information they may have. Ensure that parents are fully aware of the school's policy, and know what to do if their child is bullied, or has bullied another child. If there is a set procedure for every eventuality, parents will also feel less fearful about coming forward, and less angry if they know that any complaints that they have will be heard compassionately and that support is on offer.

Students who have a history of bullying should not be isolated in order to humiliate them, but should be actively brought into discussions in class time;

encouraged to come up with solutions for bullying issues; helped to examine feelings, values and emotions; taught how to interact on a more successful level with peers; and encouraged to deal with anger in more productive ways (for example, a highly-strung bully who lashes out after a long morning of work probably needs a good run around the playground; encourage him to join a sport in the lunch break, or consider incorporating a morning stretch and 10-minute period of callisthenics into your class structure). All these measures will empower bullies to be more responsible members of the classroom.

Similarly, recognise kids who might make obvious targets – someone new to the school, kids with learning difficulties, kids who stand out because they are different in some way, those who are more isolated than others or appear to have fewer friends, or whose body language indicates that they are unlikely to 'fight' back. Support these kids. Make sure they are supervised. Offer opportunities for them to interact more with like-minded children by putting them in groups for projects, or in suitable clubs. Give them a child to 'mentor' in order to increase confidence. Teach all children how to assert themselves in a positive way, and to stand up for themselves without resorting to violence. Teach kids about body language. Give every child the tools they need to keep bullies at bay.

Take every single report of bullying seriously, whether or not you have your doubts about its accuracy. More importantly, act quickly. Incidents that seem innocuous to adults may be devastating for a child. Assume that every report is valid and worthy of instant and full investigation.

Respond to all incidents with a two-pronged policy: discipline and protection. School staff must work with all those involved: bully, victim and bystanders. The bully should be appropriately disciplined, and offered clear guidance for dealing more effectively with similar issues in the future; in other words, taught alternative means for dealing with anger or violence issues, given moral direction and an understanding of why bullying is wrong, no matter how often this has been reiterated through class activities or school policy. Remember to deal sensitively with bullies – humiliation will always have the effect of encouraging bullying rather than stamping it out. Although no bullying should ever be condoned, it is important to realise that children who bully often have problems in the home environment or in other areas of their lives. Their motivating factor may be powerlessness or frustration. Getting to the bottom of the problem will help you to deal more effectively with the bully. Above all, treat her with respect. Bullying is possibly the most disrespectful act that any child can commit, but I fully believe (as do many educators and researchers) that the only way to teach respect is to imbue respect. Give your bully opportunities to earn some respect, and see the result.

Similarly, victims need protection. Never be tempted to ask what they could have done differently, or intimate that they are to blame in any way. Help them to work on being more resilient, to feel confident enough to stand their ground, to use more effective body language and assertiveness skills. And make it very clear that they have your full support, no matter what. Emotional support is essential.

And don't forget bystanders. Many children are traumatised by witnessing bullying incidents and genuinely do not know what to do (see page 107). Treat them with respect and ask for ideas about how they could have intervened successfully. Offer protection and support so that they do not feel that by reporting an incident they are sticking their necks out and risking becoming victims themselves.

Use every single bullying incident as a platform for learning. What happened, why it happened, what could have been done differently, what support the victim or victims need, what would be an appropriate consequence for the bully, and why bullying is wrong. The more you reinforce your basic message, the more likely it is to get through.

Remember that bullying does not necessarily lend itself to the same interventions that may reduce other types of conflict among children. Because it involves harassment by powerful children of children with less power (rather than a conflict between peers of relatively equal status), common conflict resolution strategies such as mediation may not be effective.

Ultimately, you will be dealing on a disciplinary and guidance level with a small number of children who are involved in specific bullying incidents. However, the entire school community must be engaged in order to provide the school with a culture of non-violence and no bullying. Steps must be taken to create a climate of cooperation and caring. There are many ways to do this: getting older kids involved in community initiatives and services (helping old people, working in a local dog kennel, helping in a primary school, delivering clothing for charities – anything that promotes social responsibility and compassion, and encourages interaction with all levels of society); giving them a younger child to mentor or befriend at school; undertaking school drives or fundraising activities for those who are less fortunate, and encouraging kids to choose the recipients and become involved; using plenty of group projects in order to foster interaction between cliques and different groups within the class or year; providing platforms for free speech, such as regular debates, or 'elections', complete with carefully thought through manifestos; and holding regular 'circle times' (see page 246) or class discussions about personal responsibility, cooperation and caring. All these activities can be used to reiterate the importance of supporting people in the school or the community who may find it difficult to stand up for themselves.

Some teachers may be horrified by much of this, as class time has been curtailed in many schools by several hours, and the curriculum has expanded far beyond the resources available to most educators. But remember: no child will ever learn successfully in a climate of fear, nor will children be able to concentrate or focus on core subjects if the school culture is negative. What's more, students always perform best when they are valued, respected, given responsibility, and when they feel comfortable interacting with teachers and other figures of authority – exchanging views, debating principles and ideas, expanding horizons with an understanding of the world around them. If you can put aside time for educating kids about real-life issues that affect their day-to-day lives, such as bullying, peer pressure, tolerance, race and religious issues, social responsibility, values and mores, you will create the kind of environment where children will enjoy learning, and undoubtedly go on to succeed.

Everyone must be involved

It's not just teachers and administrators who are likely to witness bullying incidents, and for any bullying prevention programme to be effective, it must be fully comprehensive. So all adult members of the school community: dinner ladies, teachers, counsellors, sports staff, nurses, coaches, secretaries, bus drivers, after school staff, 'lollipop men and ladies', governors, helpers, parent representatives and groundsmen must be advised of the school policy, given guidance about how to spot bullying, and know the procedure in and out. Everyone must be alert and ready to act quickly in line with the school's approach.

Studies have found dramatic reductions in bullying of between 2 and 80 per cent when school-wide strategies are used.

The two key messages from these studies are that:

1. There is a direct correlation between the time and quality of effort spent in developing a whole school policy and the reduction in the levels of bullying.

2. The process of developing a common understanding of the problem is as important as any other factor.

The Olweus bullying prevention programme

The first and best-known intervention to reduce bullying among school-children, the Olweus Bullying Prevention Programme, was launched by Dan Olweus in Norway and Sweden in the early 1980s. In a reaction to the suicides of several severely victimised children, Norway supported the development and implementation of a comprehensive programme to address bullying in schools. This involved interventions at multiple levels, including school-wide interventions, classroom-level interventions and individual interventions.

The programme was found to be highly effective in reducing bullying and other antisocial behaviour among pupils in primary and junior high schools. Within two years of implementation, both boys' and girls' self-reports indicated that bullying had decreased by half. These changes in behaviour were more pronounced the longer the programme was in effect. Moreover, pupils reported significant decreases in rates of truancy, vandalism and theft, and indicated that their school's climate was more positive as a result of the programme. Not surprisingly, those schools that had implemented more of the programme's components experienced the most marked changes in behaviour.

The programme is a multilevel, multicomponent school-based programme designed to reduce or prevent bullying in pupils aged 6–15. Its main focus is to improve peer relations to make the school a safe and positive place in which pupils can learn. Core programme components are implemented at the school, classroom and individual levels.

School-wide components include:

1. The administration of an anonymous questionnaire to assess the nature and prevalence of bullying at each school

2. Training for all staff

3. Formation of a bullying prevention coordinating committee
4. Increased supervision of pupils at 'hotspots' for bullying
5. Development of school-wide rules against bullying
6. Consistent consequences for following/not following the rules
7. A school-wide kick-off event
8. Parental involvement
9. Staff discussion groups to ensure understanding and motivation

Classroom components include:
1. Holding regular class meetings with pupils about bullying
2. Consistent reinforcement of school rules against bullying

Individual components include:
1. Interventions with children identified as bullies and victims
2. Discussions with parents of involved children

The core components Olweus's anti-bullying programme have been adapted for use in several other countries, including the UK, Canada and the USA. One of the first anti-bullying programmes to take place outside Scandinavia was directed by researcher Peter K. Smith and instigated in 23 schools in Sheffield, England, in the early 1990s. The schools involved were asked to develop a whole school policy on bullying that included curriculum work, such as using drama and video; working with individuals and small groups to improve social skills (for example, through assertiveness training); and playground work (i.e. improving the environment in bullying hot-spots). After four school terms, the primary schools achieved an average 17 per cent reduction in the number of pupils reporting being bullied and a 7 per cent reduction in the pupils who reported bullying others. In the secondary schools the reductions were smaller, around 5 per cent, but there were substantial increases in the proportion of bullied pupils who told a teacher about it (32 per cent) and in the proportion of bullying pupils who said someone had talked to them about it (38 per cent). Schools which put more time and effort into anti-bullying measures, and which consulted widely on whole-school policy development, had the best outcomes. Such was the success of the project in highlighting the problem of bullying that it led to the government's Don't Suffer in Silence pack, and its effects continue to have an impact on current policy in the UK.

Other key programmes

Let's look at some of the key programmes that have been implemented in schools around the world. If you like the ideas put forward, you'll find details of how to find further information in the Resources section. Some schools cut and paste various parts of different programmes according to their specific needs, and this is fine, too. As long as your anti-bullying policy is straightforward, unequivocal, firmly established, consistent and clearly communicated to parents, teachers, students and anyone else in the school environment, it matters little how you go about it. Bullying should not be tolerated: that's the message. However, there are some interesting and quite visionary ways to get the other messages across; in other words, how to teach and imbue respect; how to encourage compassion, cooperation and kindness in the school community; how to create a strong school ethos where pupils are mutually supportive; and how to ensure that students interact on a respectful level, tolerating others differences and understanding the clear result of bullying within a school community. Sometimes it takes a shock in order to get the message across – explore situations like Columbine in the USA, or one of the tragic suicides of students (see page 270), or even the cases of students who have gone on to have unhappy, criminal lifestyles because of their bullying. Either way, once you have got your message across, you can use any of the following to reinforce it.

The no-blame approach

This programme was developed in the UK by the educational psychologist George Robinson. It takes the view that bullying is an 'interaction' which establishes group identity, dominance and status at the expense of other children. It focuses on the idea that developing 'higher values', such as empathy, considerateness and unselfishness, will encourage a bully to change his behaviour and react differently to stimuli. Without apportioning blame, it uses a problem-solving approach, giving responsibility to the group to solve the problem and to report back at a subsequent review meeting.

This programme advocates the following steps, when a bullying incident has taken place:

1. Interviewing the victim, and establishing the facts and the victim's feelings. There is an emphasis on who was involved rather than on directly questioning the victim about the incidents.

2. A meeting is set up between the people who are involved, including bystanders and anyone else who colluded or joined in, but did not initiate the bullying.

3. The problem is explained – focusing on the way the victim is feeling. A poem, a piece of writing or a drawing might be used to emphasise the distress experienced. No blame (hence the name) is attributed to any particular party, and the incidents of the experience are not outlined or enhanced.

4. The idea of 'shared responsibility' is put forward, in that the teacher does not blame anyone, but indicates that she knows that the group in front of her is responsible and has the capacity to do something about it.

5. The group is asked for ideas – in other words, to suggest a way in which the victim could be helped to feel happier. There is no focus on promising to be 'better' in the future, or on changing behaviour; rather, the teacher or administrator gives positive responses to the suggestions made.

6. The teacher then ends the meeting by passing over responsibility to the group to solve the problem.

7. The group meets again, and the teacher discusses with each student, including the victim, how things have improved or changed in order to monitor the process and keep the students involved.

In general, this approach has received a mixed response. For one thing, parents of victims are often appalled that nothing has been done by the school to support the victim or to put a stop to the bullying. The focus is on the misery of the victim and how that might be alleviated, which is intended, presumably, to teach social values and conscience.

Many parents find this hard to stomach, though the outcome has been purported to be positive. The authors of this approach believe that not taking on the details of the incidents actually works by avoiding stirring up disputes and casting blame, which incites further hostility. Furthermore, they believe that apportioning blame is erroneous as the perspective of all of the children involved is bound to differ dramatically and it may well be impossible to find out the true details.

The No-Blame approach seems almost too simple and it is often very difficult for teachers to let go of the traditional ways of dealing with bullying behaviour – interrogation and punishment. However, it seems that what students and parents most want is for the behaviour to stop – and the authors of the programme believe that this type of intervention is successful in doing just that.

Shared concern

Developed in Sweden, this is a technique that aims to establish civil relations between bullies and bullied – without exploring the details of the bullying or requiring that the adversaries become friends. The teacher leads a structured series of chats, starting with the bullies, and elicits constructive agreements to help the 'unhappy' victim.

This method was published by Anatol Pikas in 1975 and was known initially as the Persuasive Coercion method. The idea is that, if properly used, it 'lifts the burden' of bullying from the victims. The author does, however, indicate that he observed some users making various changes or additions to the method, which reduced its long-term effect. For example, two or more adults have been present at the talks with individual bullies, and the second set of talks – with the group of suspected bullies – have been omitted.

Although in some ways the Shared Concern method doesn't seem to differ much from the No-Blame approach, it's worth looking at the rationale and the steps involved:

1. The problem is identified. It is important to know who is being bullied (and by whom) and whether there was a group involved.

2. Information about what is happening and the concern felt by the victim is ideally obtained through observations and reports, rather than through talking directly with the victim. This is to prevent repercussions on the victim for having 'told'.

3. A number of students are identified as either having taken part in the bullying, or as having supported it in some way. Each is seen in turn, starting (if known) with the likely ringleader.

In these meetings with individual students, it is important not to make any accusations. The meeting begins with the interviewer inviting the student to sit in a chair opposite (without an intervening desk) and waiting for eye contact before the interaction begins. The interviewer starts by sharing a concern for the person who is being victimised. Once the feelings of the interviewer have been clearly conveyed, the student is asked to say what he or she knows about the situation.

As soon as the student has acknowledged some awareness (not necessarily guilt) relating to what has been happening, they are asked directly what they can do to help improve matters.

The interviewer is not trying to 'get to the bottom of the matter' and to apportion blame but to produce a constructive response and change the situation.

Suggestions are usually elicited, but if they are not, the interviewer may make suggestions, normally ones that are not too difficult for the bully to accept. The interviewer should express strong approval for any constructive proposals, but arrange for another meeting to find out what has actually been done. Close monitoring is essential. At this meeting no threats are made nor any warnings given.

The remaining students in the group are seen, again individually, and the procedure repeated.

4. Interview with victim. The victim is seen after all the suspected bullies have been interviewed. It is essential that the interviewer begins by expressing concern, sympathy and support about what has been happening. However, questions need to be asked to find out whether the victim has been doing anything to bring on the bullying – that is, by acting as a provocative victim.

The interviewer discloses that he or she has actually talked with the bullies individually and that each of them has agreed to cooperate. The interviewer undertakes to meet again with the victim to see how things develop.

5. Further meetings are held with individual bullies (as previously arranged) to check on whether they have honoured their promises and what progress has been made.

Once it is evident that good progress has been made, a meeting with the whole group is organised. At this meeting it is usually possible to compliment the members on the progress that has been made and to elicit a suggestion from members of the group that the victim be invited to join them for a final meeting to demonstrate that the problem of bullying has actually been resolved.

6. The victim can usually be encouraged to join the group for a final meeting, with assurances that there will be no unpleasantness. If all goes well, the meeting will serve to demonstrate publicly that the bullying is well and truly over.

7. In cases where the victim has behaved provocatively, the interviewer must seek to facilitate adjustments in the behaviour of both sides, that is, play the role of mediator. The aim is to get the students to reach an agreement – ideally in writing and in an agreed form – about how each will behave towards the other in future.

The rationale is that bullies are usually insensitive to the harm they are doing to the victim because involvement in a group lends legitimacy to their bullying activities and prevents any feeling of personal responsibility. However, it is believed that, on an individual level, bullies usually feel uncomfortable. If authorities 'blame', it will create hostility and increase their desire to bully. By working with a bully (or each member of a bullying group) individually, sharing concern for the victim, a more positive response is elicited.

This method differs from the No-Blame approach because it does not in any way seek to excuse or condone the bullying, and is more direct and confrontational. In fact, it strongly encourages and expects a responsible response. The teacher or interviewer makes an arrangement with members of the bully group – the terms of which are that they do not talk to each other. In this way, group influence is weakened. Careful monitoring and follow-up are essential. There is a belief that victims are not always 'innocent', and it is important to understand what they may be doing to provoke the bullying. One may need to work directly on changing the victim's provocative way of behaving. Although the aim is to re-individualise bullies, the idea is not to 'break up' groups (students have a right to enjoy being in a group) but eventually to change their attitudes and behaviour towards the victim and other potential victims.

Advocates claim that there is now good research evidence that the method is effective in at least two cases in three. It has been used in many British, European and Australian schools with promising results.

R time (relationships to improve education)

This programme was developed in the UK by Greg Sampson, a retired primary-school headteacher, who observed that many children did not engage with one another in a positive way. There were bullies and victims; disliked, isolated, depressed and socially challenged kids; those who were demanding, and so on. He determined to improve the quality of the relationships between these children, and began his research by giving them a questionnaire to find out what they thought about themselves and their classmates.

The aim of R Time is to enable the children in the class to get on better with one another, in order to accelerate learning and raise self-esteem. Through teaching the basic skills of effective communication, it encourages kids to relate positively to one another. The belief is that a school where respect and courtesy are high on the agenda will be a community which fosters good relationships, as well as accelerating learning.

The basic steps are as follows:

1. This approach involves short 'lessons' (10–15 minutes) once a week, over a period of 30 weeks.

2. Placed in random pairs, which are 'self-selected' by the children via a series of pairing exercises, students are given a short task to complete in their pairs, working together in partnership.

3. All the tasks are easily achievable, so there is an inbuilt element of success each time. When the task is completed, the children are encouraged to thank their partner and to give positive feedback by saying something nice to their partner about how they have worked together.

4. There is a questionnaire for each year group that can be used by the school at the start and end of the programme, to enable parents and the entire school staff to get to know what children think about the school, curriculum and each other.

According to Sampson, R Time works by factoring in the following elements:

- relationship building
- enabling children to get to know one another better
- respect towards others
- listening skills
- communication skills
- cooperative working
- understanding others
- modelling respectful behaviour
- achievement and satisfaction
- nurturing classrooms
- preparing children for involvement in school councils
- supporting transition
- self-esteem and confidence building
- acceptance of others
- trust building
- emotional wellbeing
- conflict resolution
- tackling bullying
- citizenship
- drawing in the socially excluded
- bringing peace and calming
- developing confident teachers
- social cohesion
- … and the children love it

There has been some remarkable feedback, and I have personally checked with four schools that have used the method, all of which claimed to be very satisfied, and to have noticed a dramatic improvement in overall behaviour. Rob Osborne, who is part of the Educational Psychology Service in Leicestershire in the UK, and one of the founding members of the ABA (see page 251), introduced R Time as a key element of Leicestershire's anti-bullying strategy action plan in 2003, and within three years 130 primary schools in the county had either been trained in R Time or had introduced it using the available materials.

Osborne says: 'I feel that it has had a significant impact on reducing bullying in Leicestershire's primary schools. We use an annual Pupil Attitude Survey with primary schools and this has shown the level of bullying has fallen during this period. R Time is just one of a number of initiatives that we have developed but I am confident that it is R Time that has had the biggest impact.' A study of eight of the schools which introduced R Time shows that the development of positive relationships through this approach had a significant impact. It's easy to see why.

Steps to respect

This programme works on the premise that in order to address bullying effectively, educators, students and families must work together to tackle it at a school-wide level. The Steps to Respect programme provides step-by-step guidance, implementation and assessment tools, adult training and student lessons.

The programme is divided into three phases:

1. Getting the school involved, with a 'bullying prevention steering team' creating anti-bullying policies and procedures and determining consequences for bullying behaviour.

2. Training all school staff members and parents. Staff are trained to recognise bullying and to receive reports from students. Selected staff members are trained to work directly with the children involved in the bullying incidents. Families are also introduced to the programme.

3. Students are taught to recognise, refuse and report bullying. They learn and practise bullying prevention skills, including how to make friends – all a part of classroom lessons.

One of the key factors in the programme is that it is classroom teachers who teach the children the messages they need to learn to overcome bullying. The programme is based on the idea that their ability to reinforce prosocial behaviours is greatly enhanced if they are also the primary instructors of the classroom lessons. Classroom teachers are the key.

Furthermore, changing the way bystanders respond to bullying is a critical part of the programme – a bystander being defined as anyone who knows that bullying is taking place. In a nutshell, the Steps to Respect programme:

- promotes the development of empathy for children who are bullied
- fosters emotion-management skills
- improves children's recognition of bullying and their role in it
- teaches children strategies that they can use to be 'part of the solution' instead of 'part of the problem'
- involves families, using take-home handouts and letters, a brochure about what families should know about bullying, and an annual Steps to Respect letter that affirms the school's commitment to safety

It appears to work. A study in the May 2005 issue of *Developmental Psychology* evaluated the Steps to Respect programme and concluded that children who took part showed positive changes in observed playground bullying, normative beliefs and social interaction skills compared to children in the control group. Both bullying and the attitudes believed to support its execution were reduced within a relatively short period of time. The programme also reduced bystander encouragement of playground bullying. The study authors say this result is heartening because reducing the number of children who provide an audience and incitement to bullying may yield additional benefits in subsequent years.

Student councils (bully courts)

Within the framework of a sound anti-bullying policy, a court of peers decide sanctions against bullies. This method is backed by Kidscape in the UK, and they very clearly outline how best to use this method:

1. Discuss acceptable behaviour with students and agree certain basic guidelines – the 'school rules'.

2. Sign an individual contract with each student based on the agreed guidelines.

William King Elementary, Nova Scotia (Primary, Grade 6)

Before William King Elementary participated in the Committee for Children's Steps to Respect pilot in 1998, a survey showed that very few of its students knew how to recognise bullying.

During the pilot, there were so many bullying reports that staff were concerned that the problem had become worse, instead of better. However, it soon became clear that reporting had increased, rather than bullying behaviour. Sixth-grade teacher Shirley Everett said that it was a 'big, big step; kids were comfortable about coming forward'.

Everett tells the story of some boys who reported, in front of their classmates, that a group of girls in the playground had teased them and called them gay. 'The point is, these boys were so comfortable that they felt free to talk about sexual bullying in front of all the kids. The kids have to feel safe with you and have to know that there will be follow up, not only with the victim, but with the person doing the bullying. [Bullying] behaviour has to be channelled into something positive.'

3. Post the guidelines on bulletin boards throughout the school and in each classroom.

4. Call a school assembly and let the students explain the guidelines – involve all the staff, including playground supervisors, dinner ladies, etc.

5. As part of the guidelines, set up a student council (bully court) to rule on infractions.

6. This council could comprise four students: two elected by the student body and two appointed (as an honour) by the staff.

7. One member of staff should attend the council.

8. The term of office for those serving at the council might vary but one school term is suggested.

9. Unless there were an emergency, the council would convene once a week at a set time.

10. The council would be responsible for most infractions, unless they were serious enough to involve the police (i.e., assault), or there were family problems which made public discussion inappropriate.

St Francis Xavier School, Illinois (Preschool, Grade 8)

St Francis Xavier became aware through the media that school bullying had become a societal norm. This didn't fit well with the school's philosophy, which is child-centred and Catholic, so Principal Barbara Snopek and her staff decided to do something about it. They chose to implement the Steps to Respect programme because it fitted best with the school's discipline approach, which is to teach children self-discipline rather than impose it from the outside.

Snopek says that teachers are very pleased with the programme, which, according to her, is in itself a great compliment. 'It's tough to get all teachers to agree on and get behind the same programme.' Since implementation, which began with an in-service for teachers in August 2002, the school has seen many positive results. 'Children feel more confident and often come into the office breathless: "We think this is a bullying situation. Can you help us figure it out?",' says Snopek. 'Steps to Respect makes students more aware of the fact that some people have power simply because we've given it to them. This has changed – we don't see that egging on.'

The students at St Francis Xavier come from a tight-knit community and often treat each other like brothers and sisters. To help students understand the bystander role, teachers liken it to that of a sibling not hesitating to come to the defence of a brother or sister who is being bullied.

Snopek believes that one of the programme's strengths is that it 'teaches children that they need to care for each other and empowers them to say "Stop, that's bullying." [It also] gives them power to report without feeling like it's tattling... [and] teaches children that they can be part of the solution.'

11. Solutions and/or penalties would be binding on all parties, with the right of appeal.

12. The conclusions reached by the council would be written down and filed, with copies of the report going to all concerned parties.

13. School governors and parents would all receive information about the agreed guidelines and about the council, and would be invited to a council to see a mock session and to discuss the issues raised.

14. The effectiveness of the council would be evaluated periodically by students, parents and staff.

They also note that student councils work best where there is an effective whole-school anti-bullying policy, otherwise the council could simply become a way of bullying the bullies.

Further information on student councils (bully courts) is available in Kidscape's *How to Stop Bullying Training Guide*.

In terms of effectiveness, the results appear to be mixed. Kidscape first issued advice and guidance about bully courts in 1990, and a great deal of publicity ensued. It was claimed that in eight schools being monitored, reports of being bullied dropped from 70 per cent to 6 per cent. However, it has been impossible to verify these claims. Jessica Mahdavi and Peter K. Smith of Goldsmith's College in London published a case history of the effectiveness of bully courts and concluded that they can make a useful contribution to combating bullying in certain circumstances (though it appears to vary in effectiveness with age, with younger students responding better than those in later years), if the following things are included in the programme:

- a well-established and well-publicised system
- adequate staff supervision of the court process and training for those pupils involved
- a well-integrated recording system of bullying incidents
- a combination of the court system with a peer mentoring/counselling system that helps/encourages pupils to use the bully court

In other words, it can be an effective tool but, like other anti-bullying strategies, needs other kinds of interventions working alongside it.

Peer support schemes

Circle Time, peer mentoring schemes and peer support networks are only some examples of this type of initiative. Peer counselling is also operational in many schools – in a system in which older secondary-school children volunteer to go on duty in lunch hours or breaks, for example, as confidential listeners to children's problems. This is likely to be less intimidating than confiding in a teacher, but the student counsellors must be effectively trained and supported by adults, particularly when serious abuses come to light. Several studies have discussed the impact that peer support schemes can have, either on reducing bullying in schools, or on helping pupils to cope with it. In a mentoring scheme, for example, the programme is not designed to prevent bullying, but to allow mentors to learn about an incident soon after it has happened and then to encourage the younger pupil to report it, as well as providing crucial emotional support. The idea also works on the premise that when a relationship forms between a younger pupil and an older pupil, repeat incidents of bullying may be reduced.

In 1998, children and teachers from 51 schools in Britain (mainly in England but also in Scotland and Wales) were asked about using peer support to tackle bullying. The support schemes included mediation (helping discussion on school problems such as bullying and racism), mentoring (where a pupil, often older, was a positive role model for a more vulnerable pupil), befriending and counselling. When questioned about the benefits of peer support, the most frequent answer given by children and teachers was that the scheme gave users the strength to handle their bullying problems. When asked about benefits for peer supporters, the most common answers were that it helped them to acquire skills and showed that someone cared. Teachers and pupils felt that the most common benefit for the school was showing that it cares. The problems mentioned most often concerned acceptance of the scheme by both pupils and teachers and the negative attitudes of some teachers. However, the responses showed that there was a commitment to solving problems and improving the system.

Circle time

This concept has grown through various means, but is generally believed to be the brainchild of the author and consultant Jenny Moseley, who used it in employment situations. Circle Time is a popular teaching strategy in schools, where it is claimed to contribute to whole-school provision for moral, social and cultural development; to enhance pupils' personal and social skills; and to facilitate key skills necessary for citizenship and language development. Circle Time can also be associated with other aspects of school life, such

Peer support

A 1999 study by research professor Helen Cowie offered insight into the best forms of peer support. These include: befriending (going beyond a normal circle of friends to include someone who needs support); mentoring (older pupils take younger pupils under their wings); listening services (pupils are trained to listen to others' needs); workshops (older pupils can run workshops for younger pupils about issues such as friendship, being new to the school, joining clubs and other activities, as well as bullying itself); helplines (anonymous services for children who don't want face-to-face contact); and peer tutoring (an older pupil may tutor a younger child in a curriculum subject but also use this as an opportunity to help him or her with relationship problems).

An Italian study looked at the effect of a befriending scheme on bullying in two schools. In the scheme bullies and bystanders were encouraged to take responsibility for their actions. It was found that the befriending scheme did make a difference. The classes taking part in the scheme reported that there had been no increase in bullying, while classes not taking part reported an increase. The indifference of bystanders is increasingly seen as something which encourages bullying and this scheme was found to reduce that indifference and make bystanders more responsible. It also found that children's feelings of sympathy for the victim (which often decrease at this age) stayed the same or increased.

So it is clear the initiatives that use the peer group in order to support, mediate, counsel or mentor have a key role in helping to discourage the culture of bullying in the school system.

as developing a caring ethos; teaching by example; encouraging democratic values, problem-solving and prosocial behaviour; and including pupils in the formation of classroom rules. The method is now in widespread use in schools across the UK and is beginning to take hold in Australia, New Zealand, Canada and the USA. It can be used with children of any age, provided that it is used appropriately and introduced carefully. The Anti-Bullying Alliance (see page 251) has an informative and helpful list of resources for teachers who would like to use Circle Time as a tool for reducing bullying in the classroom. Their ideas for this practice are summarised below.

1. Between 6 and 18 participants is the ideal number, as larger groups tend to make it difficult for everyone to become involved. Participants are seated in a circle (with no desks!). Some schools use a 'talking' object (a teddy bear or a cushion); whoever is holding the object is the 'talker'.

2. The teacher sits in the circle with the students, at the same level. He or she has a special responsibility to ensure that the agreed rules are kept, that the emotions of individuals are protected and that suitable activities are prepared. The teacher must also be ready to draw a session to a close if pupils are persistently breaking the rules.

3. The rules are simple, but they must be discussed and agreed by all members. This is one of the first activities that should take place. The three basic rules which should be discussed are:

• only one person at a time should speak – the 'talking' object helps this rule
• you can 'pass' if you don't want to speak about something
• no put-downs

The first of these rules helps to create order and to encourage people to listen to others. The second and third help to ensure the emotional safety of children taking part: nobody should be forced to speak about something which they find embarrassing and nobody should be ridiculed for saying something in which they genuinely believe – however much others may disagree.

4. It is important to make Circle Time a positive experience, and the teacher should set the tone by taking every opportunity to make positive comments. If a negative comment is made, the teacher should encourage others to come up with solutions rather than echo a complaint. The emphasis is on problem-solving and a solution-focused approach.

5. Many circles begin with a game (guessing games may be good), or activities that take place in pairs. For example, to encourage listening skills, each one of the pair has to tell the other two or three interesting things about him or herself. Each pair then has to introduce each other, repeating the interesting things. Shopping list games can also be used to help listening. Each person has to remember the items suggested by others in the circle.

6. The main point of Circle Time is, however, the discussion, and this can take various forms. Start off with non-controversial topics that will encourage participation. For example, 'My favourite activity is...' or 'Being a friend means...'. As the sessions continue, the participants develop more confidence and will start to reveal more about themselves. The teacher should make sure that vulnerable participants are protected from put-downs. Starters such as, 'The best day of my life was...' and 'The worst day of my life...' can produce very revealing, and sometimes moving, contributions.

7. Circle Time can be used to help solve problems that have been identified by teachers or pupils (the latter may make suggestions anonymously through a postbox in the hall, for example). Problems and issues can be identified by brainstorming or by rounds such as, 'The best thing about this school is ... ' and 'The worst thing about this school is ...' Try to make sure that if a real problem is identified, at least one positive suggestion is agreed before the session ends.

8. Circle Time has an important role to play in the prevention of bullying. It can help young people develop skills such as listening and empathising; it can promote respect for others and self-esteem; it is a forum within which the nature and effects of bullying can be considered; and it can be used to develop an anti-bullying code to which all members of the school community have contributed. It can also be used to react to a particular problem. For example, if a particular group of youngsters is involved in bullying behaviour, this could be openly discussed in the circle. Or if a pupil is being socially excluded because of a perceived difference, a Circle Time discussion could be initiated which focuses on an individual's right to be different. This could be done in such a way as not to draw attention to the excluded individual but to promote reflection on the underlying causes of the isolation.

9. It is important to make Circle Time a regular part of the school week so that students begin to rely on it, and trust one another more. It will not stop bullying completely but it will help to involve young people in the development of a school policy, bring more incidents into the open and encourage a more caring atmosphere.

A 2003 paper entitled 'Going Round in Circles: Implementing and Learning from Circle Time', undertaken by the National Foundation for Educational Research (NFER) in the UK was positive about the potential use of Circle Time in schools and included many ideas for its successful implementation. All in all, in conjunction with other anti-bullying measures, it is well worth a try.

Noteworthy initiatives

It's not just on a local level that various programmes are being implemented to halt the growth of bullying in our schools. Governments, at all levels, are taking a united stand against the problem, and outside agencies have also been set up to introduce programmes to complement and support schemes. As a result, the anti-bullying movement has expanded beyond all recognition, and celebrities from all media have come forward to tell their own stories, and lend 'street cred' to the cause. The internet, too, has played a dramatic role in highlighting the issues, as well as offering virtually instant advice and support to anyone affected by bullying. It's still too soon to see a real change in bullying statistics, but with so many dedicated people and organisations involved, and the ever-increasing exposure, they should plummet. Let's look at some of the most interesting and exciting schemes worldwide. Please note that there are literally thousands of schemes in existence, and it is beyond the scope of this book to include more than a handful of noteworthy ventures. See Resources (page 293) for more information and other initiatives.

The UK

The education 'watchdog' OFSTED – set up to assess, inspect and report on all childcare facilities and schools in the UK – has recently expanded its reporting system to look at the effort that schools are making to reduce bullying and to judge whether schools are doing enough to implement the UK's national anti-bullying charter.

This charter, which was launched in 2003 by Ivan Lewis MP (see Case history, opposite), included a range of measures to tackle bullying, such as creating 'special safe places' for vulnerable pupils, and having an 'anxiety box' in which children could place anonymous complaints. The charter has several elements, including discussing, monitoring and reviewing; supporting everyone in the school community to identify and respond to problems; ensuring that children and young people are aware that all bullying concerns will be dealt with sensitively and effectively (which involves regular canvassing, awareness of sanctions, involvement in school-wide campaigns and the implementation and publication of schemes of peer mentoring, counselling, buddying, mediation, etc.); ensuring that parents and carers expressing bullying concerns have them taken seriously; and learning from effective anti-bullying work elsewhere. The charter is sent to all schools in England for signature by the chairman of governors, headteachers and a student representative, and it marks a public pledge by the school to keep its anti-bullying policy up to date, to support staff to tackle the problem 'appropriately' and reassure pupils that their concerns will be dealt with effectively.

Ivan Lewis MP, former Parliamentary Under Secretary of State for Young People, was himself bullied at secondary school, and ended two years of suffering by taking the bullies on in a fight, in which his nose was broken. He does, however, insist that violence is not the best answer to the problem. His personal experience has fired his enthusiasm for anti-bullying initiatives in the UK. When I spoke to him, he said: 'I demanded that the DfES played a greater leadership role in developing a national strategy. Hence, the Regional Conference for senior staff, the anti-bullying Charter for Action and the development of the Anti-Bullying Alliance (ABA; see below) role. However, my main message was that tackling bullying is central to, not separate from, raising school standards. It should be integral to the ethos of every school and all adults from the headteacher to the dinner lady have a duty to identify and act decisively on bullying where it is occurring. I experienced resistance from some who don't regard this as a priority educational issue and others who view government intervention as inappropriate.

'My personal experience was crucial. My first two years at secondary school were miserable as a consequence of the relentless bullying I experienced – mainly constant verbal abuse which caused me to dread going to school every day for two years. This destroyed my confidence and affected my educational performance. What is the point of being a government minister if you don't use the role to tackle some of the most difficult issues? Against advice I decided to disclose my own personal experiences as a means of reaching out to young people and challenging those who would seek to downplay the seriousness of the issue. I have no regrets.'

Anti-bullying alliance (ABA)

The Anti-Bullying Alliance was founded in 2002 by the NSPCC (National Society for the Prevention of Cruelty to Children) and the NCB (National Children's Bureau). The ABA brings into one network over 55 national organisations from the voluntary and private sectors – LEAs, professional associations and the research community – to work together to reduce bullying and create safer environments in which children and young people can live, grow, play and learn.

The ABA's functions are fourfold:

1. Promoting best practice so that adults, children and young people know how safer environments can be developed, bullying can be reduced and incidents effectively managed.

2. Policy development and advocacy working with key stakeholders to influence effective legislation, guidance and policies that secure safer environments for children and young people.

3. Information dissemination through professional networks, within the media and through an email network and service.

4. Providing a coordinated national and regional anti-bullying programme of support.

The programme began in September 2004, and built on the success of the DfES 'Make the Difference' Campaign, which provided nine regional anti-bullying conferences around the UK, the anti-bullying charter and a poster competition. In November 2004, the ABA held the first national Anti-Bullying Week. In five days, more than 44 events took place around the country to raise the profile of anti-bullying strategies, involving young people, schools, and policy makers. These included activities as diverse as an 'Art Against Bullying' exhibition in Birmingham, and a 'Big Debate' for young people in Coventry. Hundreds of schools were inspired to run their own activities at the same time.

The ABA produced a series of resources for schools, including a guide entitled 'Making Schools Safer', containing effective anti-bullying strategies, and lesson and assembly plans, as well as information about additional materials and useful contacts; plus a specially themed newsletter.

ChildLine

ChildLine is the UK's free, 24-hour helpline for children and young people. In 2005, more than 31,000 children called ChildLine about bullying, making it the most common problem counsellors dealt with. Because of their unique insight into the immediate problems that children today are facing in relation to bullying, ChildLine has been at the forefront of the anti-bullying movement in the

Wristband fiasco

Anti-bullying wristbands, which were launched in the first Anti-Bullying Week in the UK, and championed by David Beckham, Kelly Brook and Bono, among others, seemed like a good idea at the time. The thinking behind the scheme was to give young people the opportunity to make a visible commitment that they were not prepared to tolerate bullying and would stand by their friends. The success of other wristbands, such as anti-racism and anti-poverty wristbands, supported by high-profile figures, made anti-bullying a natural choice; however, according to campaigners, pupils who took to wearing a blue wristband to pledge their support for a government-sponsored anti-bullying campaign soon became the target of bullies.

Julie Oakley, founder of Bullywatch, which supports families of the victims of bullying, said: 'Kids who wear the wristbands have become natural targets. There has been a lot of interest in them because they are rare, and have become valuable. They are sought-after in the same way as new trainers. It's totally sick that something designed to help fight bullying could be used in this way – it completely defeats the object.'

Michelle Elliot, director of child protection charity Kidscape, told the *Daily Mirror*: 'We were afraid that they would make kids wearing them a target. Bullies will find any excuse – but I'm disgusted something with such good intentions should end up being abused like this.'

School pupils were quick to spot the reality of wearing the wristbands. Writing on the BBC's *Newsround* website, Rosie, 13, from London, said: 'Ugh... I'm sorry, but in one school near me, it's made it a whole lot worse. Bullies are stupid, everyone knows that, and so they came up with a stupid idea. They basically thought "Hey! Everyone who's wearing a wristband must be scared of bullying!" So they decided to bully the people wearing wristbands. So, it's made a difference, but not a good one.'

UK, undertaking research; commenting on policy papers and helping to develop useful and appropriate legislation; offering advice and support to parents, teachers and children, both on their website – through a variety of published material – and confidentially by telephone.

ChildLine in Partnership with Schools (CHIPS) was launched in 1998 and has proved extremely successful in bringing young people together to challenge problems in school. The scheme encourages young people to set up programmes, with the help of ChildLine and their teachers, to support their peers and to create safe environments in which to learn.

Some of their research is noteworthy, too. A 2003 study carried out by Christine Oliver and Mano Candappa from the Thomas Coram Research Unit at the Institute of Education, investigated the perspectives of children concerning 'what works' in tackling bullying and aimed to explore why, despite the almost universal introduction of anti-bullying policies by schools, children continue to call ChildLine in large numbers to ask for help in dealing with bullying. The views and experiences of pupils were investigated using both qualitative (focus group) and quantitative (questionnaire survey) methods. The UK government and the ABA, as well as other organisations, have used this research to change the focus of the anti-bullying movement, and to provide a comprehensive insight into the bullying issue from a child's point of view.

From the research, a set of recommendations have been made to help schools prevent bullying. These include:

- Putting measures in place so that children can participate in forming and implementing anti-bullying strategies, for example through school councils and the curriculum.
- Training teachers to incorporate children's participation in all areas of the school and monitoring their success annually. OFSTED should check that this process is being adhered to through regular inspections.
- Addressing the realities of children's experiences in anti-bullying strategies, paying attention to the importance of friendships and equipping children with the necessary emotional and social skills to help them combat problems like bullying.
- Building on friendship networks to create peer support, befriending and buddying programmes – creating supportive environments in which children can thrive.

BULLYING INITIATIVES   255

- Minimising the risks pupils face in telling teachers about bullying and giving urgent attention to making confidential sources of advice and support more widely available.
- Listening to pupils as part of a whole-school approach to tackling bullying that also involves introducing regular anonymous questionnaires to map the problem, developing a positive school ethos, making regular reviews of anti-bullying policies, and working in partnership with parents.

National anti-bullying poetry anthology

The National Anti-Bullying Poetry Anthology was launched in preparation for Anti-Bullying Week in November 2005. The book contains the winning and shortlisted poems from children and staff in primary, secondary and special schools from around the country, as well as comments from the celebrity judges and a special poem by poet Andrew Fusek Peters. These poems highlight issues around bullying, including homophobia and racism. The booklet is intended to be used both a teaching resource, for example within literacy lessons, and as a means through which to raise the issue of bullying.

Kidscape

Kidscape is the first charity in the UK established specifically to prevent bullying and child sexual abuse. Kidscape works UK-wide to provide individuals and organisations with the practical skills and resources necessary to keep children safe from harm. The Kidscape staff equips vulnerable children with practical, non-threatening knowledge and skills regarding how to keep themselves safe and reduce the likelihood of future harm. Kidscape works with children and young people under the age of 16, their parents/carers, and those who work with them. They offer:

- a helpline offering support and advice to parents of bullied children
- booklets, literature, posters, training guides, and educational videos on bullying, child protection and parenting
- a national comprehensive training programme on child safety and behaviour management issues
- advice and research
- confidence-building sessions for children who are bullied

Carmarthenshire, Wales, UK

A county in the west of Wales, Carmarthenshire was one of the first authorities in the UK to develop a firm anti-bullying policy, and to involve multiple organisations in its implementation. Children and family forums were the starting point, where the issue of bullying was brought up repeatedly. They then brought together a multi-agency group to look at the problems and to put in place initiatives that would empower children and young people. The group comprised preschool playgroup agencies; the police; voluntary agencies working with children; statutory services, such as health, education and social services; Karen Pereira, the children's partnership representative on the council; as well as youth services, parenting agencies and colleges.

They began with a conference which attracted nationwide attention, partly because it was one of the first to address the issue of cyberbullying and mobile phone bullying, but also because it drew on the resources of some of the top experts in the UK. On the basis of the opinions of professional agencies, Kidscape and the children's commissioner for Wales, they set about putting together an anti-bullying statement around which policies could be developed. Schools were emailed; organisations and agencies brought on board; and a campaign set in action. Over a thousand children were questioned during the summer holidays, through holiday clubs and play schemes, and the overall message was that children felt that when they did tell about being bullied, the bullying worsened in a high percentage of cases. Disclosure was not being handled properly.

A second conference was duly organised, and again achieved huge attention in the rest of the UK. The result? ChildLine Wales recently revealed that almost 60 per cent more children used its helplines last year because they were being bullied – the biggest ever increase the charity has seen.

Actionwork

Established in 1990, Actionwork provides a wide range of exciting shows and fun workshops all over the UK and abroad. In addition to its touring shows and workshops, it produces films with young people, and provides seminars for anti-bullying conferences, training for school governors, INSET for teachers, support for students, and creative research for government initiatives. They specialise in empowerment and peace programmes with young people, including dealing with issues such as bullying, racism, homophobia and disability. These take the form of active workshops, performance workshops, creative writing, and film and video projects. Actionwork is a member of the Anti-Bullying Alliance (ABA) and the Society for Intercultural Education and Research (SIETAR).

Box clever

This touring theatre company is dedicated to working with and for young people. Box clever provide text-based and issue-based performances and workshops. Their work on bullying has been well-received, and focuses on the idea that bullying involves everyone, not just a victim and a bully.

Australia

In Australia, the commitment to tackle bullying is set nationally. The National Safe Schools Framework sets out some national principles for a safe school environment. These include, among other things, the school ethos; student welfare; policy issues; education for staff, students and parents; the management of abuse and victimisation; the provision of support for students; and arrangements for working closely with parents. As a condition of Australian government funding to schools, school authorities were required to put the framework into effect before 1 January 2006.

PeaceBuilders

PeaceBuilders is a long-term, community-based, violence reduction/crime prevention programme for primary schools developed in the USA and Australia. Dr Gayre Christie, who worked with the Anti-Bullying network as a visiting scholar in 2000, has led the development of the programme in Australian schools. The programme is designed to help create an environment that reduces violence and establishes more peaceful ways of behaving, living and working. It incorporates many of the elements of a praise-and-reward scheme and is intended to affect all aspects of the ethos of a school. Its aims are to increase cooperation, achievement and individual success through a programme that promotes peaceful behaviour. It aims to reduce verbal and physical aggression in and beyond the school setting.

Five carefully worded behavioural guidelines are at the heart of PeaceBuilders:
• praise people
• give up put-downs
• seek wise people
• notice hurts
• right wrongs

The friendly schools project

This project was developed by a research group led by Associate Professor Donna Cross of Edith Cowan University in Western Australia. Its goal is to assess the effectiveness of a whole-school intervention aimed at preventing, reducing and managing bullying in the primary school setting. The target group for the study was year 4 students, teachers and parents across the years 2000 and 2001. The assumptions were that bullying can be reduced if children develop 'skills and values required to respond adaptively to bullying', and 'support students who are bullied, and refrain from bullying others'. It is also asserted that a whole-school approach is needed that engages parents as well as staff.

The programme involves a wide range of activities, including extensive consultation and policy development. A central feature is the Teacher Manual, outlining nine lessons which provide information about bullying, how to feel good about yourself and others, and how to cooperate with others. The lessons are intended to be practical and to address the needs and interests of children in years 4 and 5. This programme emphasises the importance of increasing cooperative behaviour among children and focuses on values that such behaviour encourages. Unlike many programmes addressing bullying, it is well informed by findings from recent research in the area.

MindMatters

This is a national mental health strategy funded by the Commonwealth Department of Health and Ageing. Part of the MindMatters programme provides classroom materials for use in a whole-school approach to dealing with bullying and harassment. It seeks to develop with students an understanding of what bullying is, and explores bullying themes through literature and drama. The programme has been promoted throughout Australia and has been used by numerous schools with some degree of success.

Peer support foundation

The Peer Support Foundation Limited provides peer-led programmes which foster the physical, social and mental wellbeing of young people and their community. The Peer Support Programme is integrated into curricula and sustained from kindergarten to year 12. It supports positive cultural change within schools by incorporating a range of strategies developed through collaboration with members of the whole school community for the specific needs of the school.

The Foundation provides:
- modules, in line with NSW curriculum
- peer-led, skills-based experiential learning programmes focusing on relationships, optimism, resilience, leadership, anti-bullying and citizenship
- student leadership training
- training and development for teachers and parents
- free consultancy to help schools raise awareness of the programme and plan for its implementation.

Well-received and evaluated, the Peer Support model has been used in many schools in Australia to good effect.

Kids help line

Kids Help Line is Australia's free, confidential and anonymous, 24-hour telephone and online counselling service specifically for young people aged 5–18. Kids Help Line has successfully raised awareness of bullying amongst children, parents and school staff, and generated considerable media attention and public debate. As a result, Kids Help Line experienced a 25 per cent increase in calls about bullying, and a 6 per cent increase in calls about relationships with peers. Over the years, several successful anti-bullying initiatives have been undertaken, including a venture with Kelloggs to provide information and advice on the back of cereal packets. Kids Help Line is involved in a great deal of anti-bullying research, and provides information, advice and support to schools and parents, and online.

Better buddies programme

The Better Buddies Programme (with Buddy Bear as its mascot) teaches children to care about the other children around them. It delivers a very positive and effective anti-bullying, anti-violence message by promoting the awareness of the existence of vulnerable children and teaching children to care for one another. Introduced to Melbourne schools in 1999, the programme has been expanded and by 2003 included schools in Tasmania, New South Wales and the ACT, South Australia, Queensland and Western Australia.

The aims of the programme include:
• reinforcing that violence isn't the solution to disputes
• assisting children in supporting their peers
• listening to and working with children in a positive, supportive environment
• developing children's social skills to enable them to get along with others
• developing children's feelings of compassion and empathy with others
• encouraging children to relate to and empathise with characters outside their immediate environment
• stimulating children's imagination and assisting them in expressing their ideas and thoughts

The national coalition against bullying

The National Coalition Against Bullying (NCAB) is an innovative initiative of The Alannah and Madeline Foundation (who are also responsible for Better Buddies/Buddy Bear). The NCAB brings together individuals from key organisations to draw national attention to the issue of bullying and to bring about a social change in the community. The idea is to empower individuals to realise that the issue of bullying is everyone's problem and each individual can make a difference. The NCAB has become a national leader in the fight against bullying, with a remarkable wealth of resources for parents, teachers and children.

New Zealand

New Zealand schools were forced at least to consider bullying in the early 1990s, when new national guidelines held them legally responsible for providing 'a safe physical and emotional environment for all students'. Since then, a number of programmes have been implemented, but no national guidelines exist for their implementation, and funding is poor.

Kia kaha

Kia Kaha means to 'stand strong'. This reflects the ethos that the whole school community must stand strong in order to eliminate bullying. Kia Kaha is a whole-school approach. It aims to help schools create environments where everyone feels safe, respected and valued, and where bullying cannot flourish. This intervention consists of an implementation book, *Kia Kaha in Your School*; a working booklet (one for primary schools and one for secondary schools) which gives a step-by-step guide to putting the whole-school approach in place; plus four curriculum programmes.

The following key concepts underpin Kia Kaha:
- All children and young people can be supported to learn new behaviours. The student who sometimes bullies will find new prosocial ways of behaving. Victims of bullying can be helped to become more confident.
- Bullying is unacceptable behaviour. There are no excuses for bullying. All forms of bullying are equally unacceptable.
- Schools and communities should adopt zero-tolerance of bullying. Every member of the community will accept this and take action to make sure this is achieved.
- A whole-school approach is needed to eliminate bullying. The whole school community must confront the issue and work together in a concerted way to establish a safe emotional and physical environment. A curriculum intervention alone will not bring about change.
- Schools should create a 'telling environment'. Every member of the school community must expect that bullying will be reported, and that it is safe to tell. Once a report has been made, this must be acted on, in the way outlined in the school policy.
- Bullying is never the victim's fault.

• Nobody deserves to be bullied.
• Schools should adopt a problem-solving (no blame) approach for intervention (see page 235). A group of students, including the student who has been doing the bullying, confront the effects of the bullying on the victim and come up with solutions to help the victim become happier and more involved.

These programmes have been developed by the Youth Education Service (YES) of the New Zealand Police, working in close association with Group Special Education. The Crime Prevention Unit provided support and financial assistance for the three primary programmes.

The general objectives of Kia Kaha are:
1. Students, parents, caregivers and teachers recognise that bullying and harassment are unacceptable and will take steps to see that it does not occur in their school.
2. Students, parents, caregivers and teachers will work together to create a safe learning environment, based on mutual respect, tolerance and a respect for diversity.

There are approximately 130 police education officers who work full-time in schools nationally, to deliver the YES programmes in partnership with teachers. In Kia Kaha their role is to:
• respond to enquiries from schools
• advise schools of the availability of the Kia Kaha programme
• take part in an initial meeting where the principal finds out more about the programme
• supply an initial inspection kit and provide the necessary Kia Kaha materials once the school decides to proceed
• assist the Kia Kaha co-ordinator with the implementation of the whole-school approach, as required
• plan the teaching programme with teachers
• teach in partnership with teachers, to the extent decided at the local level
• take part in programme evaluation
• maintain records of local schools' involvement in Kia Kaha

Cool schools

Cool Schools Peer Mediation programmes have been introduced in over 1,600 primary and secondary schools. The programme was developed from a variety of sources and a trial programme was set up by Yvonne Duncan in 1991 in 12 primary and intermediate schools in Auckland. It is supported by the ministries of Health and Education. Peer mediation and conflict resolution are part of the health syllabus in Aotearoa/New Zealand and also relate to social studies and language so the skills can be taught as part of a whole school programme. Cool Schools was created by the Peace Foundation of New Zealand, which helps to establish and maintain peaceful and non-violent relationships by teaching skills that encourage better communication, anger management, cooperation and non-violent conflict resolution.

Cool Schools programmes:
• help students develop lifelong conflict-management skills
• create win-win situations for students, teachers, parents and caregivers
• provide life skills for school, home and the workplace
• are proactive, helping to prevent bullying and conflict
• provide a better learning environment
• encourage students to develop the value of service leadership

Eliminating violence

The Eliminating Violence programme, set up by the Group Special Education department, celebrates good behaviour, developing rules and consequences, having students take responsibility for their actions and supporting children to find solutions to problem situations. The programme includes five distinct phases and is implemented over a period of at least 12 months. A high level of staff commitment is required, hence staff are balloted before the programme can commence. Trial runs in several schools have shown promising results.

South Africa

Bullying in South Africa is rife and often extremely violent. Government initiatives appear to be virtually non-existent, and not one of the federal or provincial representatives I contacted was prepared to discuss measures that could or will be introduced in the near future. This has left many children in potentially dangerous, even life-threatening, situations, as many schools refuse to acknowledge the problem and provide no support for victims or their families.

Hurt-free schools

In South African Catholic schools, where bullying was identified as a serious problem (more than 90 per cent of learners at a Johannesburg school last year said they had at some point been bullied), a programme designed to create a 'hurt-free' environment for all learners has been implemented. The programme was introduced to South Africa by American 'hurt-free schools' advocate Christina Matisse, who was invited by the Catholic-based Centre for School Quality and Improvement (CSQI) in Johannesburg to run teacher workshops in the country. These ran successfully in both Johannesburg and Durban.

The purpose of Matisse's programme – a simple, learner-friendly, comprehensive programme called 'Growing Up Safe: Creating Hurt-Free Schools' – is to support children as they grapple with the struggles of social development, by teaching life-skills that consider the 'non-negotiable' right of every child to emotional safety. The traffic light, for instance, is used as an analogy for learners to indicate whether important boundaries are being crossed by another's behaviour: red for 'stop ... bad', amber for 'getting out of control', green for 'good'. According to Colin Northmore of the CSQI, it is proving effective.

Children's movement and the children's resource centre (CRC)

The CRC was started in 1983 with the aim of helping children aged 7–14 to organise themselves into a Children's Movement that would help in building safer and healthier communities for themselves. The Children's Movement promotes respect for oneself, respect for others and respect for the environment. Its members have developed an anti-bullying campaign to take practical steps to stop bullying, to impress upon adults and communities the dangers of bullying and the need to do something practical, and to teach children to resolve conflict without resorting to violence. Although still in its infancy, the programme aims to involve children, teachers and parents, using plays, puppet shows, concerts and marches.

Canada
National strategy

The National Strategy on Community Safety and Crime Prevention is the Canadian government's commitment to deal with the problems of crime and victimisation. The National Strategy contributes funding, expertise, knowledge and tools to support grassroots community safety projects across Canada. Since its launch in 1998, the National Strategy has supported over 2,200 crime prevention projects in over 600 communities, from every Canadian province and territory.

The Strategy employs a crime prevention through social development (CPSD) approach to crime reduction – an approach that recognises the complex social, economic and cultural processes that contribute to crime and victimisation. The focus is on the underlying causes of crime: factors such as violence in the home, low literacy skills, poor parenting, and substance abuse. CPSD addresses these factors and strengthens the quality of life for individuals, families and communities. 'Protective factors', such as positive family support, are fostered, mitigating situations of risk. Since the launch of the strategy, almost 100 projects have been funded to deal with the issue of bullying, along with a host of school-based projects.

One noteworthy and particularly interesting venture is Cool Heads in the Zone, an interactive CD-ROM featuring live-action video depicting six bullying scenarios, a variety of positive interventions, and teacher-friendly resources and assessment tools. Students may explore these scenarios, imagining themselves in the role of the victim, the bystander or the bully. They will see the outcomes of their reactions to bullying situations and test a variety of problem-solving strategies. The CD is part of an early intervention and prevention programme that allows children to experience the 'real-world' emotional issues surrounding bullies, victims and bystanders.

Gambo crime prevention committee

The Gambo Crime Prevention Committee, from Newfoundland and Labrador, has worked with young people, educators, parents and community members to develop the Beat the Bully programme. Designed to empower youth to feel confident, important and worthy, this programme uses public education, storytelling and peer support to help create a community where young people feel safe. The programme is being offered to all youth in the local schools, from kindergarten through grade 12, with information and activities tailored to the various developmental levels. The project has helped to reduce incidents of bullying, victimisation and related fears, and builds on the momentum of previous youth-centred Gambo crime prevention initiatives.

Who dares to speak out?

The Centre Option Prévention T.V.D.S. of Montreal has created the 'Guets-Apens: Qui osera parler?' board game (Bullies: Who dares to speak out?) to educate children about bullying and to encourage the development of effective personal and social skills for dealing with intimidation. The game focuses on both potential victims of bullying and those who may be bullies. It is a fun, interactive way to reach young people, presenting the information in a way that is easy to understand and remember. The game allows each student to live the experience of being bullied and to identify its negative impacts. By experimenting with bullying situations in a safe environment, children learn the value of standing up for themselves, and the importance of talking with someone when they witness, or are subjected to, bullying.

Together we light the way

Together We Light The Way has been responding to the needs of schoolchildren who may later engage in antisocial behaviour. This school-based community-safety project, based on high-quality and consistent nurturing of children, has demonstrated significant progress in enhancing learning and employability skills and habits, developing non-violent responses to anger and improving attitudes towards school. The pilot sites in the Durham District School Board, Ontario, have witnessed a marked reduction in bullying and fighting and a notable increase in resilience and respectful behaviour among youth. One site has reported a 40 per cent reduction in fighting. This approach has enhanced the success of children by helping them to develop self-worth, self-respect and responsibility and connecting them to their communities in meaningful ways.

Peace circle

The Restitution Peace Project at Ecole J. H. Sissons School in Yellowknife developed a Peace Circle model to help schoolchildren learn to resolve conflict in non-violent ways, helping them to understand the underlying causes of their behaviour, and to accept personal responsibility for their actions. Educators and parents have learned new skills and strategies to manage youth without fear and coercion, and to create a positive, nurturing environment. Long-term results include improved self-esteem, enhanced relationships, increased achievement, and learned life skills for resolving conflict and gaining self-discipline. Evaluation of Phase I showed a significant decrease in unresolved playground conflicts, and an increase in the confidence of teachers and students to deal effectively with disputes.

Words hurt

In 2003 Concerned Children's Advertisers produced a strong new anti-bullying commercial, 'Words Hurt', which focuses on psychological bullying and the need to create awareness and empathy on this vital issue. Produced in partnership with Canada's National Crime Prevention Strategy, the goal of 'Words Hurt' was to create a commercial which would demonstrate in an emotive and graphic manner the painful and negative impact of this kind of bullying. The belief is that by being aware of the negative impact of their actions, kids will tap into, and act on, their feelings of empathy for the victim. Focused on girls aged between 8 and 12, the advertisement aims to show through high-tech animation techniques the effect that words and exclusionary behaviour can have on a child. By illustrating the effect of the actions of not only the bully, but also her clique, it reminds the audience that both bullies and bystanders need to take responsibility for understanding the effects of their words and their actions. Focusing on girls at this age is a pre-emptive strategy, to try to prevent psychological bullying from becoming an established behaviour. 'Words Hurt' followed on from the successful advertisement 'Walk Away', produced the previous year.

Roots of empathy

Mary Gordon, the Canadian founder of the successful Roots of Empathy programme, believes that children can be used as 'agents of change' in the promotion of peace. 'You can't teach empathy,' she says, 'but you can create the antecedents.' The idea underpinning Roots of Empathy is for a mother and her infant to visit a primary school classroom for about a third of a 27-session programme, run by a trained facilitator. The pair's interactions form the basis for discussions.

For example, the baby's frustration at its inability to stand might lead to discussion about what that emotion is, and in which situations the children feel it. The children also take things they have learned, such as the dangers of shaking a baby, home to their own parents. Independent research by the University of British Columbia found that children who had gone through the non-profit programme showed more emotional literacy, social understanding and positive peer interactions, and less aggression, than other children. They displayed less aggression with peers, and fewer antisocial behaviours such as bullying. The children were also more cooperative with their teachers. The programme Gordon founded in 1996 now runs in 500 Canadian schools. In Australia, it is about to start at 17 schools in Perth and 15 in New South Wales.

Do bullying initiatives work?

In a paper presented in 2002, Australian bullying expert Ken Rigby concluded that reductions in bullying are much greater in schools where the programmes are carried out most thoroughly. In some highly conscientious schools, reductions of up to 80 per cent were reported. However, the type of programme was also important. Interventions that used 'rules and consequences' seemed to be less effective. In Norway, for example, intervention of this nature produce negative outcomes. Among boys, reporting being bullied by peers actually increased. For both sexes, more children were reported as bullying others. In Canada, the outcomes of an intervention based on the Olweus model (see page 233) failed to produce consistently positive results. In Belgium, there was a small but significant reduction in younger children being bullied.

However, schools employing a 'problem-solving' approach appear to have fared better, with positive results (reductions in bullying) being reported in the UK, Spain, Finland and Australia. Rigby concluded that nearly all of the programmes showed some significant results. He also pinpointed the importance of beginning early, as young children can be influenced to be less involved in bullying more readily than older children. He also felt that it was important to help children to protect themselves from bullies rather than trying to stop those who bully, because victimised children were more strongly motivated to learn how to change their behaviour than were those who bully.

In 2004, David Smith, Professor of Education at the University of Ottawa, analysed data from 14 evaluation studies probing the effectiveness of whole-school anti-bullying programmes implemented in schools in Canada, the USA and Europe. Whole-school intervention programmes include specific components, namely school-wide anti-bullying policies, information kits for the school community about bullying and victimisation, curricular activities designed to instil anti-bullying attitudes, and interventions for students directly involved in or affected by bullying. Smith found the effects of such programmes were almost exclusively 'small, negligible and negative'. Only one study, drawn from Norway, showed 'medium' improvements in the level of self-reported victimisation incidents. None was categorised as large.

In the control studies analysed by Professor Smith, 57 per cent of victimisation outcomes were negligible, while 29 per cent were negative. Only 14 per cent reported 'small' positive effects. For self-reported bullying, 67 per cent reported negligible outcomes, while 33 per cent reported negative outcomes. None reported even 'small' positive effects.

Smith does not, however, advocate scrapping whole-school anti-bullying programmes. 'It's too early to throw it all out and say it's not working because these are large programmes, and they have all these different components. My guess is there are some things going on in there that work,' he said in an interview. For example, the potentially positive long-term impact of whole-school programmes on a school climate would take a while to show up in evaluation studies: 'That's going to take quite a bit of time, and only when that climate is well-developed. Then you're going to start seeing some of the impacts, and these evaluation studies simply haven't tracked programmes long enough. So this is why we can't throw these out yet. We just haven't studied them thoroughly enough.'

Another general study of anti-bullying programmes, presented by Wendy Craig, Associate Professor of Psychology at Queen's University in Canada, showed that slightly more than half reported positive results. But 15 per cent reported that bullying worsened with the programme in place. Craig said: 'Take home the message – you need to evaluate the programme you're implementing in your school. Not all programmes are successful at reducing bullying ... Some programmes cause negative results.' The most successful bullying prevention programmes included developmental and systemic perspectives. They addressed how bullying changes with age, and how children's understanding of bullying evolves with age. Such programmes also extended beyond an individual child to work with educators and administrators, and outreach to parents and community members.

Bully Police USA

Bully Police USA (*www.bullypolice.org*) actively campaigns for change to the legislation in the USA. The site hosts a wealth of information, including moving stories of children who have been seriously bullied to the extent that they have taken their own lives, as well as a multitude of facts, advice, realistic proposals and evaluations. The website was the brainchild of Brenda High, mother of Jared. Just six days after his thirteenth birthday, Jared took his own life – a case of 'bullycide', or suicide as a result of being bullied. Jared had been physically assaulted and repeatedly threatened by his tormentors at school, and provided with no support by administrators at any level. Although he was severely traumatised by his experience, he received no counselling for his emotional injuries from his middle school, no help for his physical injuries (other than the visits to the chiropractor, paid for by his parents), and no apologies from his school district. It is now believed that Jared suffered from post-traumatic stress disorder as a result of the experience, and that this led to his tragic death. Because of the bullying and the assault, Jared began to show signs of depression, which included lack of sleep and emotional outbursts.

On the morning of 29 September 1998, Jared called his father at work to say goodbye. While on the phone, Jared shot himself, dying instantly. As a healing project, Brenda began to write Jared's story,

What's the answer? The results may be mixed, but there is no doubt that a comprehensive and whole-hearted commitment to a bullying programme by the entire school community does have some effect, and that those focusing on changing behaviour and teaching skills such as problem-solving have the best results. As David Smith pointed out, programmes may take years to have a strong impact, since any programme takes time to infiltrate the school environment, the student population and their parents, and the school staff. What's more, relearned behaviour, morals, compassion and empathy are not going to be intrinsic, and must be developed in students over time. Adapting which is now published as *www.jaredstory.com*. Since 1999, the website has attracted more than a million visitors looking for information on bullying, depression and suicide, and in need of healing after the loss of a loved one.

Brenda has now become a passionate crusader. She speaks widely and offers advice to parents and educators. She has designed and continues to work on three websites that deal with bullying and suicide issues.

- *www.jaredstory.com*, which deals with bullying, depression, suicide and other issues
- *www.bullypolice.org*, which reports and grades states on their anti-bullying laws and posts current anti-bullying laws, research, news and support information for parents and/or anti-bullying activists who are dealing with bullying in schools
- *www.thewoundedchild.org*, which tells the stories of students, parents and survivors of bullying

Brenda's speciality is working to get anti-bullying laws passed or revised, and she has contributed to the passage of the Washington State Anti-Bullying Law, as well as influencing the passage of similar laws in Oklahoma and Vermont. She is aggressively working with lawmakers and anti-bullying activists in several states to get more commonsense anti-bullying laws passed in the future.

programmes as children age is also an important consideration: what works in primary schools will not necessarily work with a hardened secondary-school bully. All in all, however, there can be no doubt that doing nothing will only encourage escalation of violence. Carefully implemented plans, with the full support of all involved, can and will make a difference, along with initiatives on government level, and through individuals and corporations who are committed to making a difference.

9

A Little Extra Help

It was high counsel that I once heard given to a young person: Always do what you are afraid to do.

Ralph Waldo Emerson

EVEN THE MOST SCRUPULOUSLY ORGANISED and maintained bullying programmes can misfire or allow a child to slip through the net. Many bullies are deeply devious and expert at continuing their efforts, despite clear anti-bullying programmes, constant monitoring and supervision by teachers and staff, and scrupulous reporting by students. You may also find that you meet resistance when speaking to teachers or administrators regarding bullying incidents, whether your child is the bully or the victim; you may discover that your child continues to be bullied, or to bully others, and that there is little support on offer. Furthermore, many children are deeply traumatised by bullying, regardless of intervention and correct procedures being undertaken, and may suffer from physical or emotional symptoms long after the problem has been resolved within the school. Family support is crucial at this time, and it may also be necessary to obtain some professional help to get your child through it.

That's what this chapter is about – what to do when things don't go according to plan, and the bullying, or its effects, continue. Every child's situation, school environment and personal response will be individual to him, and there is no clear-cut method of dealing with problems that will apply to all children. Read through the chapter and work out the methods, advice and situations that are most applicable to your child and, with these tools, formulate your own strategy to get your child back on course.

Throughout this book, hundreds of ideas have been given for getting your child back on track, whether he bullies or is bullied. Once you have admitted that a problem exists, you can implement these tactics and work on rectifying the immediate dilemmas affecting your particular child – on a personal and social level. Your child may be in need of some help with social interaction, body language, problem-solving, anger management, making friends, expressing himself emotionally or learning tolerance. Your family may need a bit of an over-haul to ensure that all of its members are thriving, and that the dynamic is healthy. None of these problems is insurmountable. With determination and a little effort, you can make a big difference on many levels.

But sometimes things don't go according to plan, and you may find that the situation continues or even escalates, or that your child is ill-equipped to deal with the damage done by bullying. You may find that your child's home life is on an even keel, but that his peer network encourages him to bully, or that his school environment is not conducive to the lessons you are trying to teach at home. In this case, a little extra action may be required.

Keeping a record

I can't stress enough how important it is to keep careful records, and copies of those records. In Chapter 7 we looked at the steps that should be taken when a child is being bullied, or bullying others, and it's important that we rein-force them here. It may at times seem as if you are a one-parent army, but the more scrupulous you are in preparing your battle plans, the more like-ly you are to resolve the issues and get the support you need. So, in a nutshell:

1. Keep a diary – daily, recording even the most innocuous events. Who was involved, the time, the place, the witnesses, the 'crime' and any other details that your child or his friends can remember. Don't try to take sides, or express what you perceive to be someone else's motivation or reason for the fracas. Be completely unbiased, and document the facts only. Make a copy of your diary.

2. Write letters. Start at the bottom, with your child's teacher, and ask that the matter be kept confidential from other parents. Not all teachers are a model of discretion, and you may find that bullying escalates when other children or their parents learn that you are stirring things up by making a complaint. Make your letter factual, honest and, again, completely unbiased. Simply record the infor-mation you have to hand and ask for a response.

If you fail to get any real response from your child's teacher, it's time to move up the ladder. The headmaster/mistress or principal should be notified. With every letter you send, be sure to copy in everyone who is involved in the chain. So when you write to the head of the school, copy in your child's teacher. Furthermore, send copies of all previous correspondence to anyone involved, whenever you write to someone new. If you get no joy with the head, then move up. This is an international book, so it's difficult to assess what your direct ladder may be in your particular country or county, but you can assume that governors or the school board, education authorities, your member of parliament, and any local or federal authorities responsible for safety in schools will be part of the upward chain. Again, copy in everyone who has been involved before. This may seem pedantic and boring, but it is essential that your paperwork is in order.

3. Call in the police. Most bullying does contain a criminal element; for example, extortion, cyberbullying, mobile phone malice, physical abuse and even verbal abuse can all be reported to the police. Whether they go forward with it is something that will depend on circumstances and individual policies within authorities; however, the act of reporting a crime means that it has been officially documented, should legal action be necessary in the future. In addition, the police can caution or warn the people involved that they are breaking the law, which may just be enough to stop a bully in his tracks.

4. If you fail to get a satisfactory response, you may, depending on your position, wish to engage in legal action. This can be undertaken against a school, a council, an education authority or even the other parties involved in the bullying. It is a costly and time-consuming venture, but, to be honest, sometimes things only change when the law is challenged, and when people are prepared to stick their necks out to ensure that the law is obeyed.

Continue up the ladder until you get a response. Don't give up and consider your efforts wasted. There will be someone along the line who takes your complaints seriously, and it's essential that you continue until you find them. Record, copy and document everything, even dates and times of telephone calls and the names and departments of anyone to whom you speak.

Your child's health

An ongoing battle can be draining for anyone, and your child will be no exception, particularly if she has been the target of a bully. Try to keep her involved in a general sense, so that she knows that something is being done to help her. This reassurance is an important part of supporting a bullied child. But keep the nitty-gritty from her doorstep. She does not need to know about every hurdle you encounter, or every negative experience, or even your own frustration. It's important that she is given the freedom, with your help, to go on and enjoy her childhood with the knowledge that, having involved adults, she can now relax a little. Involving a child in a long-term campaign is unnecessary and may be detrimental to her health; indeed, she may feel guilt for having caused so many problems, embarrassment, frustration, anger and helplessness. Your job is to shield her from further distress; childhood is stressful enough without the added responsibility of undertaking what may end up being a long-term battle for retribution. Work on her self-esteem, her happiness, her friendships, and everything that may be affecting her self-image and self-respect. Show support. Be honest when requested, but don't overburden her with details that she simply does not need to know. Keep her out of personal meetings unless her presence is absolutely required. Reliving a bullying campaign can be very distressing for some children.

Emotional health

In Chapter 6 we looked at the concept of post-traumatic stress disorder, and the other effects of stress. Earlier in the book we also looked at the very real emotional symptoms that can manifest themselves as a result of being bullied. Do not assume that because the situation is being resolved, or has been resolved, all is well with your child. The effects can be far-reaching and long-lasting, and you will need to be very astute and observant to ensure that crucial symptoms are not overlooked.

Receiving support can be extremely reassuring, but your child may be suffering from a huge lack of self-confidence, self-belief and even faith in other people if she has been seriously bullied. And if you discover that your child has been bullying others, the emotional ramifications are also important to consider. A bully has issues and concerns, perhaps very deep-seated, that are every bit as detrimental as those affecting a child who has been bullied. Do not underestimate the importance of talking through the issues. Encourage your child to verbalise what he is feeling, so that emotions are not pent-up and expressed in unhealthy ways. Bullies and bullied kids alike need to have a strong line of communication with parents, and a great deal of compassion and understanding. Problems will never disappear overnight, and some experts believe that it can take months or even years to regain the status quo.

So, first of all, ensure that you are communicating regularly with your child, and that you are able to listen 'actively'.

Active listening

Listening is an important tool for all parents. It involves hearing what your child has to say, both in terms of the words he is using and the feelings between the words. It means asking questions, providing a real response to questions, offering words to help your child explain the way he is feeling, as well as a non-judgemental sounding board for thoughts, ideas and emotions. Children feel more secure when they can express themselves and know that what they are feeling is acceptable. They feel validated when they are given a respectful audience.

In brief, it is a way of talking to someone with sympathy or empathy. It is respectful of your child's thoughts and feelings, because you don't just sit there, you attempt to see the world through their eyes. What's more, you suspend your judgement and your opinions for the duration of the conversation, and commit yourself to understanding how your child sees or saw a situation. This doesn't mean you have to agree, but you do need to show willing.

In many cases, problem behaviours can be stamped out when parents are able to see and hear issues affecting their children's wellbeing. A rambling story, during which the average parent might tune out, can hold a multitude of clues to a child's emotional state. Giving problems and feelings words, identifying potential issues, showing love and acceptance, and encouraging your child to express himself all help to build self-respect. More importantly, however, children themselves learn the value of listening – a tool that will empower them in all types of difficult situations. They will also learn to return the respect shown to them by listening to you.

Active listening has two main goals: to understand what your child is thinking, from his or her point of view, and to communicate back and check your understanding with the child who is talking. You become an active participant in the conversation. It can be difficult at times, particularly when you are annoyed about behaviour, disagree fundamentally with what your child is saying, or are very busy. But it's worth the effort. Put yourself in the right frame of mind. Tell yourself that you will not only listen but you will hear your child, no matter what. Use non-judgemental questions to keep the conversation going. Avoid anything confrontational; the point is to show understanding.

Sometimes all that is required is a quiet audience, with gentle reassurance or questions at the right moments. As long as your child feels that he is being heard, you have established the type of communication that precludes serious and long-term behavioural problems.

In some instances, children may be reluctant to initiate conversations about an incident or campaign that they felt was traumatic. If so, it may be helpful to ask them what they think other children felt or thought about the event. Also, it may be easier for children to tell what happened (e.g., what they saw, heard, smelled, physically felt) before they can discuss their feelings about the event. In other instances, children will want to tell their parents the story of the trauma over and over. Retelling is part of the healing process. Children need to tell their stories and have their parents listen again and again to each and every agonising detail.

Dealing with guilt

Both bullies and bullied children can experience feelings of guilt. In the first instance, kids who have 'woken up' to the consequences of their actions may have a surge of guilt or remorse, and feel great shame. Moreover, they may feel uncomfortable about having caused their parents or families distress, regardless of the direct cause of their actions. Similarly, bullied children may also feel embarrassed and guilty that their parents have been drawn into their problem to a greater or lesser extent, and feel bad that they have caused stress or concern. They may worry that they have created the situation in some way, and feel guilty that they are unable to stand up for themselves, or rectify the problem without external help. Remember, too, that bystanders can also suffer from enormous guilt – because they were not strong or brave enough to intervene, because they did not come to the defence of a victim, or because they may have been drawn into the proceedings, possibly even against their will.

Guilt is a negative emotion and it is very, very important that you work with your child to let him know that he is not to blame, that you understand the reasons why he bullied other people, that being bullied is not a crime, and that there is no shame in being targeted by other children who have their own problems. Reassure your child constantly that you love her, believe in her, are willing and able to help, and can understand, no matter what may have occurred. If your child is able to verbalise how she is feeling, and get the reassurance she needs, she will get over her feelings – or at least accept them as being normal – that much more quickly.

Dealing with trauma

Don't underestimate the effect of bullying on everyone involved. Bystanders, bullies and victims can all be affected by the situation, to a greater or lesser degree. The incidents may occur suddenly, leaving children little or no time to prepare physically or emotionally, and may fall well outside your child's sphere of reference. Children may experience intense fear, horror or helplessness.

Parents can be instrumental in their children's recovery. Therefore, helping children recover from a trauma is a family matter. Parents need to take the lead and model positive coping. Yet parents themselves may require extra information, support and resources to assist their children. Some first steps that parents can take are to understand the impact and symptoms of trauma and how to help in the aftermath.

Trauma or distress, caused by bullying, can change the way children view their world. Assumptions about safety and security are now challenged. Children's reactions will depend upon the severity of the incidents, their personality makeup, their characteristic coping style and the availability of support. It is common for children to regress both behaviourally and academically following a trauma.

Fears, worries or nightmares are common following a trauma. Sleep disturbances or eating difficulties may occur. Children may begin to regress emotionally or act younger than their chronological age. They also may become more clinging, unhappy and needy of parental attention and comfort. Feelings of irritability, anger, sadness or guilt may often emerge. Somatic complaints such as headaches, stomachaches or sweating are not unusual. Loss of interest in school and poor concentration are some other common reactions. Symptoms of post-traumatic stress disorder (see page 192) may also manifest themselves, and it is important that you watch out for these as well.

❓ What can you do?

• Establish a sense of safety and security. It is essential that children feel protected, safe and secure in the aftermath of a bullying situation. Ensure that all basic needs are met, including love, care and physical closeness. Spend extra time to let your child know that someone will nurture and protect them. They will need a lot of comforting and reassurance.

- Validate your child's feelings. Help them understand that following a traumatic event, all feelings are acceptable. They will probably experience a myriad feelings, which could include shame, rage, anger, sadness, guilt, pain, isolation, loneliness and fear. Help your child understand that what they are experiencing is normal and to be expected.

- Allow your child the opportunity to regress as necessary. This is important so that they may 'emotionally regroup'. For example, your child may request to sleep in your bed with the lights on or you may need to drive them to school. Previously developed skills may seem to disappear or deteriorate. Bed-wetting or thumb sucking may occur. Aggression and anger may emerge in a previously non-aggressive child. Be patient and tolerant and never ridicule your child. Remember that most regression following a trauma is temporary.

- Help your child clear up misconceptions. Help correct misunderstandings regarding the cause or nature of the trauma, especially those that relate to inappropriate guilt, shame, embarrassment or fear.

- Affirm that your child is capable of coping and healing in the aftermath of a trauma. Plant 'emotional seeds' that express confidence in your child's ability to heal. Remember that the messages you give your child have incredible power.

- Seek professional assistance for your child and family as necessary. When seeking help, make sure that the professional has experience with children and has treated the traumatic effects of bullying.

- Always be honest with your child about what has happened and what may occur. Remember that following a trauma, children may lose a sense of trust about the safety and security of the world. Therefore, honesty is essential so your child can maintain that sense of trust. You may not be able to change your child's situation in the short term, or even make a real difference for many months. There is no point in telling your child that it is 'all sorted'. When it carries on, he will feel misled. Be honest, show your child that you are helping in every way you can, and be supportive through any subsequent activity.

- Respect your child's fears. Children cannot be helped by trying to argue them out of their fears by appeals to bravery or reason.

Help for bullies

One mainstream school of psychological thought is the 'social learning theory', which states that violent behaviour is brought about through learning. And there is an enormous wealth of research behind this theory, which claims that children learn to be violent chiefly through imitation of violent role models. This means that parents who rely on corporal punishment or verbal abuse to 'control' their kids are unwittingly acting as models for bullying behaviour. Secondary sources of modelled violence include older siblings, media violence, peers and even schoolteachers. In 1989, researcher Cathy Spatz-Widom published an exhaustive analysis of research addressing whether violence is trans-generational. She found substantial support for the notion that violence is created by violence. And this relationship holds true even for verbal violence, as several later researchers found. One 1991 study revealed that children who had experienced higher levels of verbal aggression at home (being sworn at or insulted) exhibited higher rates of delinquency and interpersonal aggression.

So the idea that bullies should be 'punished' when, indeed, many of them are victims themselves, is not always considered to be an appropriate means of dealing with the problem. Indeed, 'teaching' bullies to be non-violent can never work if they are then thrown back into a family system which encourages it. Many experts now believe that a more effective approach to treating school bullies is to examine the environment in which the violent responses were learned, and then to work with family members to alter the dynamics of this environment.

Because much of this type of violence, or unhealthy childrearing, has gone on for generations, it is also important not to blame the family, who may well be doing their best, given the resources at their disposal. Policies that make it standard procedure to invite parents or carers of school bullies to the school are now being considered by many authorities. The idea is that areas where parents might need support can be identified, and that parents themselves can be taught more appropriate, and less authoritarian, parenting methods. Encouraging parents to work together with their children in programmes can be much more beneficial.

If your child is bullying, do not hesitate to ask for help from your local authority, your family doctor, or your child's school. There are always resources that can be made available to willing, worried parents.

• Make sure that your child knows that you are aware of the seriousness of the situation. Allow them to cry. Saying to your child, 'Don't cry, everything will be fine,' denies the seriousness of the situation.

Professional help

In reality, the goals of therapy are to help your child regain a sense of control over his own life, and to allow a safe expression and release of feelings. The painful symptoms and behaviours will also be addressed and relieved. Misunderstandings, and issues such as blame, can also be looked at, which will restore a child's self-belief, and his hope for the future.

Siblings and friends

Dealing with bullying is very much a family issue, but not only for parents. Siblings will probably need to be involved, and friends may also be required to offer much-needed support. Make it clear that your child, whether she is a victim of bullying, a bully herself, or someone who has been drawn into the proceedings by bystanders, is undergoing a difficult time, and needs encouragement and back-up. It may be that siblings or friends will be called upon to defend your child – to give her a little extra help in situations with which she is not yet able to cope. Outline your expectations, and offer tips on how they can be of assistance. Don't embarrass your child by making her feel more of a victim than she may already believe she is. Make it clear that, in times of trouble, we need to enlist the support of everyone who cares about us.

If your child does not have a good group of friends, or a close friend on whom to rely, it is never too late to work on establishing a new network, by involving her in activities away from school. No matter how battered or underconfident she may be feeling, she will always benefit from having like-minded peers around her.

Changing schools

If you can't get anywhere with your child's school, or if, despite all interventions, he is reluctant to return, you may wish to consider changing schools.

But think carefully before you commit. For one thing, changing schools will do nothing practical to raise your child's self-respect or self-esteem, and it will not exorcise the demons of the past. If your child has been bullying, the root cause has to be explored and rectified before it will stop. If your child has been witness to regular bouts of bullying and has been traumatised, there is no absolutely guaranteed way of ensuring that this does not recur at another school, regardless of whether their bullying 'profile' is positive. If your child has been bullied, he will carry the experience with him and, until it is resolved, it will fester. If changes aren't made to the characteristics that define many bullying targets, then chances are he will find himself in the same position again.

What's more, moving schools is stressful. Starting again, meeting new friends, coming to terms with the curriculum and the routine, living with the fear that it may all start again, can be difficult for even the most robust child. It may seem like a simple solution, but it's important that you think carefully before embarking on this option.

Consider, too, these points:

1. You will need to check out the anti-bullying stance of any school to which you are considering sending your child. Don't just go on what the school says: visit the playground, watch and listen. Ask other parents. Check any government or authority reports. Set up a meeting with the head of the school and ask questions. Explain your situation; ask about how your child can be initiated with the minimum of fuss and stress. But also ask about what they might have done in a similar situation.

2. If you are considering changing from a state system to the private system, remember that there is often a considerable difference in expectations of kids, and in their academic level. You may find that your child, no matter how bright, will find it difficult to adjust. Many private schools have much longer hours, and kids are expected to turn up for lessons or music/sports events on the weekends too. Make sure that is in line with what your child can manage, and what you as a family hope to achieve as a unit.

3. Children who have been bullied are naturally wary of the experience recurring and reluctant to trust other children. This makes friendships difficult – and if your child is starting at a new school, building up new relationships is crucial. Before any bullied child is moved, he will need some help to get over any emotional hurdles. Body language and self-esteem will all need to be improved, as, perhaps, will personal skills.

4. If you have a choice of schools, try to choose one where your child knows at least one or two other kids – perhaps from extracurricular clubs or weekend

activities. Starting completely fresh can be very daunting, and may set your child back emotionally – which can encourage the bullying cycle to begin all over again.
5. Remember that moving schools does not guarantee a better existence. You may need to make some compromises. In the UK, the best schools are heavily oversubscribed, so moving your child may involve accepting a school in a rougher area (which may bring its own disciplinary issues), one with lower standards and results, or one that involves a long journey to reach. If your child is feeling a little fragile, none of these is a particularly welcome change; furthermore, you do not want to compromise his long-term educational success by sending him to an inferior school. No one wins in that situation.

All in all, I suggest thinking twice before changing schools. It's unlikely to have a dramatic effect, and can often cause as much harm as good. Of course, the choice may be offered to your child, and if he is adamant that change is the only option, you may wish to proceed. But leave options open – make sure you have a fall-back position, if things don't work out.

Home education for your child

In the UK, more than 50,000 families choose to educate their children at home; in fact, research by Durham University indicates that some 150,000 kids are schooled at home (which represents about 1 per cent of the 5–16 age group). It is an option that is growing in popularity, too, and some experts believe that it may increase to as much as 3 per cent of all kids by 2012. In the USA, it is estimated that 850,000 children are home-schooled. Figures are up by more than 500 per cent in Australia and New Zealand over the past decade.

Many parents swear by home education, and believe that it offers far more than mainstream schooling. Benefits include:

- Developing a closer relationship with parents, siblings and other family members.
- Fewer distractions (without a classroom of children, who may be disruptive).
- Working at an appropriate pace for your child, rather than the average needs of the classroom body.
- Working to an elastic time frame – more time for things that interest your child, for example the ability to go a little further afield on a regular basis, with 'field trips', trips to museums, galleries, other cultures, exhibitions and fairs.

• Less wasted time. At home it takes roughly one and a half hours a day to teach a first-year child what he would learn in the average seven-hour day in school, according to Dr Raymond Moore, author of many books on home education. This is because the teacher must assign 'busy work' to most of her pupils while she fills out administrative paperwork, handles disciplinary problems and gives extra attention to pupils with special needs. This allows a child more time to play, explore and invent – and to use his imagination.

Many parents enjoy the opportunity to teach their own values, rather than allowing their children to be overly influenced by their peer group; in a school where discipline and bullying is a problem, this can be a paramount consideration. Studies by Cornell University Professor Urie Bronfenbrenner suggest that, at least until age 10 or 12, students who spend more time with other children their age than with their parents tend to rely on other children for their values. The result? They tend to have a lower sense of self-worth, of optimism, of respect for their parents, and, ironically, even of trust in their peers.

Results can be significantly better. Departments of education in such states as Alaska, Tennessee and Washington in the USA have conducted studies that found the typical home-schooled student comes out ahead on virtually every significant measurement.

Many parents consider educational development as a part of everyday family and social life, so children are encouraged to view learning as resulting from all experiences. Baking can be used to teach fractions and nutrition, for example; a trip to the shops can teach money management, sums, percentages and much more. What's more, the fact that children schooled in the home have more contact with adults, and often have more opportunity to watch adult interaction, rather than relying on peers for the development of social skills, can show marked improvement their socialisation, which can be superior to that of children in a school environment.

But remember, there are drawbacks, too.

You will need to ensure that your child does get plenty of time with children of his own age. Although adult interaction can be excellent and serve a useful purpose, children do need to learn to establish relationships with their peer group. Having said that, there are now various organisations and associations that bring home-schooled children together for different activities and events. Home-schooling advocates assert that this allows children

Special schools

Some parents are involved in, or opting for, schools that are set up specifically to help bullied children. Some of these schools are short-term educational programmes, designed to encourage self-confidence, boost social skills, allow kids to work in an unpressured atmosphere with like-minded children who have also undergone the same difficulties, supply counselling or therapy where necessary, and regain their interest in their educational goals.

One such school is the Red Balloon in the UK, which was set up by Carrie Herbert, an educational consultant, who believes that some children are so traumatised by bullying at school that they need an educational 'intensive-care unit' in order to recover – a school geared to their needs in size, atmosphere and staff–pupil ratios. A trained teacher who set up a consultancy advising schools on bullying and harassment, Herbert also had a niece who was badly bullied at her private school. Although she was able to change schools, Herbert was concerned about the number of children who dropped out of the system completely and who deserved a chance to learn, but were prevented from doing so. Some children do not have a home-teaching option; nor are some parents equipped to offer it.

Herbert's teaching, and that of her colleagues, is very individual, as some children have been out of the education system for long periods due to the problems they have experienced. It involves drama, music and other forms of expression that help children to communicate their concerns and experiences. Despite the children's previous problems success rates are pretty spectacular. Most of their students have returned to mainstream school, gone on to sixth-form college or further education (university included), or started work in local industries. Their attendance rate is also excellent.

In Kent, in the UK, parents felt 'forced' to establish their own school for victims of bullying, and the Cooperative Independent College in Broadstairs was set up independently, charging students a small weekly sum because education authorities have refused funding. The College was founded by Corron Osborn – whose daughter Julia, 13, is a pupil – and Cindy Petford. Julia, who was bullied for two years and once had her hair doused in petrol and set alight, said 'They were beating me up almost every day and making my life hell. But this school's brilliant because I can just concentrate on work'.

who are home-schooled ample opportunity to interact with other children their own ages.

Similarly, exercise is an important consideration – keeping a child stimulated, physically active and learning can be a challenge for most parents, and it is important that they maintain physical fitness – and not just alone. Team sports have an important function in childhood development.

It can be time-consuming, and there is, in most countries, little support for parents who choose to school at home.

A home-schooled child is usually limited to only one teacher and, at best, siblings as classmates. Certainly this reduces the number of unique ideas being shared and explored. Therefore kids may lack exposure to the diversity of beliefs and backgrounds that they would encounter at school – and which reflect the reality of society. Parents may only teach areas in which they are skilled, thus leading to more pronounced strengths and weaknesses in their child's abilities.

As a child moves to secondary school, the level of knowledge needed to teach them appropriately increases. Research by Michael Romanowski found that 'most students need a teacher who has expertise in the subject to provide the appropriate level of instruction or to deal with the complexities of particular academic areas'. In schools, as the child moves on to the secondary level, there are teachers for each content area; in the home there is only the parent.

In addition to limited knowledge, it may be difficult for the parent to balance the duty of teaching and other day-to-day tasks. Researcher Raymond Moore claims that, 'Procrastination has to be a major problem in a home setting. It is easy to start a little later or delay learning so the parent or guardian can run an errand. Some parents give in too easily to the complaints of their children and change things to meet the desires of the child. This lack of structure is a major negative to learning'. Romanowski agrees, adding that 'the baby crying, the phone ringing, or the siblings fighting can all cause an academic programme to suffer'.

It also may be hard to separate the home and school when it comes to areas such as discipline. Moore points out that 'not every parent or guardian has the ability to teach or the resolve to stay with it. Knowing materials and having resources to use still does not provide everyone with the skills to teach young minds. As kids get older, they also display a natural rebellion to parents which adds to the inability to learn.'

Another concern regarding home schooling is that children will be limited in what resources are present to help facilitate their learning. Everything has a price and the amount of income a family has can create serious barriers for the child's education. As Romanowski points out: 'Limited resources affect their ability to provide adequate educational opportunities and equipment, such as computers; field trips and other experiences that cost money, such as entrance fees to museums; science materials such as microscopes and other laboratory facilities; access to tutors to teach courses such as Spanish or to other needed specialised professional assistance; and simple everyday school materials.'

Consider, too, that schools offer much more in terms of extracurricular activities, and many of these take place during the course of the day, in lunch breaks, for instance. Sports, orchestras, choirs, school plays and other drama, and a variety of clubs can usually not be supplied in the home environment, or within the time left over!

Much home schooling is also unregulated.

So there are pros and cons to home schooling. You may feel that you have little choice because of your child's situation, but be very careful not to choose this option without addressing the reasons why your child has been bullied – or is bullying. Running away from the problem, or providing your child with an 'alternative' reality, will not help her in the long run. She'll still have to go out into the big bad world at some point in her life, and she must be prepared for it – and part of that is learning to deal with children who bully, or with the impetus to bully herself.

Laws within countries all vary with regard to home education, but you can be fairly certain that it is almost always legal. There are a variety of websites that can help you work out what you can and can't do (see Resources). As long as you work within the law, and are happy to take on the challenge, it may well be an option that will work for you and your children.

Suicide and bullying

An extreme response to bullying is, sadly, suicide. Many children would rather give up entirely than face a life being bullied, and many do not feel that they have anyone to turn to. Suicide statistics show that in the UK between 15 and 25 children kill themselves each year because they are being bullied at school.

UK charity Kidscape's 'Long-term Effects of Bullying' study, published in 1999, stated: 'Forty-six per cent of the respondents (bully victims involved in

Signs of depression

Depression is often not recognised. In younger children and in adolescent boys, it may seem that the child is simply angry or sullen. If this lasts more than a week or so with no relief, and if there are other signs of depression – changes in appetite, activity level, sleep pattern; loss of interest in activities that normally give pleasure; social withdrawal; thoughts of death or punishment – it should be taken seriously.

Signs of developing depression include:
- unhappiness
- gradual withdrawal into helplessness and apathy
- isolated behaviour
- drop in school performance
- loss of interest in activities that formerly were sources of enjoyment
- feelings of worthlessness, hopelessness, helplessness
- fatigue or lack of energy or motivation
- change in sleeping habits
- change in eating habits
- self-neglect
- preoccupation with sad thoughts or death
- loss of concentration
- increase in physical complaints
- sudden outbursts of temper
- reckless or dangerous behaviour
- increased drug or alcohol abuse
- irritability, restlessness

the survey) had contemplated suicide. Twenty per cent attempted suicide, some more than once.'

No matter how you look at it, that makes worrying reading.

In the USA, statistics show that suicide is the third leading cause of death among the 15–25 age group and the sixth leading cause of death among those aged 5–14. The numbers attributed directly to bullying are unknown, but given that bullying is one of the most pervasive and stressful events for a child, there can be no doubt that it is at least very influential in many cases.

Remember that a traumatic event in a child's life may seem minor to an adult, but it can be enough to push them over the edge into severe depression or a complete inability to cope.

? What can you do?

Never take any talk of suicide lightly, no matter how innocuous the circumstances may seem. Get some professional help immediately.

- But don't just leave it to the 'professionals'. Take a risk and get involved. If you suspect your child has suicidal thoughts or is showing signs of suicidal behaviour, ask him directly if he is considering it. Tiptoeing round the problem may mean missing the one opportunity you had to address it.
- If you suspect your child may be suicidal, do not, under any circumstances, leave her alone.
- A child who is being bullied may not always come clean, or even admit to or be willing to discuss the matter. You will need to be on guard. There are too many stories of teens who have taken their own lives because of bullying, and too many parents who had no inkling that there was any problem at all.
- Remember to consider your child's perception as being all-important. Adult standards do not apply to children's feelings. If there is considered to be a problem, then there is one.
- Encourage open, honest communication with your children. If your child trusts you enough to come to you with a problem, take time to listen immediately.
- Talk about suicide in an open manner. Children need to be given a chance to discuss suicide by voicing their thoughts and opinions. Candid discussion is particularly important when a teen suicide has occurred in a community.
- Let your child know about hotline telephone numbers and crisis intervention services. If they are in a state and can't face talking to a family member or friend, these services can be invaluable.

Bullying is prevalent and it is debilitating for everyone involved. Whole families can find themselves under pressure when just one member is affected, and there are many cases where professional support and individual advice may be necessary to get through the difficult periods. Whatever you do, don't sweep bullying under the carpet. You've bought this book, so you've acknowledged the problem. Within these pages you should find all the information you need to set it to rights, but, if all else fails, there are many, many organisations and support groups which can offer assistance. Whatever anyone might tell you on your journey to help your child, bullying is not a part of growing up, or something that all kids need to go through on the road to adulthood. It can be beaten, and with the collective efforts of concerned parents and educators, that vision can become a reality. The best advice I can offer is to start now, and use every resource available to you. We all want healthy, happy kids, and knocking bullying on the head is the first step towards achieving that – for all.

Resources

There is a wealth of useful organisations set up specifically to help families and teachers who are dealing with a bullying problem. I've listed some of the best here, but there are many others. For international websites, see page 309.

UK

ChildLine

ChildLine offers a free and confidential 24-hour helpline for children, as well as an impressive website with information, advice, research and publications on all aspects of bullying. You'll also find details of their CHIPS (ChildLine in Partnership with Schools) scheme, as well as videos, other supporting materials and a wealth of information on peer support schemes.

Helpline: 0800 1111

Website: *www.childline.org.uk*

For details on CHIPS telephone 020 7650 3230 or email *lfeather@childline.org.uk*

Kidscape

A charity that offers training, resources, a helpline and leaflets for dealing with bullying. Kidscape can also provide a wealth of information about prevention strategies and initiatives; in particular, see their literature on bully courts.

2 Grosvenor Gardens

London

SW1W 0DH

Helpline for parents (Mon–Fri; 10am–4pm): 020 7730 3300

Website: *www.kidscape.org.uk*

Anti-Bullying Alliance (ABA)

The ABA brings together 65 organisations into one network with the aim of reducing bullying and creating safer environments for children and young people. The Alliance's national co-ordination team is based at the National Children's Bureau. Their website provides a wealth of useful information, and includes details of the many programmes organised for bullying awareness week.

National Children's Bureau

8 Wakley Street

London

EC1V 7QE

Tel: 020 7843 1901

Website: *www.anti-bullyingalliance.org*

Anti-Bullying Network

The Anti-Bullying Network is based at the University of Edinburgh, and is funded by the Scottish Executive. While they don't offer a helpline, they do offer support and advice through their literature, and give a great overview of anti-bullying strategies. Adults working in Scottish schools may also contact them for advice by telephone. Their website is extremely useful.

Moray House School of Education
University of Edinburgh, Holyrood Road
Edinburgh EH8 8AQ
Tel: 0131 651 6103
Email: *abn@education.ed.ac.uk*
Website: *www.antibullying.net*

ParentlinePlus

Offers a free confidential helpline to parents and carers. Also provides a secure email helpline via the website. The website provides advice and information on bullying .

Tel: 0808 800 2222
Website: *www.parentlineplus.org.uk*

Don't Suffer in Silence

This government agency has a number of well-thought-out campaigns and a clever and informative website with different sections for teachers, kids and parents. The key message of the strategy is that pupils should report bullying to someone they trust and not suffer in silence.

DFES
Improving Behaviour and Attendance Division
Department for Education and Employment
Sanctuary Buildings, Great Smith Street
London SW1P 3BT
Tel: 0870 000 2288
Email: *anti.bullying@dfes.gsi.gov.uk*
Website: *www.dfes.gov.uk/bullying*

Bully Free Zone

Bully Free Zone was established in 1996 to provide a service for children and young people who had issues around bullying. They aim to offer a peer mediation service, and to advance education on the subject of bullying, while helping those who are affected, through a telephone helpline, written advice, school and youth organisation consultancies, policy work, setting up and running peer support schemes, and working with groups of young people.

23 Palace Street
Bolton, BL1 2DR
Tel: 01204 454958
Email: *office@bullyfreezone.freeserve.co.uk*
Website: *www.bullyfreezone.co.uk*

Bullying Online

Bullying Online was founded in 1999 and is now one of the best and most comprehensive sources of bullying information for parents, children, teachers and anyone else affected. The site deals with individual emails from sufferers, parents and bullies themselves. There is a wealth of information about many of the initiatives discussed in this book, including the No Blame method, and Circle Time. What's more, you'll find plenty of information on legal implications, sample letters for concerned parents, and much, much more. Well worth a visit.
Website: *www.bullying.co.uk*

Bully Online

This website is one of the best available, with statistics, information, advice, excellent links, strategies, prevention policies and much, much more. Make this your first port of call. The website has grown from a few pages to more than 450 over recent years, and is now one of the world's most renowned sites dealing with bullying of all descriptions.
Website: *www.bullyonline.org*

NSPCC

The National Society for the Prevention of Cruelty to Children has a well-grounded, effective approach to child welfare and their approach to bullying is no exception. They have an excellent website with plenty of advice and information for all parties concerned, plus many fact sheets that can be ordered or downloaded.
Weston House, 42 Curtain Road
London EC2A 3NH
Tel: 020 7825 2500
Child protection helpline: 0808 800 5000
Email: *help@nspcc.org.uk*
Website: *www.nspcc.org.uk/helpline*

Schools Out!

This organisation tackles homophobia (and subsequent bullying) in schools.
BM Schools Out! National
London WC1N 3XX
General email: *secretary@schools-out.org.uk*
Website: *www.schools-out.org.uk*

PSU Connections Programme

This programme uses bullies to care for younger children to change behaviour.
Adriene Codelia
Family Services Units
207 Old Marylebone Road
London NW1 5QP
Tel: 020 7402 5175

Actionwork

This organisation arranges anti-bullying events for young people – by young people! They visit schools and other organisations to teach kids about bullying issues through entertainment, including drama and music. Actionwork call themselves an international peace, film, theatre, education and anti-bullying organisation.

Actionwork, Anti Bullying Conference (ABC)

Bully Web I Power I, PO Box 433

Weston Super Mare BS24 0WY

Tel: 01934 815163

Email: *info@actionwork.com*

Website: *www.actionwork.com*

Box Clever

Box Clever is a writer-led, multi-disciplinary company that creates contemporary theatre with and for young people. They have written and performed a number of plays about 'hate', including bullying and victimisation.

12.G.1 The Leathermarket

Weston Street, London SE1 3ER

Tel: 020 7357 0550

Email: *admin@boxclevertheatre.com*

Website: *www.boxclevertheatre.com*

YoungMinds

YoungMinds aims to raise awareness of the importance of children's mental health, and the importance of recognising when a child is troubled and providing adequate support for these children before their problems escalate out of control. They have an excellent website with a wealth of advice and information about bullying, and are one of the founding members involved in the ABA.

48–50 St John Street

London EC1M 4DG

Tel: 020 7336 8445

Email: *enquiries@youngminds.org.uk*

Website: *www.youngminds.org.uk*

Stonewall

Stonewall actively campaigns against homophobia of all descriptions, and has a good, informative website for parents and pupils who are bullied for their sexual orientation. Their resource section will be useful for teachers dealing with the problem.

46 Grosvenor Gardens

London SW1W 0EB

Tel: 020 7881 9440

Email: *info@stonewall.org.uk*

Website: *www.stonewall.org.uk*

The Samaritans

Samaritans is available 24 hours a day to provide confidential emotional support for people who are experiencing feelings of distress or despair, including those which may lead to suicide. They train schools to deal with bullies, and have an excellent team of volunteers who can advise children and/or their parents on all aspects of dealing with bullying.

Tel: 08457 90 90 90 (UK); 1850 60 90 90 (ROI)

Email: (all urgent enquiries or requests for help) *jo@samaritans.org*; (non-urgent enquiries): *admin@samaritans.org*

Website: *www.samaritans.org*

Lucky Duck

Lucky Duck Publishing was established in 1988 to provide written materials that supported training services offered by the company throughout the UK. These include a huge number of anti-bullying and bullying-prevention strategies, most of which are discussed in some detail in this book (Circle Time, for example). Contact them for details of training programmes and useful books, or just visit their informative website.

SAGE Publications Ltd

1 Oliver's Yard

55 City Road

London

EC1Y 1SP

Tel: 020 7324 8500

Email: *publishing@luckyduck.co.uk*

Website: *www.luckyduck.co.uk*

YWCA

YWCA runs youth and community projects offering more than 150 programmes across England and Wales, giving young women aged 11 to 30 support, information and the opportunity to learn. They help young women to challenge violence or abuse, learn new skills, finish their education and improve their health and self-esteem. Their website has an informative section on girls and bullying, which is well worth a read.

Clarendon House

52 Cornmarket Street

Oxford, OX1 3EJ

Tel: 01865 304200

Email: *info@ywca.org.uk*

Website: *www.ywca.org.uk*

The Children's Legal Centre

The Children's Legal Centre is an independent national charity concerned with law and policy affecting children and young people. They offer advice and a number of publications regarding bullying, children and the law.

The Children's Legal Centre
University of Essex
Wivenhoe Park
Colchester, Essex CO4 3SQ
Tel: 01206 872 466
Education Law Advice Line: 0845 456 6811
Email: *clc@essex.ac.uk*
Website: *www.childrenslegalcentre.com*

Home Education UK

A helpful organisation with information on all aspects of home education, including links to external organisations and those offering extra-curricular activities for home-educated children. Plenty of research and ideas on the site, plus contact details for all local authorities.
Email: *support@home-education.org.uk*
Website: *www.home-education.org.uk*

R Time

The R Time website provides details of the programme (see also page 239), as well as general information and advice on bullying, practical solutions to problems and help for schools to develop relationships between children, and improve citizenship. Their resources are aimed at parents and teachers.
55 Garth Crescent
Binley, Coventry
CV3 2PP
Tel: 07946 333321
Email: *greg@rtime.info*
Website: *www.rtime.info*

CALM (Campaign Against Living Miserably)

Helpline for boys and young men aged 16–35 years, suffering from depression and low self-esteem. Offers counselling, advice and information
Tel: 0800 58 58 58 (7 days a week 5pm–3am)
Website: *www.thecalmzone.net*

Australia

PeaceBuilders

PeaceBuilders is a community-based, violence reduction programme, designed to help establish more peaceful ways of behaving, living and working in families, schools, organisations and communities.
Email: *info@peacebuildersoz.com*
Website: *www.peacebuildersoz.com*

The Friendly Schools Project

The Friendly Schools Bullying Intervention Project aimed to assess the effectiveness of a whole-school intervention aimed at preventing, reducing and managing bullying in the primary school setting. This led to the Friendly Schools and Families programme, which is based on six years of scientific bullying research by staff from the Child Health Promotion Research Unit (CHPRU) at Edith Cowan University. The programme supplies plenty of information to help schools get started, and lots of research and statistics backing up their approach.

Building 18, Child Health Promotion Research Unit
School of Exercise, Biomedical and Health Sciences
Pearson Street,
Churchlands
WA 6018
Tel: (08) 9273 8140
Email: *friendlyschools@ecu.edu.au*
Website: *www.friendlyschools.com.au*

Lifeline's MindMatters

MindMatters is a programme funded by the Australian Government Department of Health and Ageing. Its focus is promoting well-being in all Australian schools, and particularly in secondary schools. Lifeline and MindMatters work collaboratively to create communication pathways between schools to implement MindMatters and national Lifeline services including Just Look and Just Ask.

Lifeline helpline: 13 11 14
Website: *www.lifeline.org.au/pages/mindmatters.php*

Connecting Kids

Connecting Kids Company is a non-profit organisation which has been providing student wellbeing programmes for school communities for eighteen years, working collaboratively with schools to create friendly, supportive communities.

46 Taylor Street
(PO Box 17)
Ashburton, VIC 3147
Tel: (03) 9885-8956
Email: *office@connectingkids.org.au*
Website: *www.connectingkids.org.au*

Peer Support Foundation

The Peer Support Foundation Limited provides peer-led, school-based programmes which foster the overall wellbeing of young people and their community. The programme is integrated into curricula and continues from Kindergarten to Year 12. It encourages positive change within schools through a range of strategies developed by members of the whole school community for the specific needs of the school.

2 Grosvenor Place, PO Box 498
Brookvale, NSW 2100
Tel: (02) 9905 3499
Email: *peeroz@peersupport.edu.au*
Website: *www.peersupport.edu.au*

National Coalition Against Bullying

The National Coalition Against Bullying (NCAB) is an innovative initiative of The Alannah and
Madeline Foundation. It brings together people from key organisations to draw attention to
the issue of bullying and to promote a tolerant, inclusive, balanced society. The Coalition
aims to raise awareness of the seriousness of bullying in Australian society. Through expert agencies, they work to develop and implement school, work and community-based anti-bullying
programmes.
85 Canterbury Rd
Canterbury, VIC 3126
Tel: (03) 9830 2577
Email: *ncab@amf.org.au*
Website: *www.ncab.org.au*

The Alannah and Madeline Foundation's Better Buddies Program

The Alannah and Madeline Foundation's mission is 'Taking care of the little things'. The Better
Buddies Program teaches children to care about the other children around them. The program
introduces and enhances primary schools' Buddy systems. It delivers a very positive and effec-
tive anti-bullying, anti-violence message.
5 Canterbury Road,
Canterbury, VIC 3126
Tel: (03) 9830 7460
Email: *betterbuddies@amf.org.au*
Website: *www.buddybear.com.au*

Kids Help Line

Kids Help Line is Australia's only free, confidential and anonymous, 24-hour telephone and online
counselling service specifically for children and teens. Kids Help Line has helped to raise aware-
ness of bullying and has generated considerable media attention and public debate. They have
a good website, with useful links, information and strategies to reduce the impact of bullying.
PO Box 2000
Milton, QLD 4064
Tel: (07) 3369 1588
Counselling line: 1800 55 1800
Email: *admin@kidshelp.com.au*
Website: *kidshelp.com.au* (see their website for a direct email counselling service)

Lawstuff

A great website with advice on children's legal rights in relation to bullying, run by the National Children and Youth Law Centre. Advice can be obtained by email, via the website's internal form.
National Children's and Youth Law Centre
32 Botany Street
Randwick, NSW 2032
Tel: (02) 9398 7488
Email: *ncylc@unsw.edu.au*
Website: *www.lawstuff.org.au*

Bullying. No Way!

Bullying. No Way! is a website created by Australia's educational communities. It aims to create learning environments where every student and school community member is safe, supported, respected, valued and free from bullying, violence, harassment and discrimination.
Website: *www.bullyingnoway.com.au*

Home Education Association (HEA)

A useful organisation that can help you get started on home education; plenty of links, resources and a membership programme.
4 Bruce Street
Stanmore, NSW 2048
Tel: 02 9500 7664
Email: *secretary@hea.asn.au*
Website: *www.hea.asn.au*

Bullying in Schools

This site is run by Dr Ken Rigby, one of the pioneers of anti-bullying research, prevention and programmes. It offers a wealth of information – and not just for Australians. Well worth a visit.
Website: *www.education.unisa.edu.au/bullying/*

Lifeline's Just Look

Lifeline's Just Look is an online national database of health and community services offered throughout Australia. It offers a free, confidential 24-hour service.
Lifeline Helpline: 13 11 14
Website: *www.justlook.org.au*

Australian Community Safety & Research Organisation Incorporated (ACRO)

ACRO has developed a series of innovative programmes to develop leadership skills through mentoring, where young people can work in partnership with adults to share knowledge and skills. Their Youth Panels scheme is highly regarded, as are their buddy programmes and youth camps.
Website: *www.acro.com.au*

Emotional Literacy Australia

This informal group comprises individuals and organisations who aim to raise the profile of the fundamental social (interpersonal) and emotional (intrapersonal) skills which are the foundations for wellbeing, resilience, learning and healthy relationships. Excellent ideas, links and information on various programmes that work.

Wellbeing Australia

PO Box 1031

Spit Junction, NSW 2088

Website: *www.emotionalliteracyaustralia.com*

Response Ability

A resource and support project that aims to help prepare trainee teachers, journalists and nurses for their roles in youth suicide prevention. The project provides a range of useful resources for professionals in these fields, including guidance on reporting suicide in the media.

Hunter Institute of Mental Health

Hunter New England Area Health Service

PO Box 833

Newcastle, NSW 2300

Website: *www.responseability.org*

New Zealand

Kia Kaha

Kia Kaha (meaning stand strong) is a whole school approach to eliminate bullying. It is run by the Youth Education Service of the New Zealand Police. It aims to help schools create environments where everyone feels safe, respected and valued. It has been widely adopted in New Zealand and, by all reports, is very successful.

Contact: Your local police station

Website: *www.police.govt.nz/service/yes/nobully/kia_kaha*

Keeping Ourselves Safe (KOS)

KOS is a positive personal safety programme that aims to provide children and young people with the skills to cope with situations that might involve abuse. Like Kia Kaha, it is run by the police department. A good website with lots of information.

Website: *www.police.govt.nz/service/yes/resources/violence/kos.html*

Kidsline New Zealand

Kidsline is New Zealand's only 24-hour helpline for children. Children can ring on the 0800 number at any time, to speak to a trained counsellor. Between 4 and 6pm on weekdays, kids can also speak to a Kidsline 'buddy' who will be an older student (year 12 or 13), trained to help. They also offer an email advice service, and a highly organised and useful website.

Tel: 0800 KIDSLINE (0800 543 754)

Website: *www.kidsline.org.nz* (you can access their email service through the site)

0800 NO BULLY

0800 NO BULLY is a 24-hour information line giving helpful advice about taking action to stop bullying.

Tel: 0800 NO BULLY (0800 66 28 55)

Eliminating Violence

The Eliminating Violence programme is a whole-school programme that focuses on reducing bullying in schools (see page 263).

Ken Begg

Co-ordinator, Eliminating Violence Programme

Canterbury

Special Education

Ministry of Education, Canterbury

Email: *ken.begg@minedu.govt.nz*

Cool Schools

The Cool Schools Peer Mediation programme has been introduced to over half of all New Zealand schools, with resounding success. It helps students develop conflict-management skills.

Tel: Yvonne Duncan (09) 373 2379

Email: *coolschools@fps.pl.net*

The Peace Foundation

The Peace Foundation (Foundation for Peace Studies Aotearoa/New Zealand) offers innovative programmes, services and resources that are used in many schools, homes and communities – both in New Zealand and overseas – to help create a more peaceful society. It helps to establish and maintain peaceful and non-violent relationships by teaching skills that encourage better communication, co-operation and non-violent conflict resolution. Hosts an excellent website with a wealth of information for parents, children and teachers.

PO Box 4110

Auckland 1

Tel: (09) 373 2379

Website: *www.peace.net.nz*

Child Development Foundation (CDF)

The Child Development Foundation (CDF) is a charitable educational trust established to develop, implement, monitor and promote educational programmes that are directed towards the development and enhancement of personal and social skills.

PO Box 109697

Newmarket

Auckland

Tel: (09) 520 6512; 0800 438 233

Email: *admin@reachingcdf.org.nz*

Website: *www.reachingcdf.org.nz*

New Zealand Home Education (NZHE)

An organisation for parents who wish to educate their children at home. Plenty of information, advice, legal help, resources and links on their website.

Website: *www.home.school.nz*

No Bully

An excellent website, loaded with information for teachers, parents and children, which was created by New Zealand Telecom and the New Zealand Police.

Website: *www.nobully.org.nz*

Youthline

No longer just a helpline for kids and teens over the age of 12, Youthline aims to 'understand the wider social and economic contexts which young people are growing up in'. Teens can use their free helpline, email for advice, or visit the website for a host of information, resources, advice and links – all designed with today's teens in mind.

Youthline Help: 0800 37 66 33

Email: *youthline@youthline.co.nz*

Website: *www.youthline.co.nz*

What's Up

A free, confidential, nationwide telephone counselling service for all school-age children in New Zealand. Available between noon and midnight, seven days a week.

Tel: 0800 WHATSUP (0800 942 87 87)

South Africa

Hurtfree Schools

An American programme that has been practised widely in South Africa with some success; for case histories, information, advice, teaching packs and any other help, contact:

HURT FREE Schools and the Rainbow of Safety

22 Fairway Drive

Amherst, New Hampshire

03031 USA

Tel: +1 603 672 3348

Website: *www.hurtfreeschools.org*

The Children's Movement and the Children's Resource Centre (CRC)

The Children's Resource Centre was started in 1983 to help children to organise themselves into a Children's Movement. Today the CRC have more than 50 Children's Groups throughout South Africa with a membership of more than 5000 children between the age of 7 and 14 years. They have a good website, plenty of advice for teachers and children, as well as an anti-bullying programme.

3 Milner Road, Rondebosch, 7701, Cape Town
P.O. Box 408, Rondebosch, 7701, Cape Town
Tel: +27 21 6866898/3
Email: *crcchild@iafrica.com*
Website: *www.childrensmovement.org.za/program.htm*

Staysafe: Youth Crime Prevention

The StaySafe Discussion List provides a platform for networking and information sharing relating to crime prevention, with a specific focus on the youth. The website serves as a store-room of useful resources including a news clipping service, a database of service providers, down-loadable resources and links to other relevant online sources of information.
Suite 3
4 The Crescent
Westway Office Park, Westville
Tel: 031 265 0890
Email: *val@ipt.co.za*
Website: *www.staysafe.co.za*

Canada

Bullying Awareness Network

The Bullying Awareness Network is an initiative of the Ottawa Anti Bullying Coalition (O-ABC), which offers a community-based approach to the prevention of bullying and victimization. The network provides a variety of resources and services, including codes of conduct, anti-bully-ing guidelines, best practice guidelines, youth programmes, communication links and anti-bul-lying programmes, plus a database of information, research and updates.
Website: *www.bullyingawarenessnetwork.ca*

Canadian Public Health Association

Provides an assessment toolkit for harassment, bullying and peer relations at school. A good web-site, with plenty of links, information, research and initiatives, plus a 'safe school' study.
400–1565 Carling Avenue
Ottawa, ON, K1Z 8R1
Tel: (613) 725 3769
Email: *info@cpha.ca*
Website: *www.cpha.ca/antibullying*

Bully Beware

Developed in British Columbia, this excellent and informative site is devoted to bullying pre-vention and provides tips and strategies on how to deal with bullies. A wealth of information on programmes, research, statistics, support groups and news, as well as the newest and most effective initiatives.

Bully B'ware Productions
1421 King Albert Avenue,
Coquitlam, BC
V3J 1Y3
Tel: (604) 936 8000 or 1 888 552 8559
Email: *bully@direct.ca*
Website: *www.bullybeware.com*

Cyberbullying
An excellent Canadian website with information and advice on how to deal with cyberbullying in its many forms.
Website: *www.cyberbullying.ca*

Canadian Safe School Network
The Canadian Safe School Network (CSSN) is a national, charitable organisation dedicated to reducing youth violence and making schools and communities safer. They offer details of many resources and programmes for schools, plus a website with information aimed at teachers, parents and children. They also offer the 'Cool Heads in the Zone' CD Rom.
111 Peter Street, Suite 617
Toronto, ON, M5V 2H1
Tel: (416) 977 1050
Email: *info@canadiansafeschools.com*
Website: *www.cssn.org*

Roots of Empathy
In 1996 Mary Gordon founded Roots of Empathy, a not-for-profit, evidence-based classroom programme that has dramatically reduced levels of aggression and violence among schoolchildren while raising their social emotional competence and increasing empathy.
215 Spadina Avenue
Suite 160
Toronto, ON, M5T 2C7
Tel: (416) 944 3001
Fax: (416) 944 9295
Email: *email@rootsofempathy.org*
Website: *www.rootsofempathy.org*

Gambo Crime Prevention Committee – Beat the Bully
The Gambo Crime Prevention Committee has developed the Beat the Bully programme with young people, educators, parents and community members. This programme uses public education, storytelling and peer support to help create a community where young people feel safe, confident and worthy.
Tel: (709) 674 0074

The Fair Play: Teaching Skills of Empathy to Young Children through Music and Drama

A bilingual theatrical and musical presentation to help develop a language of emotions and encourage empathy in young children.

Tel: (902) 888 8458

Bullies: Who Dares to Speak Out?

This board game aims to educate children about bullying and help them to develop personal and social skills for coping with intimidation. The game focuses on both potential victims of bullying and those who may be bullies themselves.

Tel: (514) 425 2697

Together We Light the Way

This school-based community-safety project is based on nurturing children to enhance learning, skills and habits, develop non-violent responses to anger, and improve attitudes toward school.

Tel: (905) 666 6381
Email: *canon-brenda@durham.edu.on.ca*
Website: *www.togetherwelighttheway.com*

Peace Project

The Restitution Peace Project developed a Peace Circle Model to help schoolchildren in the Northwest Territories and Nunavut learn to resolve conflict in non-violent ways, helping them to understand the underlying causes of their behaviour, and to accept personal responsibility for their actions.

Tel: (867) 873 3477

National Strategy on Community Safety and Crime Prevention

A strong organisation with a good website, hosting details of provincial and national programmes available for teachers and other educators.

National Crime Prevention Centre
Department of Justice
St Andrew's Tower
284 Wellington Street
Ottawa, ON, K1A 0P8
Tel: (613) 941 9306
Email: *info@prevention.gc.ca*
Website: *www.prevention.gc.ca*

Kids Help Phone

A 24-hour telephone counselling service for children of all ages, with a variety of different programmes for schools, as well as a referral and information service. They also offer online advice.

300–439 University Avenue
Toronto, ON, M5G 1Y8
Tel: 416 586 5437
Toll-free line: 1 800 668 6868
Email: *info@kidshelp.sympatico.ca*
Website: *www.kidshelpphone.ca*

The Canadian Association of Home Based Education

A useful organisation with links to resources, information on legal issues, provincial legislation, ordering textbooks and other skills-based tools, and plenty of advice.
Website: *www.flora.org/homeschool-ca/achbe/index.html*

Canadian Children's Rights Council

This organisation provides an overview of legal issues surrounding bullying. Their website is an excellent source of information for parents and educators.
Suite 905
357 Eglinton Avenue West
Toronto
ON, M5N 1Z3
Tel: 416 410 6858 (if you are calling long-distance, they will return your call free of charge)
Email: *info@canadianCRC.com*
Website: *www.canadiancrc.com*

USA

There are many US organisations dealing with bullying; these are just some of the programmes and initiatives you may find interesting.

Center for the Prevention of School Violence

This US organisation hosts web forums on school violence prevention issues. Good material and some excellent anti-violence posters and stickers.
Website: *www.ncdjjdp.org/CPSV/*

Steps to Respect

For information on the Steps to Respect approach to bullying, plus a wealth of other resources, contact the committee for children.
568 First Avenue South, Suite 600
Seattle
WA 98104 2804
Tel: 800 634 4449 ext. 6223
Website: *www.cfchildren.org*

Take a Stand. Lend a hand. Stop Bullying Now!

This national anti-bullying programme is the largest government-organised effort to stop bullying. The website offers plenty of research, resources and tips on ways to prevent bullying, and ways to respond if your child is being bullied. The website has many interactive features for kids, too.

Email: *comments@hrsa.gov*
Website: www.*stopbullyingnow.hrsa.gov*

Take Ten

Take Ten aims to reduce violence and bullying in schools by encouraging children to take time to consider their actions and words. Their useful website is well worth visiting.

Phone: 574 631 9424
Email: *taketen@nd.edu*
Website: *www.nd.edu/~taketen/index.html*

Operation Respect

Operation Respect is a non-profit organisation working to transform schools, camps and organisations focused on children and youth, into more compassionate, safe and respectful environments. They offer a host of different programmes for various age groups.

Operation Respect
2 Penn Plaza, 5th Floor
New York, NY, 10121
Tel: 212 904 5243
Email: *info@operationrespect.org*
Website: *www.dontlaugh.org*

Broken Toy Project

Strong, visual presentations undertaken throughout the US and Canada about bullying from seasoned speaker and ex-victim Thomas Brown.

Email: *brokentoyproject@columbus.rr.com*
Website: *brokentoyproject_1.tripod.com*

Useful Websites

Cyberbullying

For a good source of information (aimed at both parents and children) and advice, visit: *www.mcgruff.org/Grownups/cyberbullying*

For details of facts, news, research and advice, visit: *www.cyberbullying.org*
Another useful site with legal information, advice and prevention information, aimed at specific age groups can be found at: *www.stopcyberbullying.org*

Dr Kenneth Rigby's Bullying Pages

Information on Dr Rigby's research into the efficacy of bullying intervention programmes.
Website: *www.education.unisa.edu.au/bullying/intervention*
Worth a look too is his book (edited by Peter K. Smith of Goldsmiths College, London, and written with Debra Pepler of York University, Canada), *Bullying in Schools: How Successful Can Interventions Be?*, published by Cambridge University Press.

Shared Concern

Details on this method of intervention, written by Dr Ken Rigby.
Website: *www.education.unisa.edu.au/bullying/concern.html*

Bullying.Org

A schoolteacher and his students developed *Bullying.Org* to help other children deal with the issues of bullying and teasing. The group volunteered once a week during their lunch break to discuss these issues and contribute their own thoughts, feelings, experiences, poems and drawings to the site. One of the most exciting features of this site is the large selection of films and music on bullying from young people around the world. Visitors will find all forms of entertainment available through WAV, MP3 or Real Audio/Real Player and may submit their own files. In addition, the site offers an extensive list of resources available to help educate youths and parents on this issue.
Website: *www.bullying.org*

Stop Bullying Now

An American website based on social worker Stan Davis's approach to stopping bullying. Plenty of research, ideas, plans and advice for their implementation, and more. Stan is also a certified Olweus bullying prevention trainer (see page 223).
Email: *stan@stopbullyingnow.com*
Website: *www.clemson/edu/olweus*
For details of the Olweus Bullying Prevention programme, including information on how to learn more, visit: *www.stopbullyingnow.net/olweus_program*

National Healthy Schools Standard

This initiative is hosted by the Health Development Agency in the UK, and aims to help schools provide a healthy environment that is conducive to learning.
Website: *www.hda-online.org.uk/html/improving/nhss.html*

BBC

This excellent site includes information on bullying for parents, students and teachers.
Website: *www.bbc.co.uk/schools/bullying*

Index

Boxed sections are indicated by *italics*
Main sections are indicated by **bold** type

A

abuse *184*
Actionwork (UK) 257, **296**
adolescents 78, 185, 191, 208
aggression 142, **147–52**, 158, 212
aggressive bullies 36
Alannah and Madeline Foundation (Australia) 260
anger 28, 38, 62, 102, 150–1
Anger Coping Programme (US) 150–1
anonymous reporting 228, 229, 233, 250
Anti-Bullying Alliance (ABA, UK) 241, 251–2, 257, **293**
anti-bullying initiatives
    best programmes **226–33**
    effectiveness of **268–71**
    international initiatives **257–68**
    Olweus Programme **233–4**
    other key programmes **235–49**
    UK initiatives **250–7**
    see also Resources **293–311**
Anti-Bullying Network (UK) 247–8, 257, **293–4**
anti-bullying strategies
    bullyproofing your child **102–5**
    changing schools 282–4
    counteracting negative self-image **84–6**
    dealing with guilt 278–9
    dealing with trauma 279–80, 282
    fostering emotional health **276–7**
    fostering social skills and friendships **96–102**
    home education **284–8**
    improving problem-solving skills **84–8**
    keeping a record **274–5**
    overall plan **81–3**
    practical steps for parents of bullies **158–63**
    professional help 79, 282
    siblings and friends 282
    special schools *286*
    supporting your child 276
    talking and listening to your child 83–4, **105–7**, 130–1, 134–5, 208–9, 211, **277–8**
    teaching resilience **88–94**
Anti-Bullying Week (UK) 253
assertiveness *90–1*
attachment **71–2**, 93
Australia 12, 74, 76, 247, 268, 284
    initiatives and resources **257–60**, **300–4**

B

Baumeister, Roy 135–6
Beat the Bully (Canada) 265–6, **308**
Beckham, David 253
Belgium 268
Better Buddies (Australia) 260
Birkinshaw, Sue 45
Blatner, Dr Adam 145–6
Bono 253
boredom 180, 189
Bosworth, Kris 148
Box Clever (UK) 257, **296**
Bradshaw, Professor Jonathan 221
Bronfenbrenner, Professor Urie 285
Brook, Kelly 253
bullies
    age differences 17–18
    characteristics 18, **20**

dealing sensitively with 230
gender differences 16, 17, *19, 132–3*
help for *281*
importance of empathy **144–7**
influence of parents **20–5**
influences, other **25–32**
insecurity of 138–40
Is your child a bully? **32–4, 125–9**
motivation *35*
need for power **155–8**
peer pressure **152–5**
perception of others 22, **142–3**
practical steps for parents of
   158–63
risk factors *31*
self-esteem question **134–6**
temperament of 25, 140–1
types of **36–9**
violence and aggression in **147–52**
bullying
difference between play and 42–4
different types of **44–55, 110–19**
by family members 54
hotspots *43*
ignoring *106*
myths that sustain *58*
and post-traumatic stress disorder
   192–3
scale of the problem 11–12, 15–16
stress and 166, 186–7
by teachers 52–3
see also bullies; anti-bullying initiatives; anti-bullying strategies
Bully Police (USA) *270–1*
bully-victims 37–8
Bullywatch (UK) 253
bystanders **107–10**, 229, 231, 242, 247

C

Canada 47, 48, 234, 247
initiatives and resources **265–8,
   307–10**
Candappa, Mano 254
Carmarthenshire initiative *256*
Centre for School Quality and
   Improvement (CSQI, South Africa)
   264
Charter for Action (UK) 251
Childline (UK) 79, 252, 254–5, 256,
   293
Childline in Partnership with Schools
   (CHIPS, UK) 254
childrearing *see* parents
Children's Movement and the
   Children's Resource Centre (CRC,
   South Africa) 264, **306**
choices, giving children 218–19
Christie, Dr Gayre 257
Circle Time (UK and others) 245,
   246–9
City University, London 168
Coloroso, Barbara 107
   *The Bully, the Bullied and the
   Bystander* 38
Columbia University 207
Columbine High School 235
Commonwealth Department of Health
   and Ageing (Australia) 258
confrontation *120*
Cool Schools (New Zealand) 263, **305**
Cooperative Independent College,
   Broadstairs 286
Cornell University 285
counselling services 79, 282
Cowie, Helen 247
Craig, Wendy 269
Crime and Disorder Act (UK 1998)
   113
Cross, Donna 258
crying 62, 282
cyberbullying 41, 43, 51–2, 114–15,
   117

D

Dato, Dr Robert 166–7, 178, 182
   Dato Stress Inventory 167
depression, signs of *289*
Developmental Psychology 242
DfES (UK) 252
disabilities 64
discipline and punishment 22, *29*, 141,
   158, 203–4, **209, 212–19**, 230

family rules *222–3*
divorce 182–3
Dodge, Kenneth 148
Doherty, William J. 182
'Don't Suffer in Silence' pack (UK)
   234
Duke University 142
Duncan, Yvonne 263
Durham University 284

E
École J.H. Sissons (Canada) 267
education **176–8**
   home education **284–8**
   see also schools
Educational Psychology Service,
   Leicestershire 241
Eliminating Violence (New Zealand)
   263, **304–5**
Elkind, David
   The Hurried Child 179–80
Elliot, Michelle 253
emotional bullying 112–13
emotional environmental factors
   93
emotional health **194–6, 276–7**
emotional vocabulary 88, *210–11*
empathy 23, 100–1, 109, 143, **144–7,**
   267–8
Eslea, Mike 45
Everett, Shirley 243
exclusion bullying 46–7
exercise 184, 287
extortion bullying 50, 110–11, 161

F
fagging 50–1
false victims 63
families and home
   broken families 182–3
   bullying at home 24, 54, 130
   creating healthy family life
      220–3
   discipline and punishment **209,**
      212–19
   emotional factors *93*

family rules *222–3*
giving children an outlet 219–20
importance of home environment
   199–200
spending time together 139, 163
support by siblings 79, 282
see also parents and parenting
Field, Tim 112–13, 160, 192
Finland 268
Floyd, Nathanial 65
Friendly Schools Project (Australia)
   258, **300**
friends 79, 101–2, 221–2
   befriending scheme 247

G
Gambo Crime Prevention Committee
   (Canada) 265–6, **308**
gangs 38, 133
girls who bully 16, 17, *19*, 36, *132–3,*
   138, 267
Goldsmith's College, London 245
Gordon, Mary 267–8
growing up too soon **178–81**
guilt 106, 108, **278–9**

H
hazing (initiation rites) 50–1
Hazler, Richard 18, 35, 59
happy slapping 52, *116*
Harrington, Dr Richard 182–3
Hendessi, Mananda 19
Herbert, Carrie 286
High, Brenda *270–1*
High, Jared *270–1*
Hoffman, Dr Martin
   Empathy and Moral Development
      144
home *see* families and home
home education **284–8**
homicide 156
homosexuality 47–8, *243*
Hostile Hallways report (US) 49
humour 32, 104
Hurt-Free Schools (South Africa) 264,
   306

I

'I' statements 90, 103–4
ignoring bullying *106*
insecurity 71–2, 138–40
Institute of Education 177–8
Institute of Psychiatry 168
interests and leisure **101–2, 181–2**
internet 118–19, 250
isolation bullying 46–7

J

jealousy 139–40
Jenson, Alan 178
Jones, Gail 41
Joseph, Dr Stephen 186–7
Juvonen, Dr Jaana 26

K

Kaiser Family Foundation (US) 83
Katz, Adrienne 65–6
Kellogs 260
Kia Kaha (New Zealand) 261–2,
   304
Kids Help Line (Australia) 259–60,
   302
Kidscape (UK) 75, 76, 242, 245, 253,
   255, 256, 288, **293**
Kumpulainen, K. 148

L

latch-key kids 21, 180
legal action 275
leisure activities **101–2, 181–2**
Lewis, Ivan 250, 251
lifestyle, modern 176
Lochman, John E. 142, 150–1
Loomans, Diane
   365 Positive Activities for Kids
   28
Luce, Professor Terry 212

M

Mahdavi, Jessica 245
Make the Difference campaign (UK)
   252
material bullying 50

material possessions 172–3, 221
Matisse, Christina 264
Maudsley Hospital 168
meals together 220
Menninger Clinic, Houston 149
mental disorders *201*
Mental Health Foundation 169
mentoring 157, 230, 246, 247
MindMatters (Australia) 258–9
Mintel 172
mobile phones 51–2, 114, *115, 116,*
   117–18
Moore, Dr Raymond 285, 287
MORI-NSPCC poll on children 168,
   171, 177
Moseley, Jenny 246
motivation of bullies *35*
Myron-Wilson, Rowan 71

N

National Anti-Bullying Poetry
   Anthology (UK) 255
National Children's Bureau (NCB, UK)
   251
National Coalition Against Bullying
   (NCAB, Australia) 260, **301**
National Foundation for Educational
   Research (NFER, UK) 249
National Institute of Child Health and
   Human Development (US) 175
National Safe Schools Framework
   (Australia) 257
National Society for the Prevention of
   Cruelty to Children (NSPCC, UK)
   11, 168, 171, 177, 184, 251, **295**
National Strategy (Canada) 265
NCH (UK) 52, 115
New Zealand 12, 284
   initiatives and resources **261–3,**
   304–6
Nickelodeon (US) 83
'No', saying 91, 154
No-Blame Approach (UK) **235–7**
Northmore, Colin 264
Norway 233

O

Oakley, Julie 253
Office for National Statistics (UK) 168
OFSTED (UK) 250, 254
Ohio University 18
Oliver, Christine 254
Olweus, Dan 27, 36, 63, 75, 76, 107, 226
Olweus Bullying Prevention Programme **233–4**, 268
Oregon Social Learning Center 148
Osborn, Corron 286
Osborn, Julia 286
Osborne, Rob 241
Oxford University 11

P

Palmer, Professor Stephen 168
parents and parenting
bullying by 54, 93
busy parents 173–6
childrearing factors *23*
elements of parenting 129–30
fostering self-esteem **200–7**
involvement in anti-bullying programmes 226
is my child being bullied? **76–8**
living through our children 171
parental expectations 169–71, 215–16
parents of bullies **20–5**, *21, 29,* 32–3, **125–63**
parents of victims **65–71**, 79, **119–23**
physical affection **207–8**
stressed parents 172–3
talking and listening to your child 83–4, 99, **105–7**, 130–1, 134–5, **208–9, 277–8**
see also anti-bullying strategies; families and home
passive bullies 36–7
passive victims 62–3
Patterson, Gerald 148
Peace Circle (Canada) 267, **309**

Peace Foundation (New Zealand) 263, **305**
PeaceBuilders (Australia) 257–8, **300**
Peer Support Foundation (Australia) 259, **301**
peers
exclusion by 101
fitting in with 96–8
peer pressure **152–55**, 184, 186
peer support schemes 245–6, *247*
and stress 94, *185*
Pennsylvania State University 172
Pepler, Dr Debra 153
perception/cognition 73, 98–9, **142–3**
Pereira, Karen 256
perpetual victims 63
Peters, Andrew Fusek 255
Petford, Cindy 286
physical affection 207–8
physical bullying 44–5, 111
physical punishment 209, **212–13**
Pikas, Anatol 237
police 111, 113, 115, 116, 275
New Zealand 262
popularity of bullies 26, 126
post-traumatic stress disorder *192–3*, 279
power 35, **155–8**
praise 205–7, 215–16
pre-school children 189
primary school children 77, 190
problem-solving skills **84–8**
professional help 79, 282
provocative victims 63–4, 238, 239
Public Order Act (UK 1986) 113

Q

Queen's University, Canada 269

R

R Time (Relationships to improve education, UK) 239–41, **298**
Race Relations Act (UK 1976) 113
racial bullying 47, 55, **113–14**
Randall, Peter 64
reactive victims 37

Red Balloon school *286*
regression 280
relationship bullies 37
resilience, teaching 88–9, 92, 94
Rigby, Ken 12, 74, 76, 268
Robinson, George 235
Romanowski, Michael 287, 288
Roots of Empathy (Canada) 267–8,
  308
Ross, D. 62
Rudolph, Karen 94

S
St Francis Xavier School, Illinois *244*
Sampson, Greg 239–40
SATs (Standard Attainment Tests)
  177–8
schools
  changing schools 185, 282–4
  changing the school climate *157*
  effect of bullying on 16–17
  influence of environment on bullies
    25–6
  making contact with **120–2**, 160
  special schools for bullied children
    286
  see also anti-bullying initiatives;
  teachers
self-esteem
  of bullies 27–8, 30, **134–6**
  in the family 93
  importance of **200–2**
  overemphasis on 144, **203–4**
  realistic praise **205–7**
  of victims 61, 72
self-image **94–6**
Selman, R.L. 98
sexual bullying 47–8, *49, 243*
Shared Concern (Sweden) **237–9**
Sheffield anti-bullying programme 234
Sheras, Dr Peter 59, 76
Shure, Myrna 85
siblings
  bullying among 25, 54, 130
  source of support 79, 282
Sigman, Dr Aric 175

Simmons, Rachel
  Odd Girl Out 19
Slee, P.T. 74
Smith, Professor David 269, 270
Smith, Peter K. 9–10, 71, 234, 245
Snopek, Barbara 244
social cognition/perception 73, 98–9,
  142–3
social skills **98–101**
sociopathic tendencies 161
South African initiatives and resources
  263–4, 306–7
Spain 268
Spatz-Widom, Cathy 281
special schools for bullied children *286*
Spivack, George 85
Steps to Respect (US) 241–2, 243, 244,
  310
stress
  assessing your child **194–6**
  and bullying 27, 73, **166**, 276
  causes **169–87**
  extent of problem **165–9**
  peers and 94, *185*
  post-traumatic stress disorder
    192–3
  symptoms **187–91**
  in young children *167*
Student Councils (Bully Courts) 242–5
submissiveness 92
suicide 41, 55, 75, 75–6, 83, 156, 193,
  235, *270–1*, **288–90**
superiority and control *27*
Sweden 233, 237

T
teachers 42, 45–6, 79, 159, 228, 232,
  242, 248
  bullying by 52–3
  parents' contact with **120–2**
  Professional Association of Teachers
    177
teenagers *see* adolescents
telephones/mobiles 51–2, 114, *115,
  116*, **117–18**
television **30–2**, 143, 181 *bis*

Thomas Coram Research Unit 254
Together We Light the Way (Canada)
  266, **309**
trauma 279–80, 282
  post-traumatic stress disorder
    192–3
Twemlow, Dr Stuart 53

U

UK initiatives and resources **235–7**,
  250–7, 268, **293–9**
University of British Columbia 268
University of California 26
University of Illinois 94
University of Michigan 16
University of Ottawa 269
University of Tulsa 212
University of Warwick 186
USA 247, 284, 289–90
  initiatives and resources 234,
    310–11

V

Vanderbilt University 148
verbal bullying 37, 42–4, **45–6**, 187
vicarious or surrogate victims 63
victims
  age differences 17–18, 77, 78
  characteristics 58–60, 123
  factors contributing to victimisa
    tion **65–71**
  impact of bullying in later life 73,
    75–6
  influence of parenting styles 65–71

Is my child being bullied? **76–8**
lack of friendships *74*
perceived weakness 60–2
protection for 231
signs of 76–8
types of **62–4**
victim mentality 61, 63, 73
vulnerability 65
Who do children talk to? *79*, 83–4
word 'victim' 109
violence
  in bullies **147–52**
  in the home 65, 126
  in society 183–4
  on television/films **30–2**, 181

W

websites, useful **309–10**
Who Dares to Speak Out (*Qui osera
  parler*? Canada) 266, **309**
Wigmore, Caroline 177
William King Elementary, Nova Scotia
  243
Words Hurt (Canada) 267
wristband fiasco *253*

Y

York University 221
Young Minds 169
Youth Education Service (YES, New
  Zealand) 262
Youth Justice Board 213
Young Voices (UK) 11, 65, 66
YWCA 19

OTHER RODALE BOOKS
AVAILABLE FROM PAN MACMILLAN

1-4050-9334-X 978-1-4050-9334-7	Grow Up!	*Clare Paterson*	£8.99
1-4050-0675-7 978-1-4050-0675-0	The Secret Life of the Dyslexic Child	*Robert Frank and* *Kathryn E Livingston*	£10.99
1-4050-7732-8 978-1-4050-7732-3	How to Help Your Overweight Child	*Karen Sullivan*	£12.99
1-4050-6729-2 978-1-4050-6729-4	When Difficult Relatives Happen to Good People	*Dr Leonard Felder*	£10.99
1-4050-8812-5 978-1-4050-8812-1	Pregnancy Questions & Answers	*The Editors of* *BabyCentre.co.uk*	£14.99
1-4050-4182-X 978-1-4050-4182-9	The Doctor's Book of Home Remedies	*Dr Stephen Amiel*	£20.00

All Rodale/Pan Macmillan titles can be ordered from the website,
www.panmacmillan.com, or from your local bookshop and are also available
by post from:

Bookpost, PO Box 29, Douglas, Isle of Man IM99 1BQ
Tel: 01624 677237; fax: 01624 670923; e-mail: *bookshop@enterprise.net*; or visit:
www.bookpost.co.uk. Credit cards accepted. Free postage and packing in the United
Kingdom

Prices shown above were correct at time of going to press.
Pan Macmillan reserve the right to show new retail prices on covers which may differ
from those previously advertised in the text or elsewhere.

For information about buying *Rodale* titles in **Australia**, contact Pan Macmillan
Australia. Tel: 1300 135 113; fax: 1300 135 103;
e-mail: *customer.service@macmillan.com.au*; or visit: *www.panmacmillan.com.au*

For information about buying *Rodale* titles in **New Zealand**, contact Macmillan
Publishers New Zealand Limited. Tel: (09) 414 0356; fax: (09) 414 0352;
e-mail: *lyn@macmillan.co.nz*; or visit: *www.macmillan.co.nz*

For information about buying *Rodale* titles in **South Africa**, contact Pan Macmillan
South Africa. Tel: (011) 325 5220; fax: (011) 325 5225;
e-mail: *marketing@panmacmillan.co.za*

RODALE   MACMILLAN